IMAGES
of America

BEARTOOTH MOUNTAINS

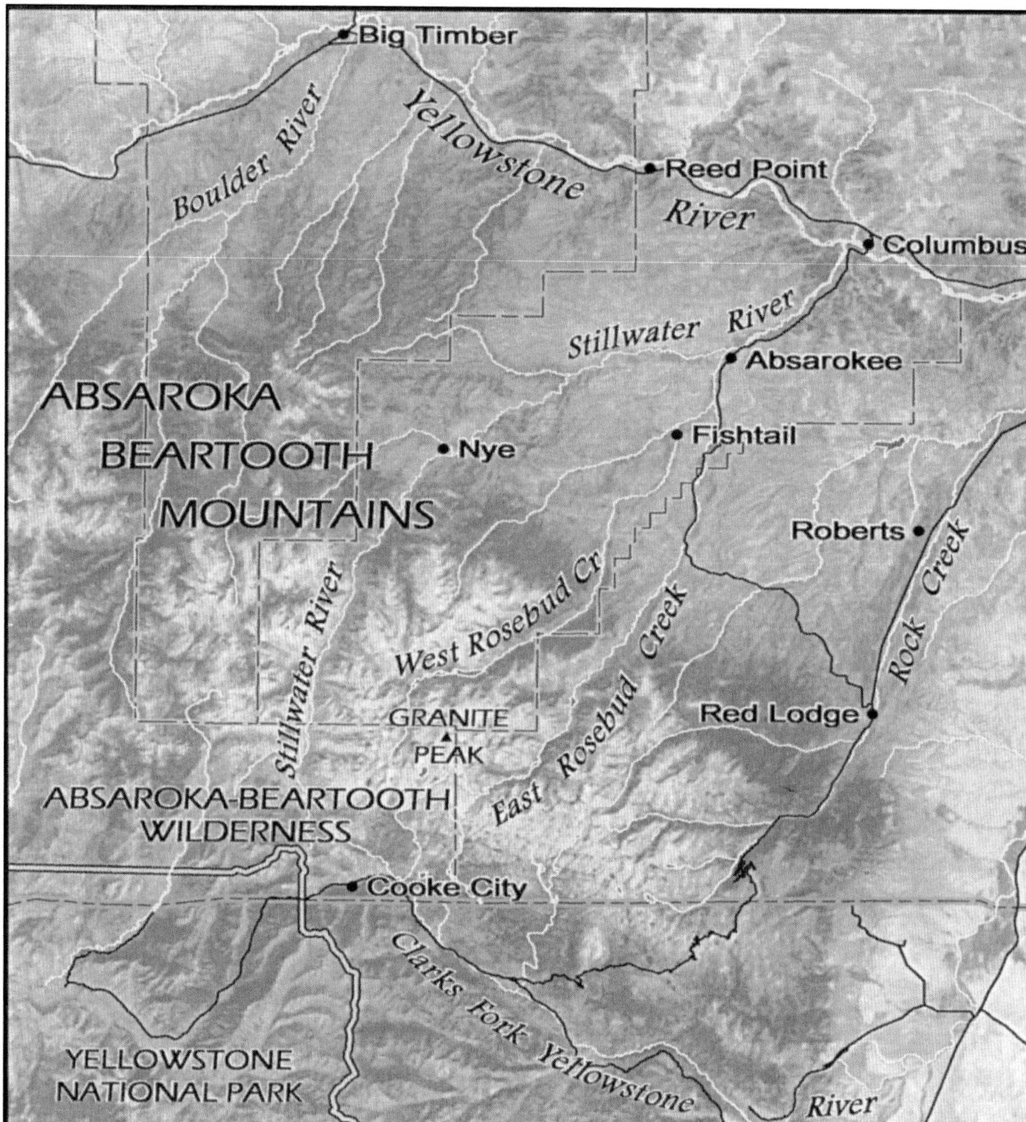

The Beartooth Mountains are technically a section of the Absaroka Mountains. The Beartooths range from the Boulder River in Montana southeast to the canyon of the Clarks Fork of the Yellowstone in Wyoming. The mountains also skirt along a small portion of Yellowstone National Park. (Courtesy of Bill Johnston, DOWL HKM.)

On The Cover: This photograph by Kenneth Dupee "K.D." Swan is a 1938 vista of Wounded Man Lake in the Beartooth Mountains. Upon graduating with a forestry degree from Harvard University, Swan was appointed as forest assistant in Montana in 1911. By 1913, he began to work for the Northern Region Forest Service Headquarters in Missoula, Montana, as a topographic draftsman. He became that organization's first photographer and was instrumental in establishing their photograph storage system. (Courtesy of US Forest Service [USFS], Beartooth Ranger District.)

IMAGES
of America

BEARTOOTH MOUNTAINS

Patty Hooker

ARCADIA
PUBLISHING

ISBN 978-0-7385-9331-9

Published by Arcadia Publishing
Charleston, South Carolina

Printed in the United States of America

Library of Congress Control Number: 2011946112

For all general information, please contact Arcadia Publishing:
Telephone 843-853-2070
Fax 843-853-0044
E-mail sales@arcadiapublishing.com
For customer service and orders:
Toll-Free 1-888-313-2665

Visit us on the Internet at www.arcadiapublishing.com

To those whose dreams and lives are enriched
by the Beartooth Mountains

Contents

ACKNOWLEDGMENTS

The daunting task of writing this book fell into my lap on the eve of finishing my first Arcadia title, *Columbus and Stillwater County*. With that experience under my belt, and with thc guidance and suggestions of many, I felt up to task. Steadfastly, Penny Redli, with the Museum of the Beartooths of Columbus, gave her suggestions and opened her doors to the archives and photograph collections, most notably the Annin Collection. Donna Madson, of the Carbon County Historical Society and Museum in Red Lodge, was accommodating, allowing use of computers and databases. With staffers Dana Walquist and Cathy Wiltgen and historic preservation officer Scott Lauf, I covered many bases. A treasure trove of photographs, particularly the Helen Brooke Herford Collection, was found at Montana State University Special Collections in Bozeman, and archivist Kim Allen Scott let me set up shop and scan away. With Rita Esp from the Crazy Mountain Museum in Big Timber, I worked quickly and efficiently as she deftly pulled photographs for me to scan. Ralph Saunders was also in the forefront of this project, suggesting background reading materials and map information and acting as a general sounding board. Ralph, along with Bill Johnson of DOWL HKM, created the custom insert map. Tom Highberger, retired from the Beartooth Ranger District, was most helpful on a wide range of topics, while his wife, Denise, masterfully created a travois sketch for use in the book. Terry Jones, with the Beartooth Ranger District, gave me ardent information on photograph-enhancing techniques as well as providing photograph materials. Mike Bergstrom, archeologist for the Custer National Forest, patiently fielded questions and lent photographs. From the Big Timber Ranger District, Bill Schwartz and Carl Ronneberg gave me a delightful tour of the district's restored ranger station and photograph selections. Professionals Eileen Wright, from the Montana State University in Billings Special Collections; Jon Ille, of Little Big Horn College; and John Boughton, with the National Historic Register program, provided photographs and information. Deb Hronek, friend and Joliet librarian, assisted me with tasks, suggestions, and proofreading. Linda Dutcher was most helpful with information and photographs from the Yellowstone Bighorn Research Association. Numerous residents shared their local knowledge, including Wanda Wilcox, Marilyn Weast, Allen Nelson, Nancy Branger Okerman, Jack Hash, Doris Donahoe, Jim and Sue Klessens, Marlene Donelson, Don Cowles, Brian Sullivan, Art Veatch, and Sam Johnson. Mavis Carrithers shared photographs of her father, David Kjell, on a trail construction crew.

INTRODUCTION

First, there were the mountains . . . but not just any mountains—a shear mass known as the Snow Mountains or Snowy Range and eventually coined the Beartooth Mountains. While Earth is estimated to be about 4.5 billion years old, igneous rocks in the Beartooths, mostly granite, are about 3.9 billion years old—some of the oldest rocks on the planet. The Beartooths were powered upward from the surrounding landscape as the Pacific plate slid underneath the North American plate, upon which Montana lay. A period of major igneous activity occurred, resulting in volcanic deposits that blanketed the southern Beartooths. The Beartooths received the sculpting of valleys, cirques, horns, and arêtes 1.6 million years ago, when the grinding action of retreating glaciers carved out their present massive grandeur.

It is said that trails tell the story of an area. Over 11,000 years, prehistoric Indians set the stage, traveling the Beartooth environs on game trails in search of migrating animals or shelter, leaving behind their occupation sites as evidence. Generations followed the trails, and they were eventually named after the last Native Americans to use them. The Bannock Trail, used by many tribes, traversed from Snake River country through the southern portion of the Beartooths to hunting grounds. In 1877, a portion of this trail, to the Clarks Fork River, was used by the fleeing Nez Percé on their epic escape to avoid the military. This portion became known as the Nez Percé Trail. The Mountain Trail led from Livingston east across the Boulder River to the Stillwater River, then skirted the Beartooth foothills to connect with the Meeteetse Trail. The Lodge Pole Trail was also associated with the Mountain Trail, with a section known as the Skookum Joe Trail, named after mining prospector "Skookum Joseph" Anderson. Trapper Osborne Russell traveled these arteries in 1837 in the first verified crossing of the Beartooths. These open routes enabled gold seekers, like Lou Anderson's prospecting party in the late 1860s, to the heads of Hellroaring, Buffalo, and Slough Creeks. Despite the lands being on the Crow reservation, miners filed into the Boulder River area and Cooke City area, staking claims. Their presence was undoubtedly a factor in the US government removing this portion of land, 1.5 million acres, from the Crow reservation in 1882 and opening it for settlement. Major mine developments occurred in the New World mining district on Republic Mountain near Cooke City and in the Boulder mining district. As trails became wagon roads, the mining camps of Independence, Contact, and Cooke City thrived to service this industry. The mining record is an example of the boom-and-bust nature of the national economy; with the Depression of 1893, they faded away.

However, new mining production was initiated during World War II. A national crisis involving a shortage of chromium ore supplies spawned widespread building and expansion in several portions of the Beartooths, most notably in the Mouat and Benbow mines. But this development waned as the economy no longer demanded the ore. Mouat mine was recharged again, however, when Stillwater Mining Company discovered palladium and platinum there in the early 1970s. Stillwater has expanded, with a mine near the East Boulder River that has been in operation since 2003. In the late 1890s, coal was mined, and the towns of Red Lodge, Bearcreek, and Washoe exploded with miners trying to keep pace with the needs of locomotives, smelters, and industry.

Geographers and geologists were next on the trail, organizing expeditions, scaling peaks, and exploring vast regions, mapping and recording the Beartooths. Edward Douglas, the geographer in charge of the US Geological Survey of Montana in the late 1890s, made the first recorded attempt to climb Granite Peak in 1889. The diaries of Thomas Jaggar, who was hired by geologist Arnold Hague, provide insight about the greater Yellowstone area and include an account of being led down the wrong trail, the treacherous Clarks Fork precipices. In 1898, geologist James P. Kimball hired photographer Andres Wilse, who stumbled upon present-day Grasshopper Glacier. The Kimball expedition gave a legacy of namesakes upon the Beartooths.

Fascinated by the peaks of the Beartooth Mountains, one of the largest areas over 10,000 feet in North America, man has been lured to ascend them for generations. One such soul was Fred Inabnit, a mountaineer in every sense, who spent 20 summers in the high country and attempted to reach Granite Peak five times but was unsuccessful. Seasoned forester Elers Koch and his party had the honor of being the first to place "Old Glory" upon the dome of Granite Peak on August 29, 1923. Koch considered the ascent of Granite Peak one of his greatest achievements.

Cattlemen and shepherds took an early foothold in the Beartooths, trailing livestock to the mountain meadows and grazing allotments. Many recall when the high country carried thousands of sheep; now only namesakes of creeks, drainages, and benches echo these early agriculturists. By 1900, many established ranches turned to another sort of revenue. The term *dude* was coined, and accommodations were built. The dude ranch industry was created. Word of these vacations spread until the Northern Pacific Railroad stepped in to help the fledging dude ranch industry. Publicity shots and advertising brochures were created for prospective vacationers, and the railroad benefited with increased passengers. Dude ranches sprouted up in many strategic, scenic locations. In some cases, the operations have survived generations and are still family-owned and active today.

Dr. John Carl Siegfriedt organized the Black and White Trail Association around 1915. Originally, it was to connect Red Lodge with Cody, Wyoming, but efforts were redirected, and by 1919, portions of road were constructed from Bearcreek to Cooke City, with the ultimate goal of access to Yellowstone Park. When money ran short, Siegfriedt did not lose sight, enlisting Red Lodge newspaperman Oliver Shelley and Congressman Scott Leavitt to help. After years of hard promoting and lobbying, Montana senators Thomas Walsh and Burton Wheeler secured federal funding under the 1931 Park Approach Act. By September 1931, road construction was underway on the highway over the Beartooth Mountains. The road was officially opened on June 14, 1936.

Technically, the Beartooth Mountains are a section of the Absaroka Range, named for the children of the large beaked bird: the Appasalooka, or Crow, people. However, some Beartooth aficionados consider the Beartooth Range to include all of the mountainous territory between the Yellowstone and Clarks Fork Rivers. In this book, the boundaries will be roughly delineated by Thomas Turiano's term "the Eastern Beartooths:" the Clarks Fork River of the Yellowstone, the Boulder Canyon area, and edges of the Montana and Wyoming border. However, both the Beartooths and the Absarokas include the territory of the area's crown jewel, the Absaroka-Beartooth Wilderness. The roots of the Forest Service run deep in this area, with the first national reserve, the Yellowstone Park Timber Reserve, established with the Forest Reserve Act of 1891. The entire Beartooth Mountain Range was included in this reserve following the last ceding of lands by the Crow tribe in 1892. The forest family tree officially began in 1902, when the Absarokee and Yellowstone Forest Reserves were established from the Yellowstone Park Reserve.

One

Native Americans, Place Names, and Events

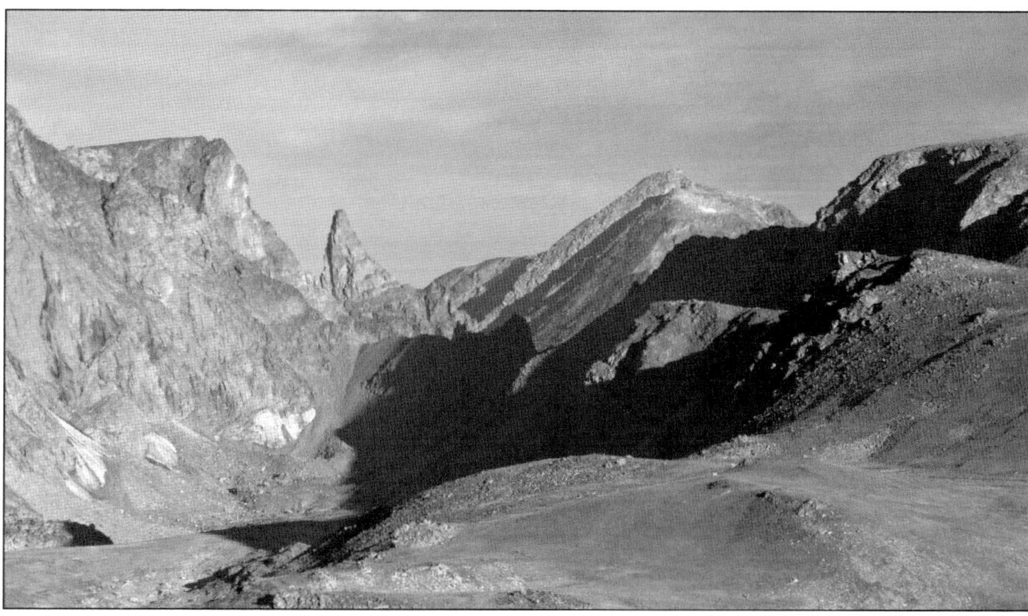

A road sign along the Beartooth Highway indicates that a spire jutting to the west like a fang near Thunder Mountain is the "Bearstooth." According to materials gathered by Crow tribal historian Dr. Joseph Medicine Crow, the term "bearstooth" stems from *Dak Pit Chay Igotush*, meaning "Bear's Small Teeth," referring to the jagged mountain's resemblance to the teeth of a bear. The Crow word *Daxpitcheeihte*, meaning "The mountains are like bear's teeth," is also used. Dr. Medicine Crow also notes that some referred to a particular rock formation as Dak Pit Chay Itagotush, meaning "Bear's Tusk" or "Bear's Small Tusk." Dr. Medicine Crow believes it is feasible that the Crow description of the particular rock formation resembling a bear's tusk or fang may have been used to describe the general area. (Courtesy of Terry Jones.)

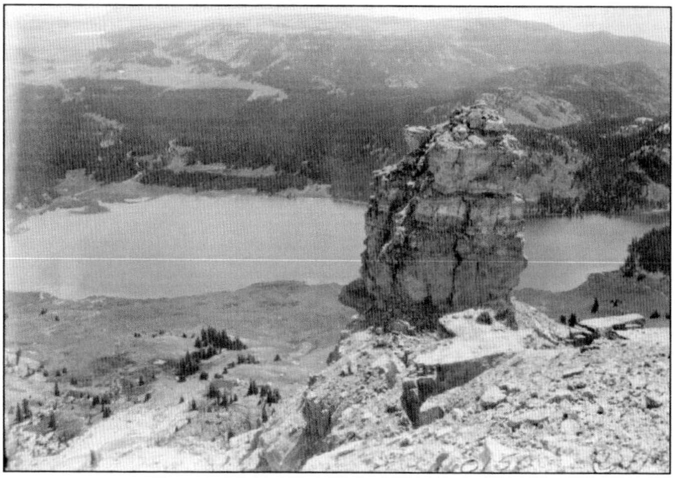

Early promotional materials labeled this pinnacle, near Beartooth Lake, the "Bearstooth." Also promoted was the moniker Nah Pit Sei, coined by the Arts and Crafts Guild of Red Lodge. This term, according to the guild, was a more "balanced and pronounceable" name for Bearstooth, based upon their finding Crow root words for bear's tusk or bear's tooth. (Courtesy of Carbon County Historical Society & Museum.)

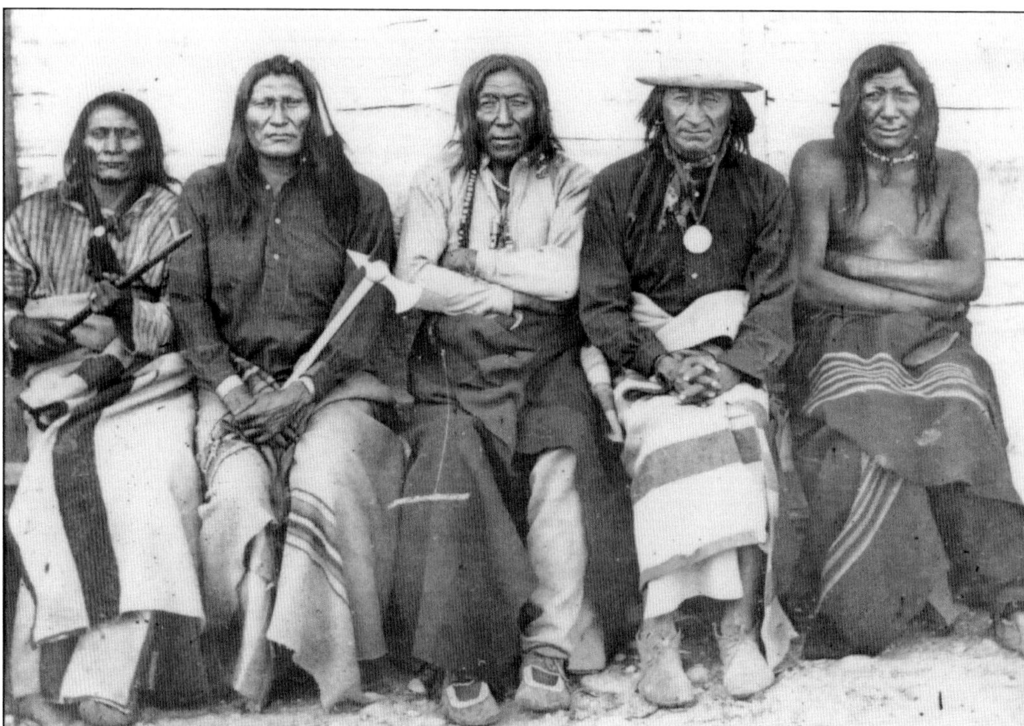

Poor Elk (left) and Blackfoot, or Sits in the Middle of the Land (second from left), photographed here in 1872 at Fort Parker, were among the 11 Crows who signed the Fort Laramie Treaty of 1868. With the signing of this treaty, the Beartooth Mountain region was included in the eight-million-acre Crow reservation, which was a reduction from the 38 million acres set in the 1851 treaty. The eight-page treaty also set the blueprint for future Crow life. (Courtesy of Crazy Mountain Museum.)

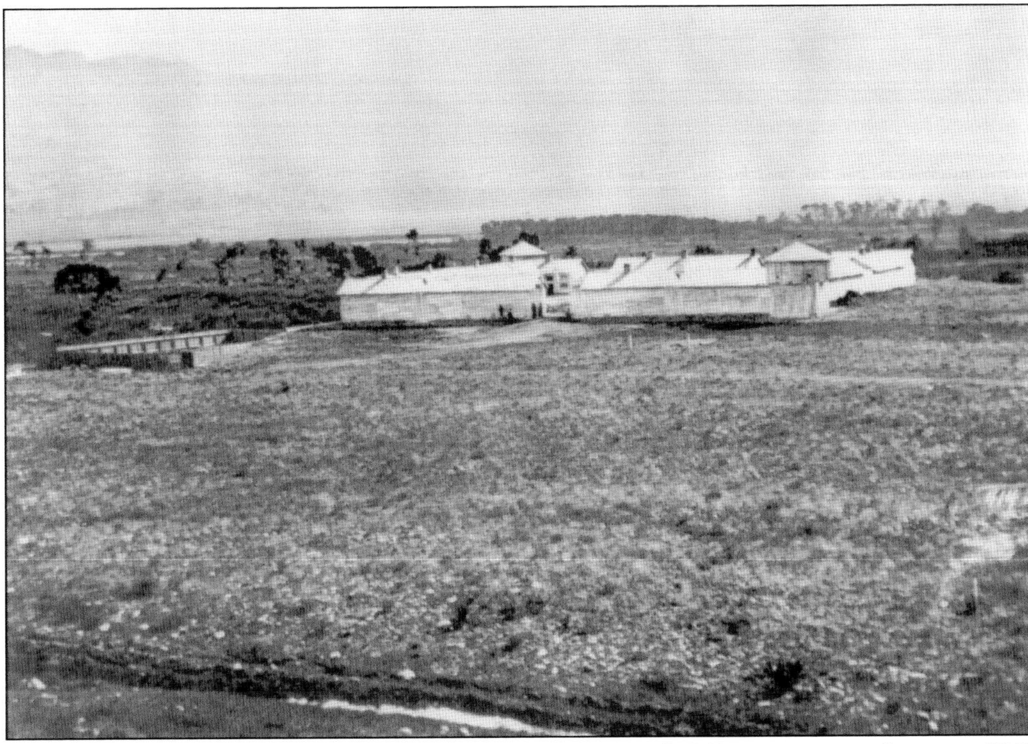

In accordance with the signing of the Fort Laramie Treaty of 1868, construction began in 1869, near Mission Creek, on the first Crow Agency. Named Fort Parker after Ely S. Parker, then commissioner of Indian Affairs in Washington, the agency included an agent, a physician, carpenters, a farmer, an engineer, and blacksmiths, as well as a school. It was more commonly called the Mission Agency. After an 1872 fire, it was rebuilt with adobe brick. (Courtesy of Crazy Mountain Museum.)

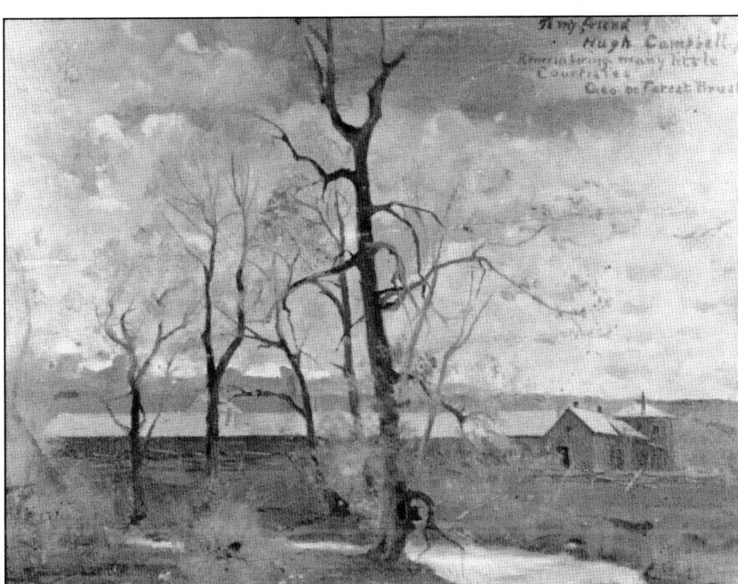

The Crow Agency was relocated south of Absarokee in 1875 to a site overlooking the East Rosebud River. It was hoped this land was more suited for agriculture and farther from whiskey traders. However, perhaps the real motive for relocation was pressure from the increasing mining and agricultural interests in the western portion of Crow land, who demanded a reduced reservation. (Courtesy of Museum of the Beartooths.)

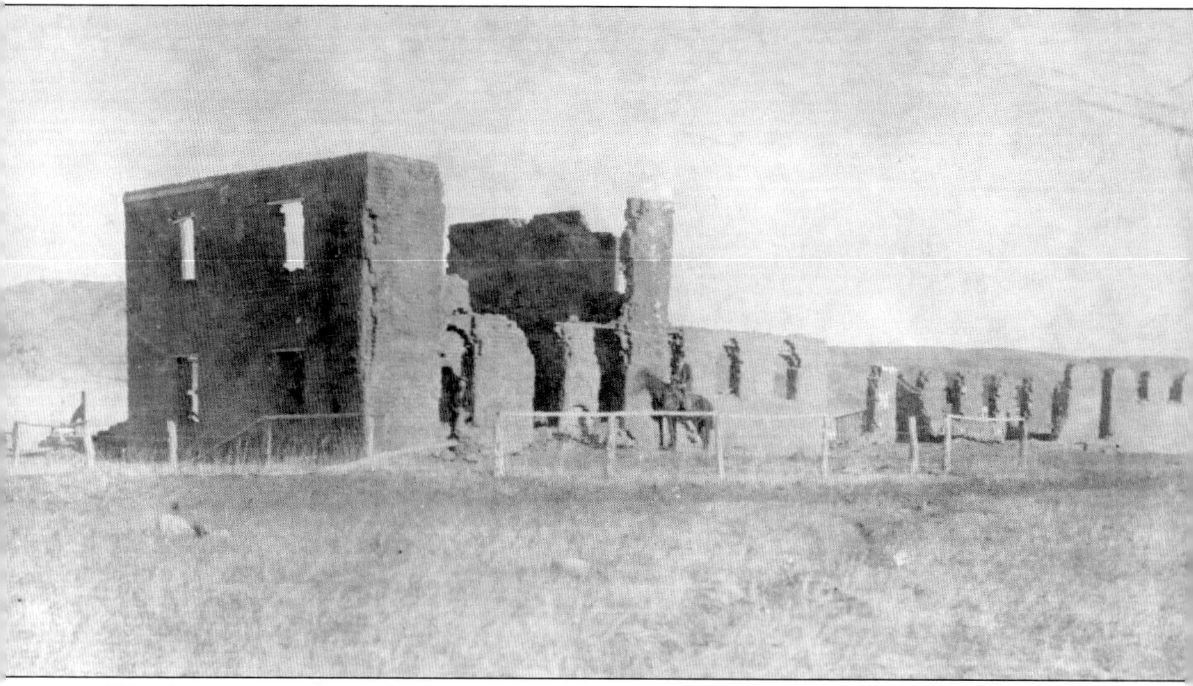

The Crows were relocated again in 1884–1885 to their present-day agency along the Little Big Horn River near Hardin. This 1895 photograph shows the ruins of the second Crow Agency, which had been witness to plenty of activity. In 1876, Crow scouts, including "Curley," were recruited here for the campaign against the Sioux and Cheyenne resulting in the Battle of Little Big Horn. The next year, six Crow scouts and a French guide were hired by Col. Samuel Sturgis of the 7th Cavalry and sent to the Clarks Fork River in search of the Nez Percé as they made their attempt to flee to Canada. Sturgis remained at the agency for a week, waiting for the return of the scouts. When they did not return, fearing that the Nez Percé were fleeing east out of Yellowstone Park, he took his force to the mouth of Clarks Fork Canyon. (Courtesy of Museum of the Beartooths.)

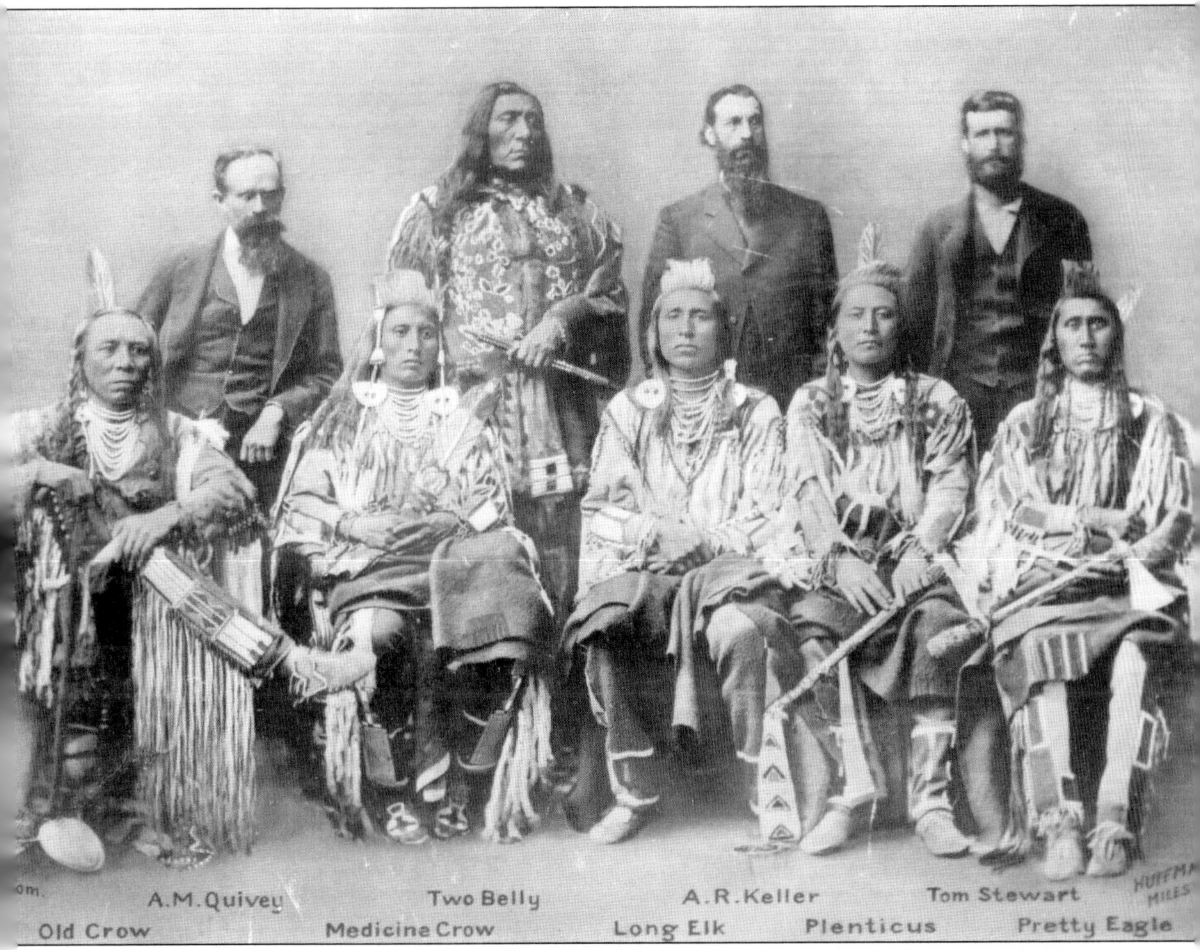

This 1880 Crow delegation, along with the two interpreters and agent shown here, traveled by stage from the Crow Agency via Virginia City to the rail station in Salt Lake City and onward to Washington, DC. On the agenda, arranged by Crow agent A.R. Keller, was a meeting with Pres. Rutherford B. Hayes, who hoped to convince the Crow to locate to another reservation or at least reduce a portion of their land for the railroad. During the monthlong tour, stops were made at the Capitol, Mount Vernon, and a zoo. On April 11, 1882, one and a half million acres, including a major portion of the Beartooths, was ceded to the US government. Pressure for even more Crow land continued, and the Tripa Commission was appointed to negotiate a 400-foot right-of-way for the Northern Pacific Railroad to cross the Crow reservation. This was approved by Congress on July 10, 1882. In 1892, one point eight million more acres were removed from the Crow reservation and opened to homesteading. (Courtesy of Museum of the Beartooths.)

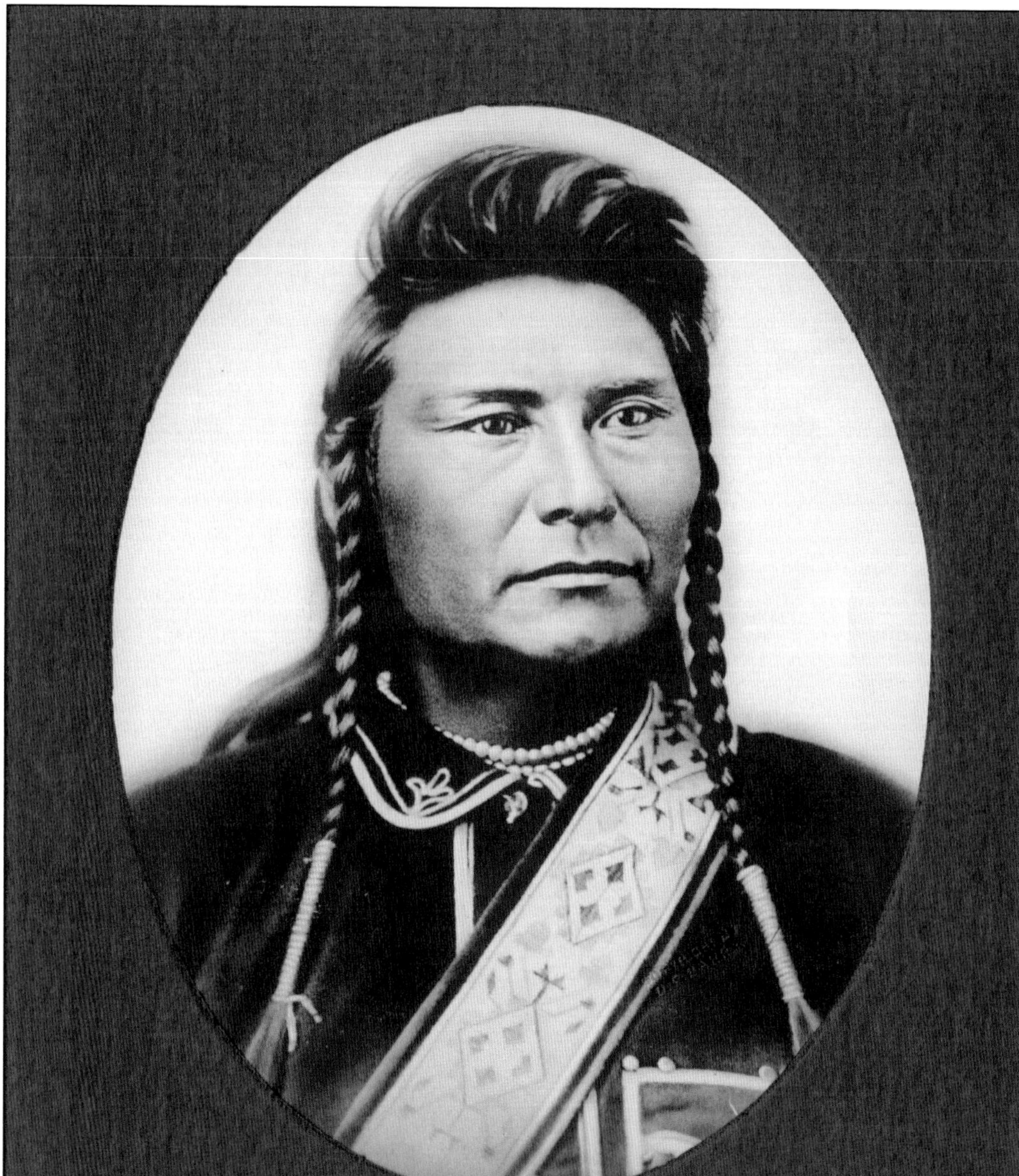

In the summer of 1877, Chief Joseph, seen here in a portrait by Frank Jay Haynes, led his band of 800 Nez Percé men, women, and children, under the military guidance of Looking Glass, from Wallowa Valley in Idaho towards Canada. They entered the Beartooth region of the Clarks Fork Canyon after a melee in Yellowstone Park in which they took tourists captive and killed two. By evasive tactics and strategic use of the terrain, they managed to evade both Gen. Oliver Otis Howard and Col. Samuel Sturgis, killing several prospectors on their way through Clarks Fork Canyon. Their epic 1,700-mile journey was stopped 40 miles short of the Canadian border by Gen. Nelson Miles. It was here that Joseph delivered his surrender speech, saying, "I will fight no more forever." (Courtesy of Montana State University at Billings Special Collections.)

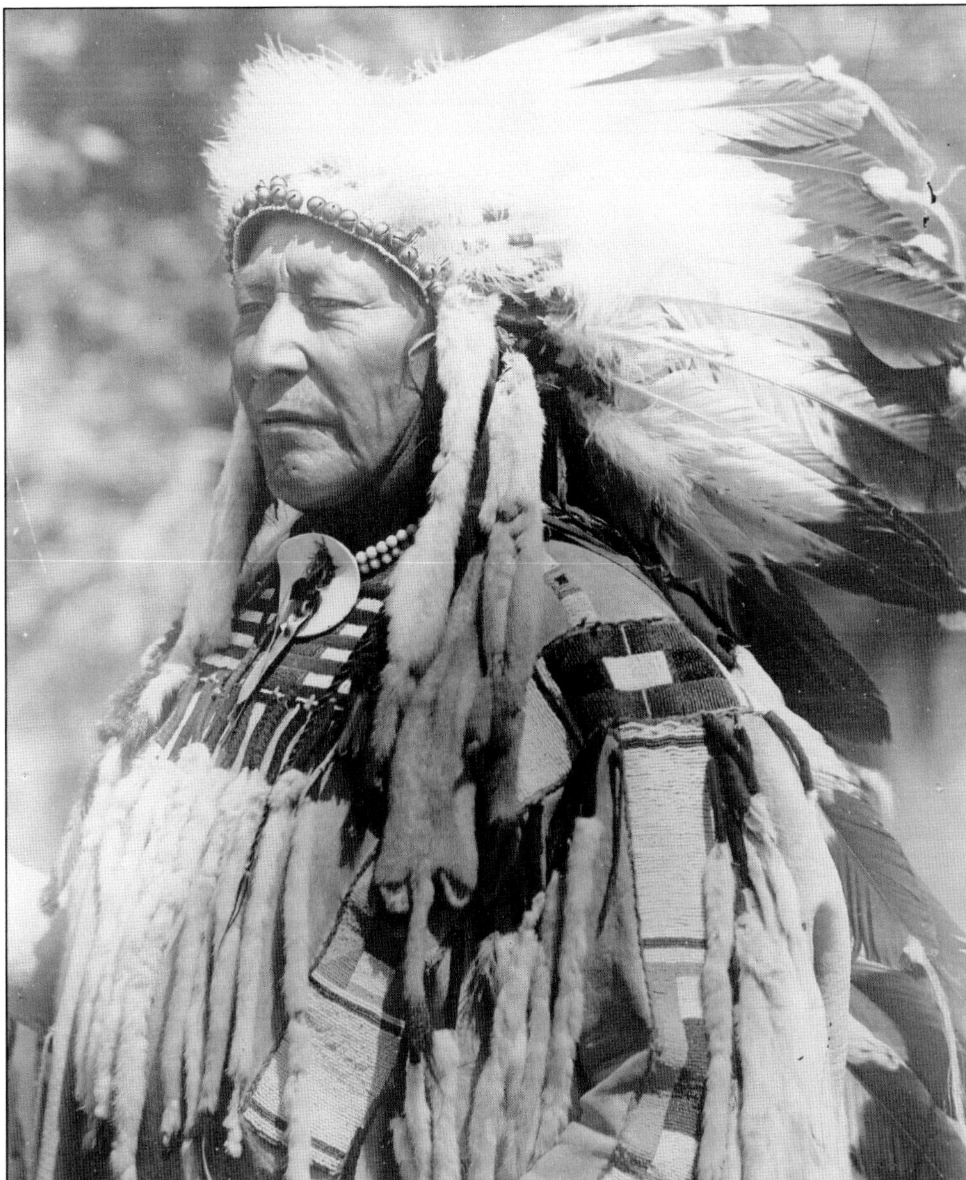

Plenty Coups, who lived from 1848 to 1932, was given the birth name Chíilaphuchissaaleesh, or "Buffalo Bull Facing the Wind." As a young man, his grandfather changed his name, christening him Alaxchiiaahush, or "Many Achievements." As a young boy at tribal gatherings in the Beartooth Mountains, Plenty Coups dreamed of belonging to the Fox warrior society. Joining it early in his career, he became a feared warrior. But Plenty Coups is best remembered for his tribe leadership in its transition from the "buffalo days" to reservation life. He was one of the first Crow leaders to farm, harvesting hay in 1880–1881 with Chiefs Medicine Crow and Pretty Eagle at the second Crow Agency. He represented all American Indians at the Burial of the Unknown Soldier in Washington in 1921. As a memorial, Plenty Coups and his wife, Strikes the Iron, made an agreement with the US Department of the Interior to set aside their land for park and recreation, thus creating Plenty Coups State Park. Upon his death, the Crow people designated him as their last traditional tribal chief. (Courtesy of Museum of the Beartooths.)

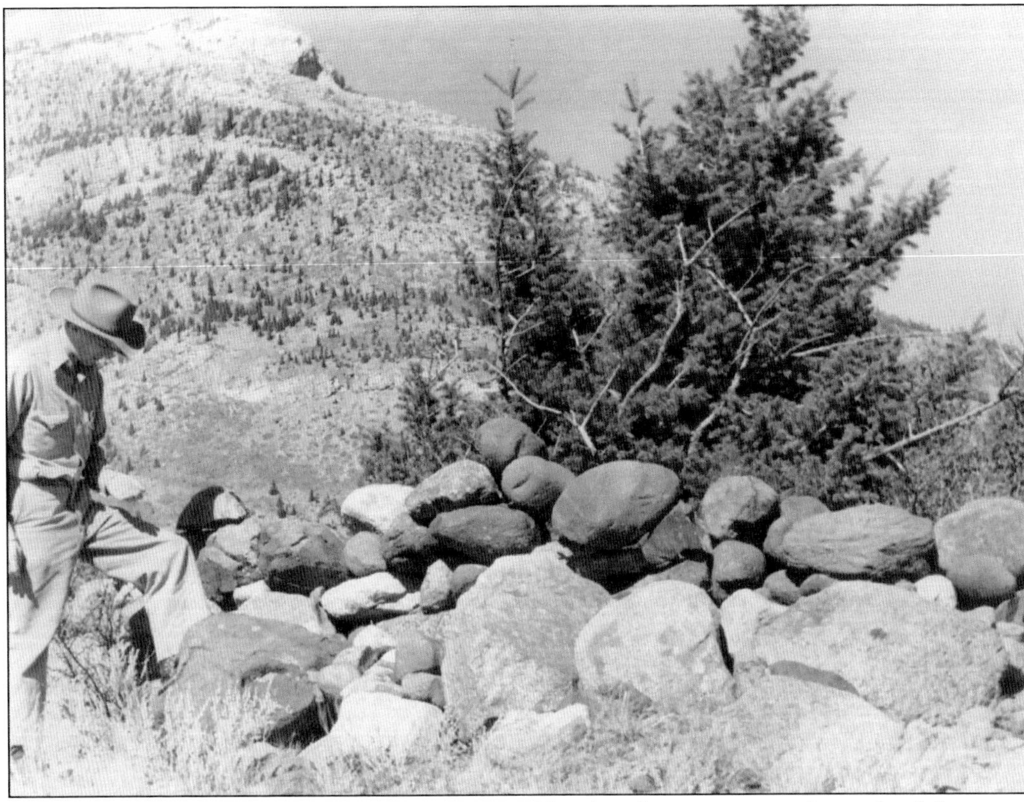

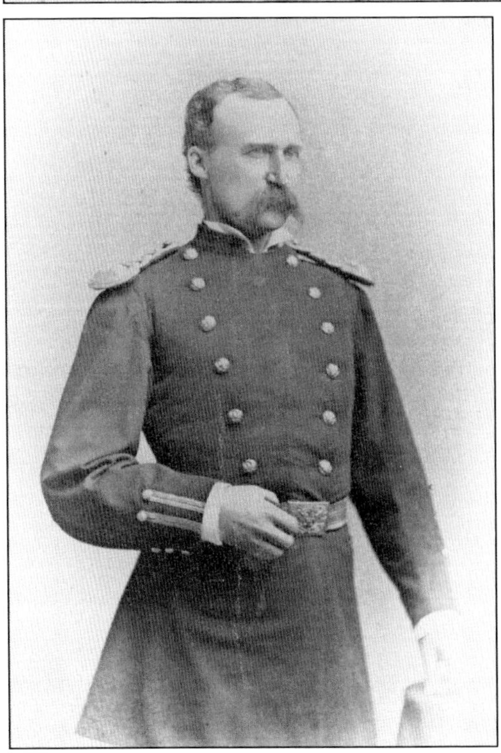

This fortification, one mile south of the Natural Bridge, was built by Lt. Hobart Bailey and 30 of his men in September 1878 to prevent Bannock Indians from fleeing from their Fort Hall, Idaho, reservation towards the Arapaho Trail. Instead, they fled through another corridor near Clark, Wyoming, and their journey ended in a battle on Bennett Creek with Gen. Nelson Miles. (Courtesy of Pioneer Museum–Bozeman.)

In the battle between Bannock Indians and General Miles near Bennett Creek, 11 Bannocks were killed and 31 were captured. Capt. Andrew S. Bennett, the creek's namesake, pictured here, also died in the battle. "Frenchy" Bethune, also known as "Little Rock," who was serving as a scout and lived with the Bannocks, betraying them by reporting their approach to the Crow Agency, was killed as well. Littlerock Creek is named for him. A Crow named Two Crows is another known casualty. (Courtesy of Waukesha County Historical Society & Museum.)

Two

MOUNTAIN ROUTES

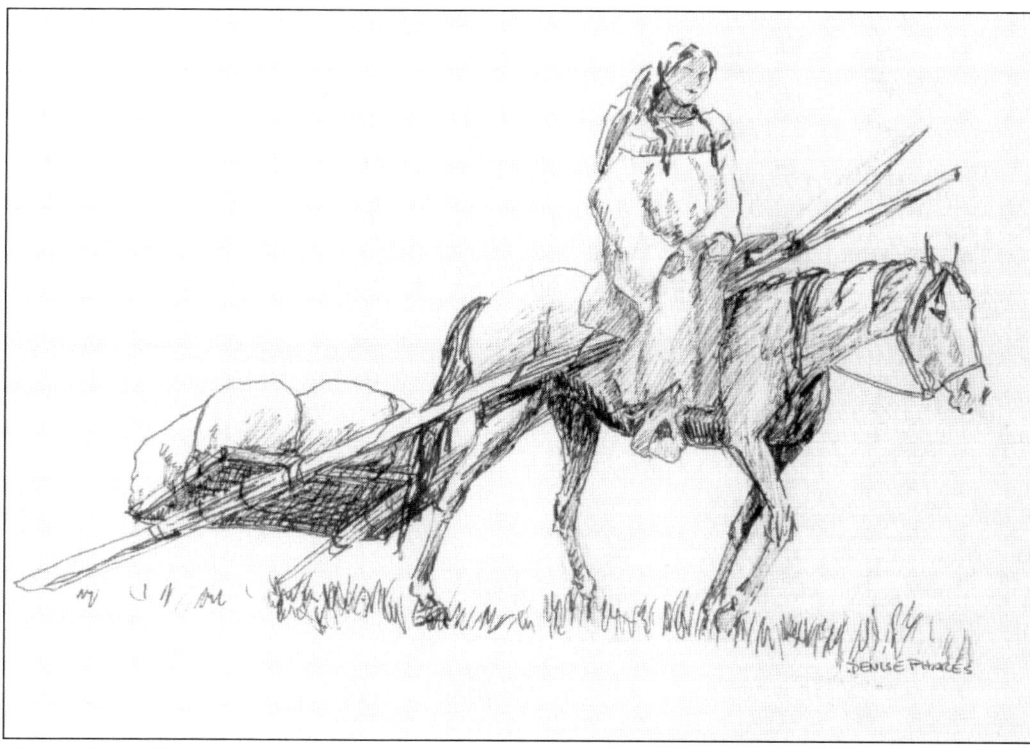

Generations of Native Americans traveled the corridors of the Beartooth Mountains. The Bannock Trail, or Great Trail, led from Idaho to the southern edge of the Beartooths before dropping to the Clarks Fork River and reaching the eastern plains, where the buffalo roamed. The Mountain Trail passed east from Livingston through Boulder River's drainages to Stillwater River, skirting the Beartooth front to eventually connect with the Meeteetse Trail east of Red Lodge. This trail led to Trail Creek, part of the Great North Trail. Meeteetse Trail was later used as an Army supply line and a stage and mail line connecting Billings, Red Lodge, and Meeteetse, Wyoming. (Courtesy of Denise Phares.)

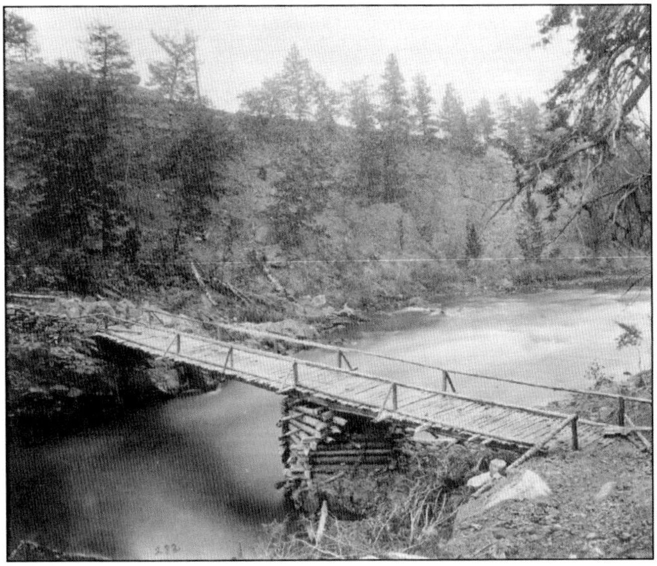

John Baronett, also known as "Yellowstone Jack," pursued several different careers, including soldier, miner, guide, and sailor. In 1864, he was an early gold prospector near what is now Yellowstone, building this bridge across the Yellowstone River that gave prospectors and suppliers from the mining development of Cooke City access to the Yellowstone area. Photographed by William Henry Jackson in 1871, the bridge was partially burned by the Nez Percé in their 1877 flight. (Courtesy of Yellowstone National Park, No. 7516.)

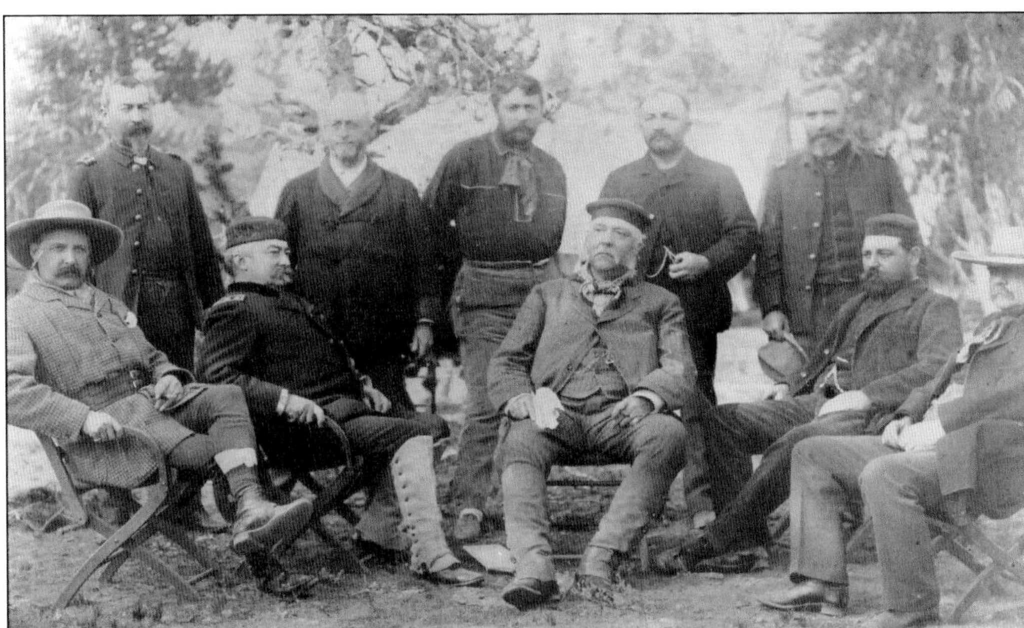

Pictured with Pres. Chester Arthur (center right, seated) is Gen. Philip Sheridan (center left, seated), who entered the Yellowstone region in 1882 on an inspection tour of Fort Washakie and the Wind River country. Leaving Cooke City on August 26, Sheridan hired a guide, thinking he could save three days' travel. The party passed Beartooth Butte and followed the Line Creek divide, eventually reaching the mouth of the Clarks Fork River. Portions of the current Beartooth Highway follow Sheridan's trail. (Courtesy of Parmly Billings Library.)

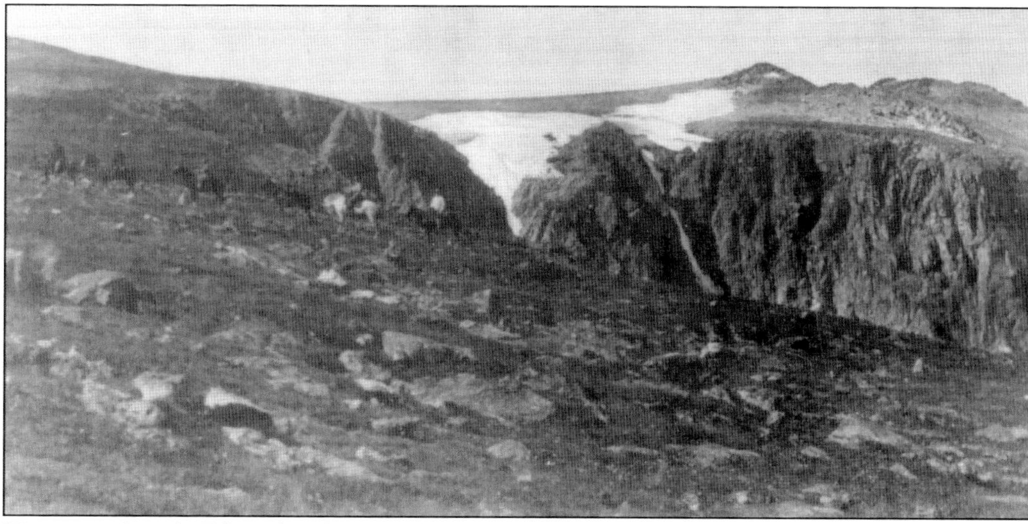

Hunter and guide Edward Earl Van Dyke blazed a trail with his father in 1883 from Cooke City to Red Lodge. The trail began at Mirror Lake, about 25 miles south of Red Lodge, circled the lake basin, and crossed over the Rock Creek divide to the Clarks Fork River. Van Dyke had a cabin near Wolf Creek but usually picked up his hunting parties at the railroad depot in Columbus. Teddy Roosevelt was a member of these hunting parties before he became president. (Courtesy of Special Collections, Montana State University Library, Bozeman.)

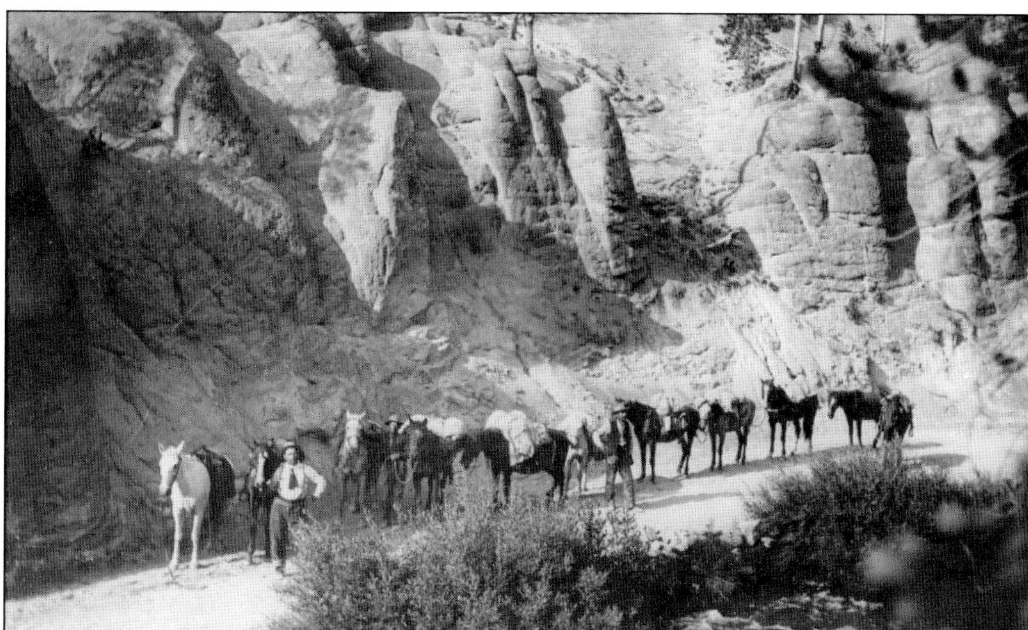

From left to right, pioneers Dan Bedford, George Lathom, and Bert Chambers file through Lodge Pole Pass in 1893. This approximately 30-mile route from Lodge Pole Creek near Nye to Myers Creek traversed the Deer Creeks to the East Boulder River, moving westward to the Livingston area. Traveling this trail in 1902, Malcolm Mackay saw signs of wolf, grizzly bear, and elk en route to his destination in Mammoth Hot Springs. (Courtesy of Museum of the Beartooths.)

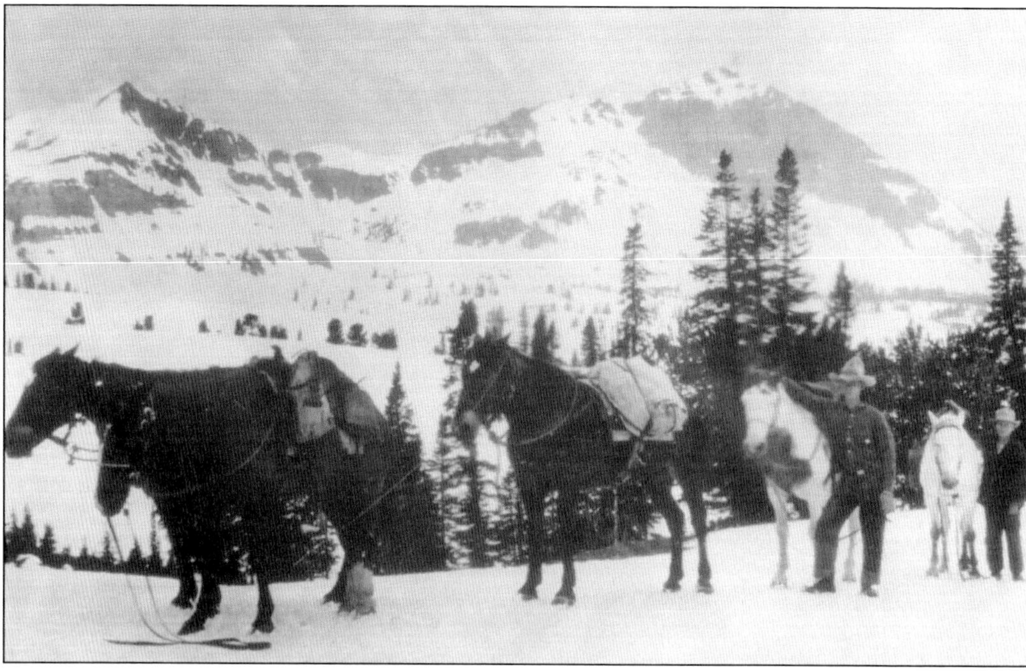

Stanley Peterson (left) and Russell Olson, with Wolverine Mountain in the background, pack for the Forest Service on the Nye–to–Cooke City trail. While there is no hard evidence of its exact path, this 40-mile trail is mentioned numerous times. In the 1880s, mail was carried from the Nye mining camp along the Stillwater River. Carriers would travel by snowshoe in the winter, skiing their way to the top, where, in some accounts, stages would retrieve the mail and bring it to Cooke City. (Courtesy of Museum of the Beartooths.)

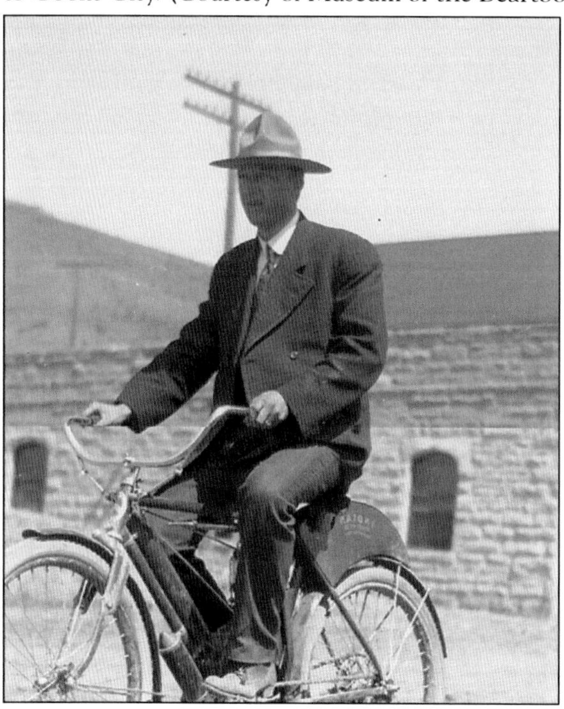

In 1906, Dr. John Carl Siegfriedt arrived in Bearcreek, Montana, from Iowa to practice medicine. Around 1915, he organized the Black and White Trail Association with himself as president. He was mayor of Bearcreek for several terms, and his goal was to build a road from Red Lodge to Cody, but promotional projects and events for the road were put on hold as America entered World War I. (Courtesy of Special Collections, Montana State University Library, Bozeman.)

By the close of the war, Dr. Siegfriedt's intentions for the Black and White Trail had changed, and he now wanted to build a road from Bearcreek to Cooke City for access to Yellowstone Park. By 1919, a total of 2,100 feet of trail was in condition for auto travel. T.V. "Red" Hatcher, the assistant engineer pictured here, laid out 12 or 13 switchbacks beginning from Bearcreek—Scotch Coulee—up the east side of Mount Maurice. (Courtesy of Carbon County Historical Society & Museum.)

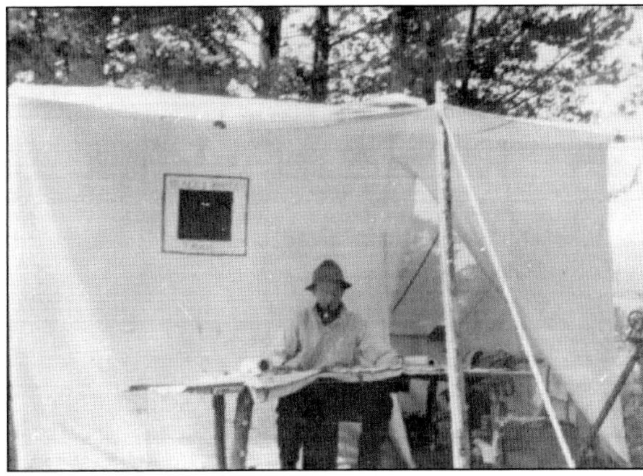

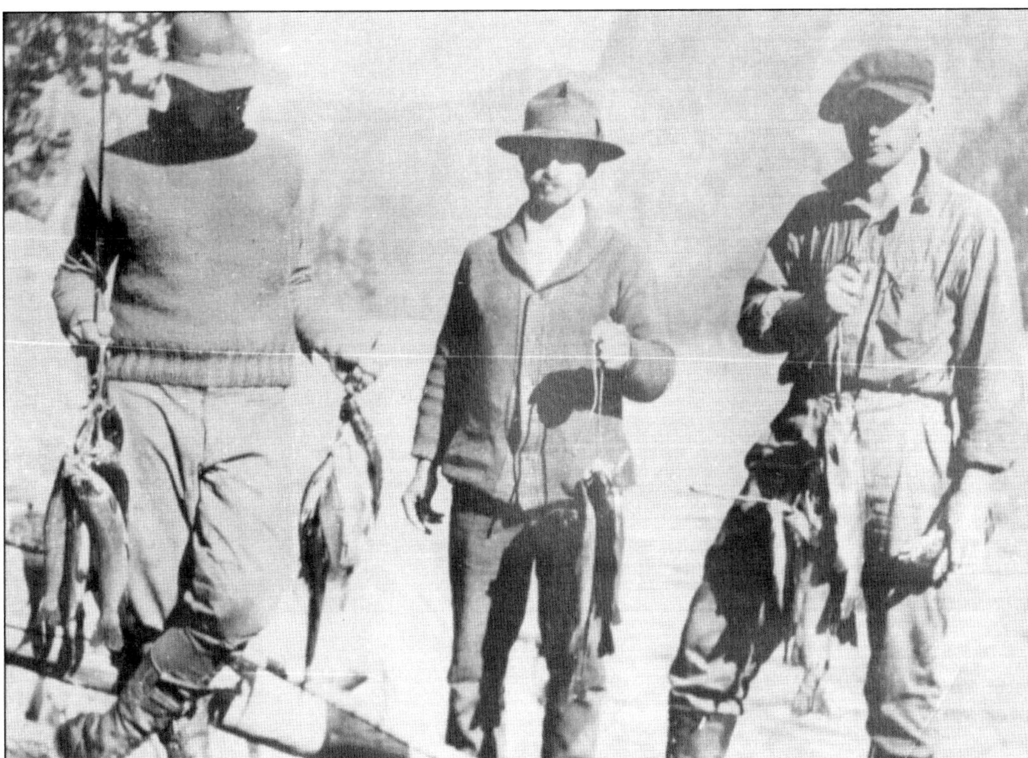

By the spring of 1920, Dr. Siegfriedt had raised enough money to run a reconnaissance survey to Cooke City from the east side of Mount Maurice, going through Line Creek Plateau and past Beartooth Lake down to the Clarks Fork River into Cooke City. The route provided good fishing for the survey crew, including, from left to right, transit man Walter Columbus, packer Melvin Martin, and Fred Annula. Due to a lack of proficient funding, the Black and White Trail was abandoned. (Courtesy of Carbon County Historical Society & Museum.)

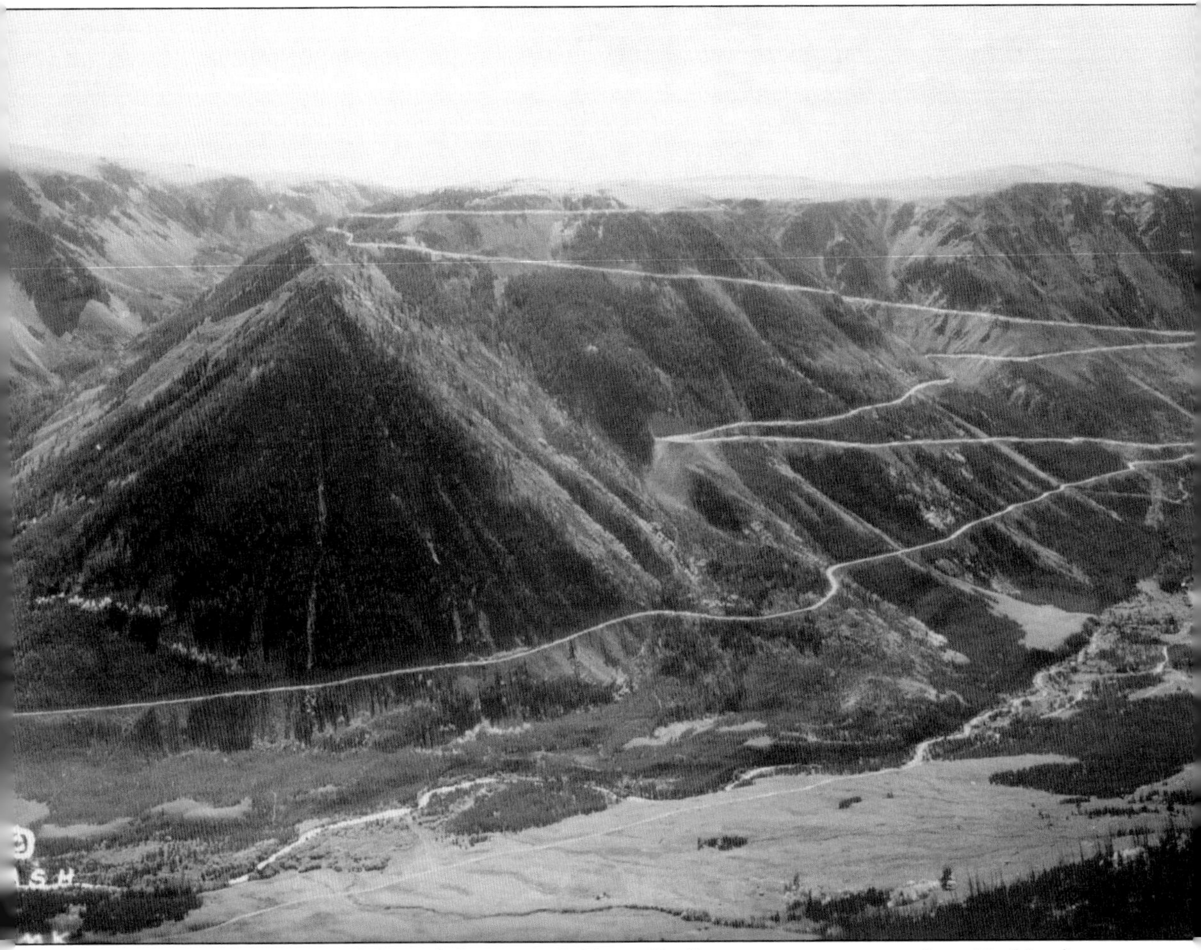

Dr. Siegfriedt's dream did not fade. He and Oliver Shelley, a newspaperman from Red Lodge, were determined to get federal funding. By 1927, a field survey was conducted. Congressman Scott Leavitt reviewed several route options, including the current route up the Rock Creek drainage, at an estimated cost of $1.14 million ($14.4 million today); a second route down the Stillwater valley to Big Timber, at $985,000; and a third route down the Clark Fork valley to Cody, Wyoming, at $915,000. He selected the first—the higher, more scenic route pictured here, which followed up Rock Creek just south of Red Lodge and utilized a series of six spectacular switchbacks to wind to the top of the Bearcreek Plateau and westward on to Cooke City. (Courtesy of Carbon County Historical Society & Museum.)

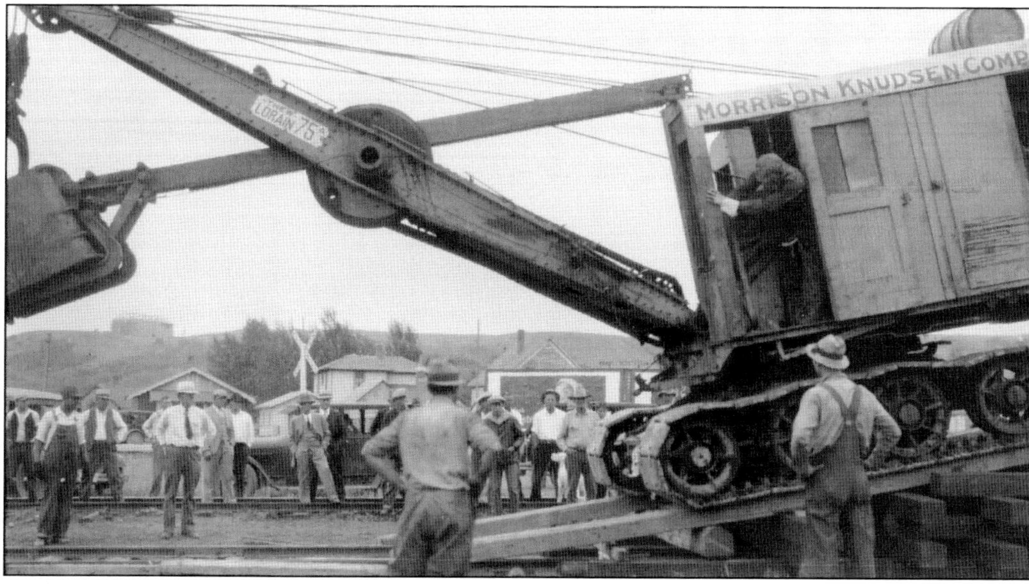

With Congressman Leavitt's help, the Montana delegation of senators, Thomas Walsh and Burton Wheeler, secured funding under the 1931 Park Approach Act signed by Pres. Herbert Hoover. By September 1931, road construction was under way, and the Morrison-Knudsen Company offloaded this Lorain 75 diesel shovel in Red Lodge. (Courtesy of Carbon County Historical Society & Museum.)

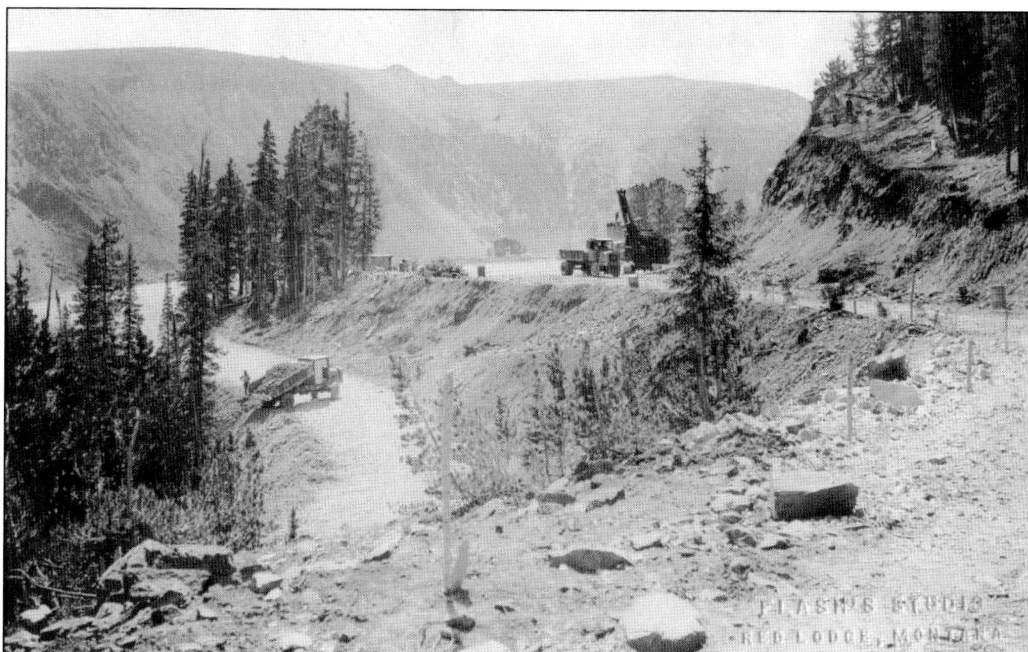

The work was divided among three contractors, with Morrison-Knudsen responsible for 11.93 miles of switchbacks from Quad Creek southwest of Red Lodge to Twin Lakes, McNutt & Pyle contracted for 25.16 miles, and Winston Brothers, of Minnesota, covering the last 18 miles to Yellowstone National Park. Morrison-Knudsen set up construction camp near the present-day M-K campgrounds along Rock Creek. (Courtesy of Carbon County Historical Society & Museum.)

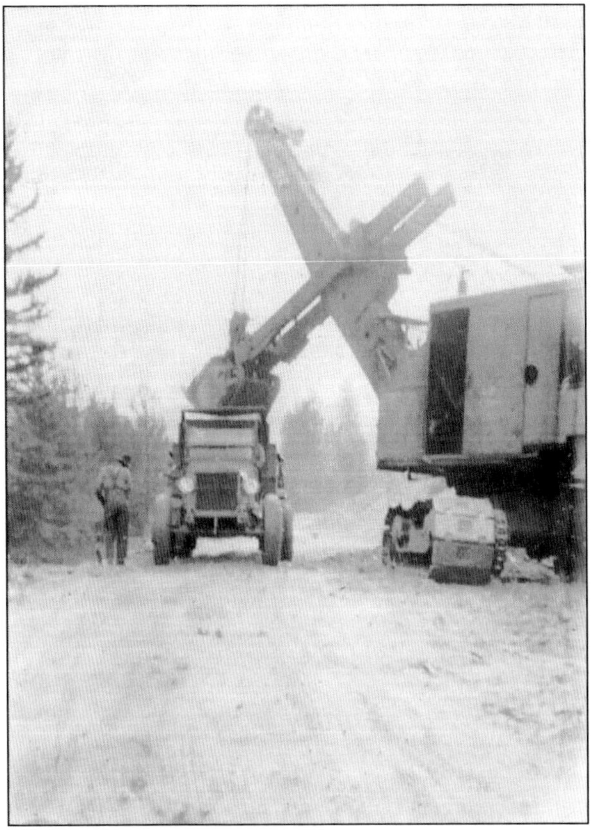

In 1934, skilled men such as these, here operating a caterpillar RD8 and a diesel shovel, were paid $1 per hour, while unskilled workers made 60¢. In bad winter weather, an additional 10¢ per hour was paid. Construction accidents took the lives of two workers. Glen Welch, a McNutt & Pyle employee, was killed when a powder blast discharged prematurely, and Waino Timonen, a Red Lodge native employed by Morrison-Knudsen Company, died when he fell into the pulley system of a rock crusher. (Both, courtesy of Carbon County Historical Society & Museum.)

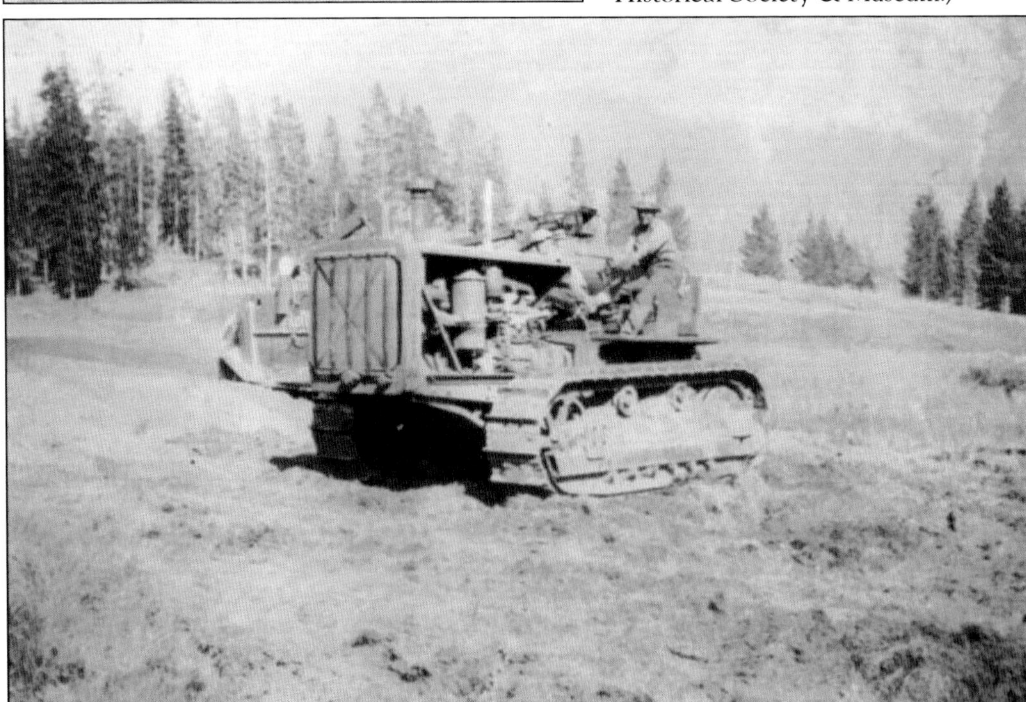

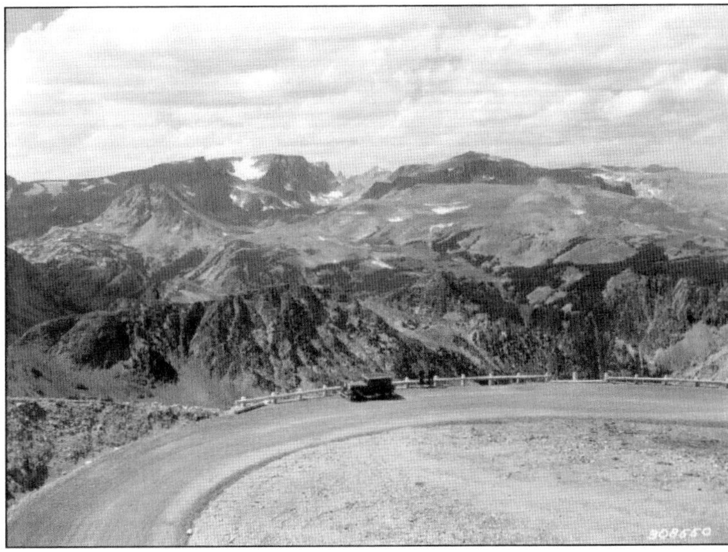

Beartooth Highway, a 68-mile corridor beginning south of Red Lodge and ending near the Northeast Entrance to Yellowstone National Park, rises to 10,947 feet at Beartooth Pass in Wyoming. The road officially opened on June 14, 1936. A 54-mile section of the highway has been awarded All-American Road status and celebrated its 75th anniversary in 2011. (Courtesy of USFS, Custer National Forest.)

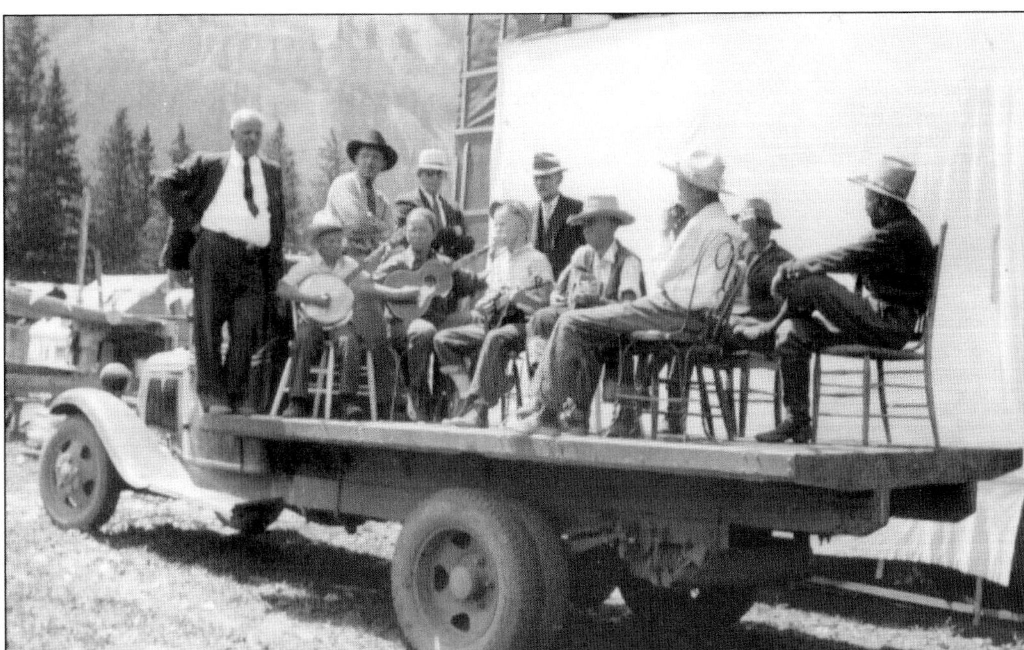

An informational meeting about the highway featuring musical accompaniment was held in Cooke City in 1935. Present are, from left to right, Dr. Siegfriedt, Bob Herlevi (playing banjo), C.W. Post (standing with cowboy hat), Vern Waples (with guitar), Oliver Shelley (standing with hat), Sigrud Tervo, unidentified, Matti Koski (sitting with guitar), two unidentified, and "Pack Saddle Ben" Greenough. (Courtesy of Carbon County Historical Society & Museum.)

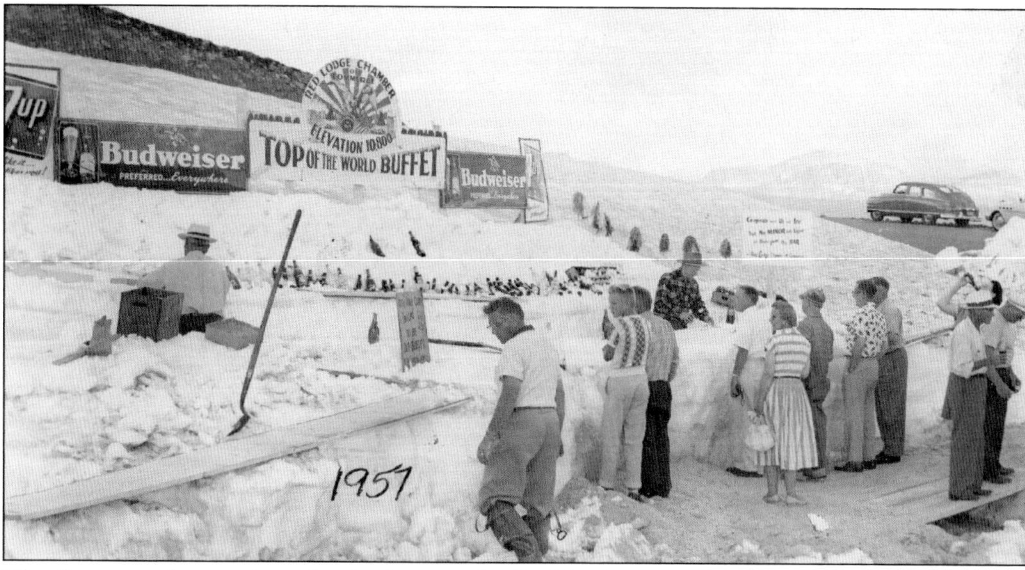

The first surprise serving of refreshments by Red Lodge organizations to travelers over the Beartooth Highway began in 1947. This tradition celebrating the highway featured the Top of the World Bar, which was carved from snow on the pass. The one-day event attracted many, but the tradition ended in 1985. (Courtesy of Marlene Donelson.)

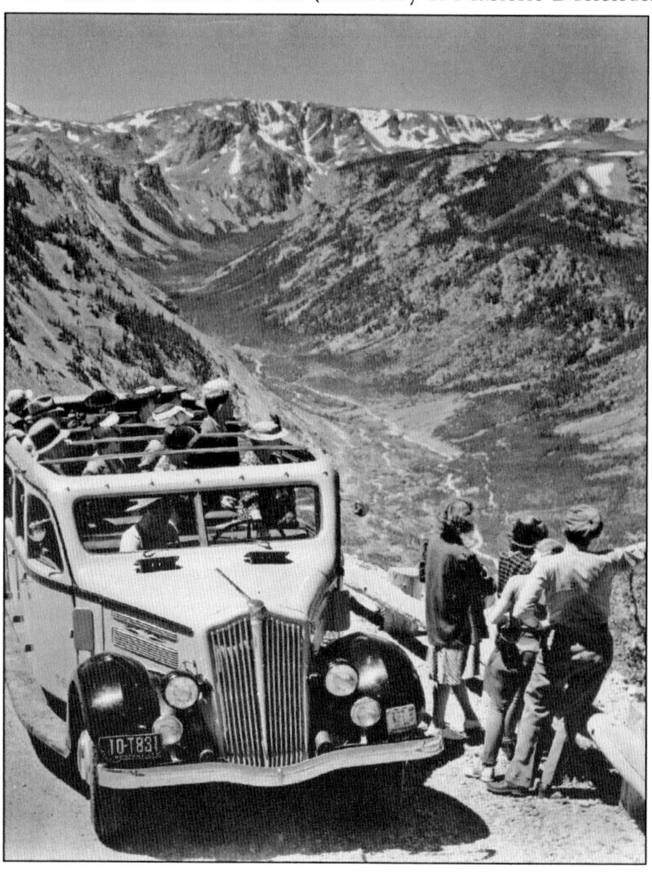

On August 1, 1915, the first automobiles were allowed in Yellowstone Park, and as a result, tourism came to the Cooke City area as travelers passed through on the Beartooth Highway. A growing number of visitors took advantage of the Yellowstone Park touring bus seen here. (Courtesy of Carbon County Historical Society & Museum.)

Three

MEN AND MOUNTAINS

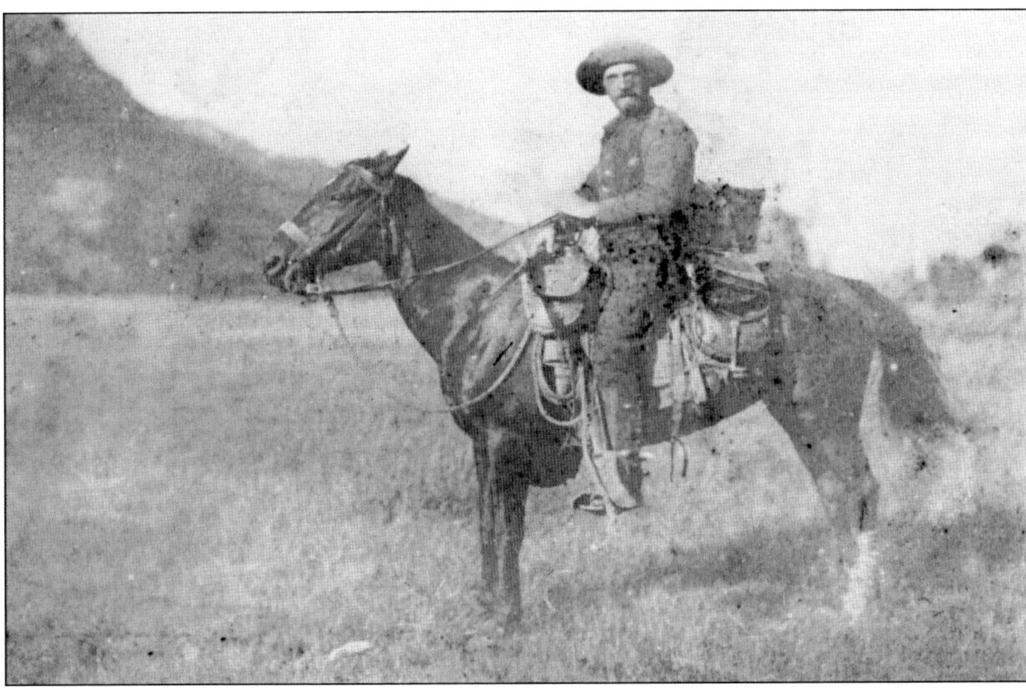

The greater Yellowstone and Beartooth region was surveyed by geologist Arnold Hague from 1883 to 1897. In an effort to fully comprehend the region, he organized a small party in 1893 to study the volcanic fields in the eastern area. Thomas Jaggar, a Harvard geology graduate, assisted him and wrote a detailed diary. Upon departing Bozeman, the party traveled up the Boulder River, stopping at Solomon City, a mining camp at an elevation of 8,000 feet near the Independence mine. His diary chronicles visits to Cooke City, where supplies were cached and purchased. He also explored the mining area and climbed Republic Peak. Explorations eventually led them to the Clarks Fork Canyon, where Jaggar's trusty steed, Bessy, fell with him. After explorations in the Absaroka Mountains, the party returned to Bozeman, where Jaggar was disgusted "to come out of the back wood to this tourist place." (Courtesy of Yellowstone National Park, No. 9274.)

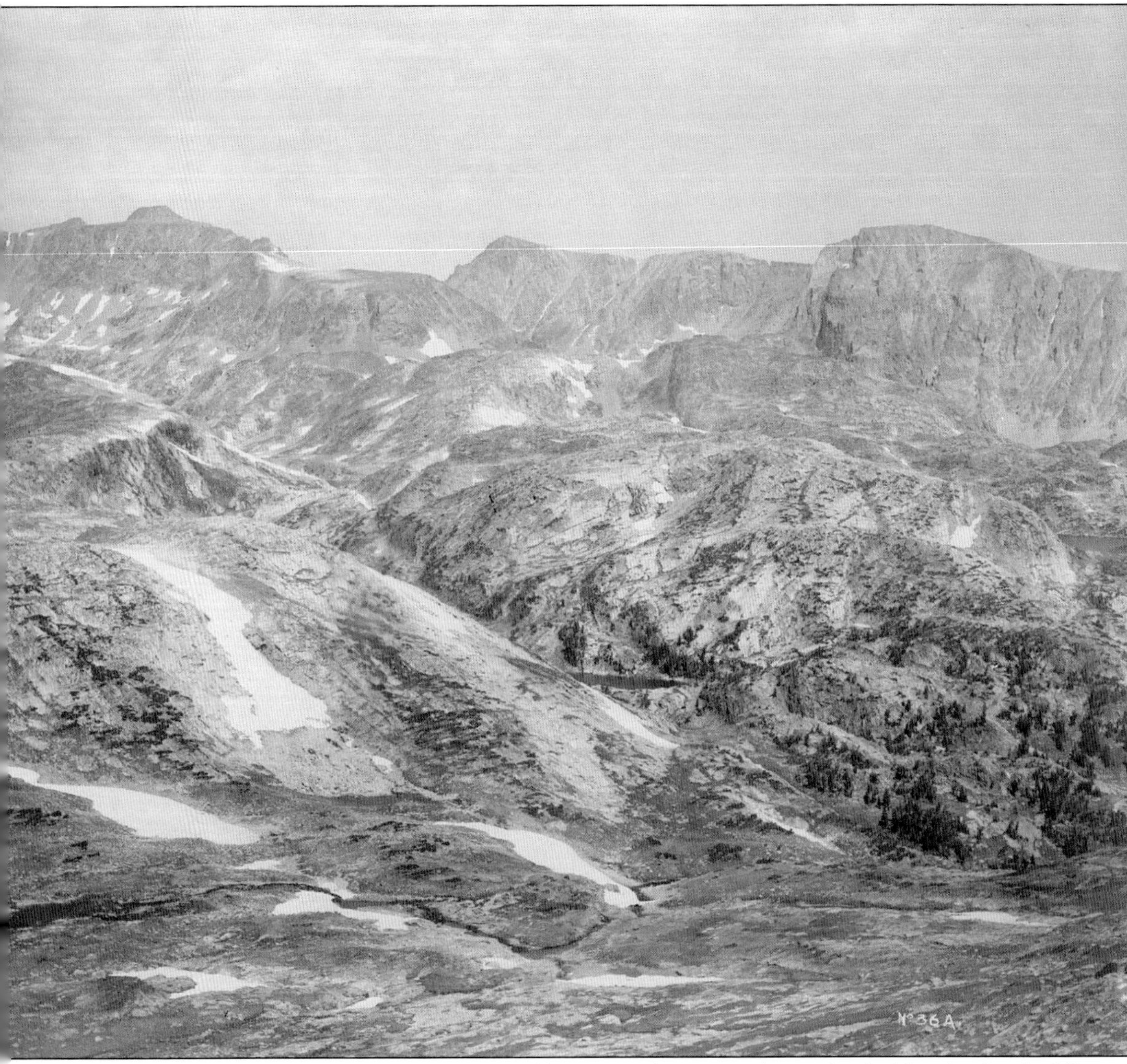

In 1898, geologist James Putnam Kimball organized an expedition funded by the Rockefeller family and the Rocky Fork Coal Company to the Beartooths, then known as the Granites, to discover veins of extractable minerals and complete a topographic map between Cooke City and Nye, Montana. Although geologist William Holmes had been in the region some 20 years prior, Kimball's party was the first to meticulously record its activities. Outfitted in Bozeman with eight saddle horses and nine pack animals, the party reached Cooke City on July 24, 1898, to begin their

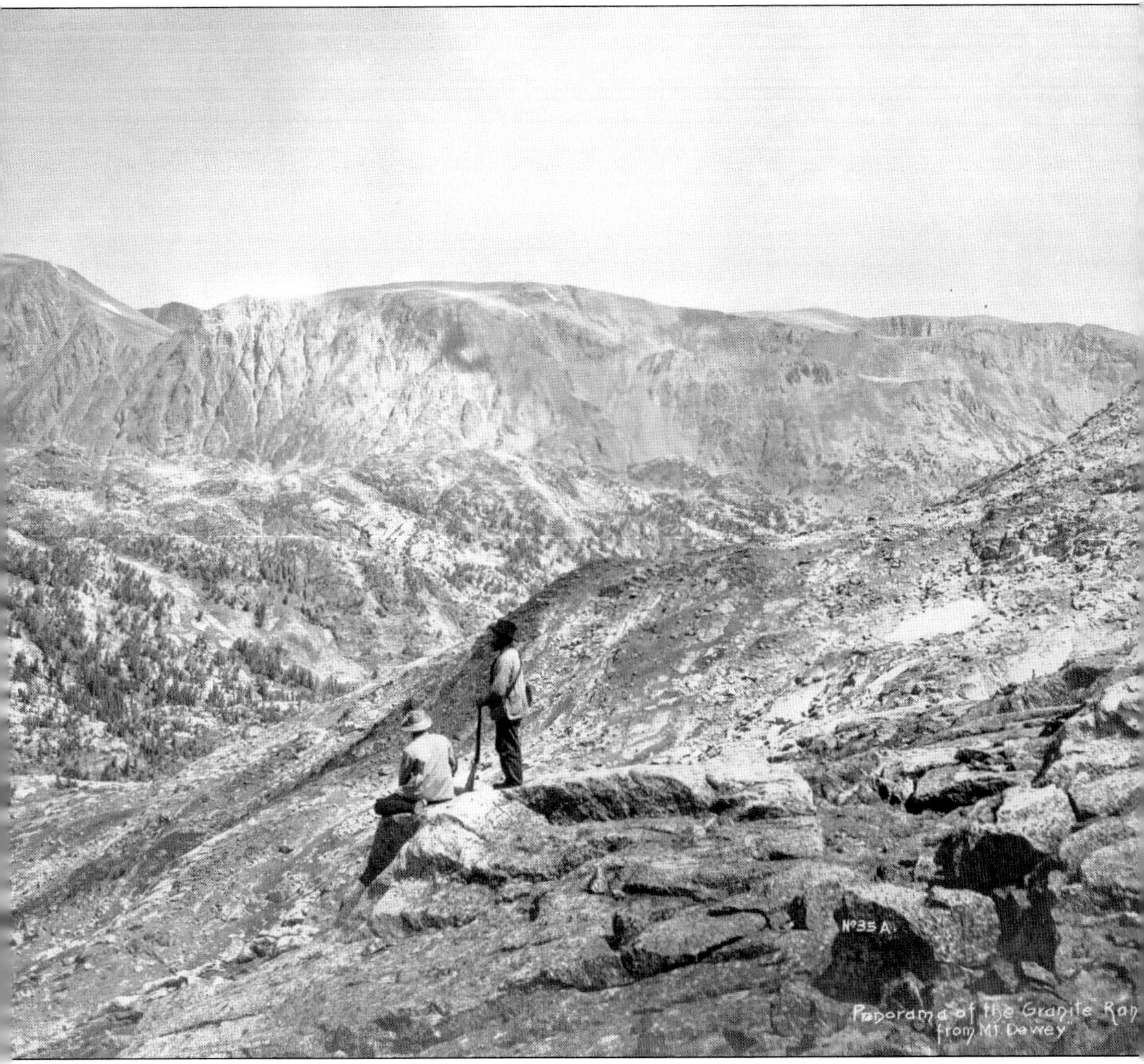

chronicles of peaks and passes. Kimball, who regarded the Beartooths as "terra incognita and a mystery," ventured into the unknown week after week. Several attempts to reach the summit of Mount Dewey were thwarted due to bad weather. However, a few party members reached the apex, and Andres Wilse took this panorama of the mountains. They named the peak Mount Dewey in honor Kimball's friend Adm. George Dewey, who was serving in the Spanish-American War. (Courtesy of Montana Historical Society.)

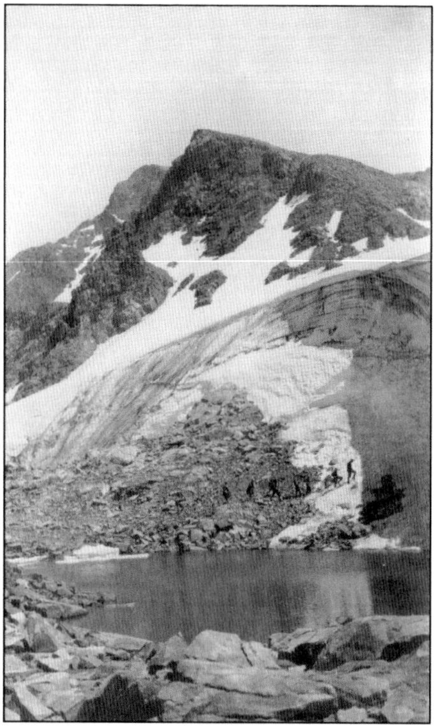

Andres Wilse, who had a photography business in Seattle, was offered the job of mapping and photographing with the Kimball expedition. While climbing a 12,000-foot peak to take the measurements of a watercourse, he discovered a glacier with "stripes that went sideways across it, they were piles of dead grasshoppers." He filled a flask with some samples and caused quite a stir in camp. He later named it Mount Wilse, and it is now known as Grasshopper Glacier. It is estimated that the grasshoppers were 200 years old and had become embedded in the ice when swarms were migrating and got caught in a storm or chilled, depositing them on the forming glacier. Today, preserved grasshoppers are difficult to find. The glacier, at 11,000 feet, is approximately one mile long and a half-mile wide and is receding from a length of more than four miles. (Left, courtesy of Special Collections, Montana State University Library, Bozeman; below, courtesy of Library of Congress.)

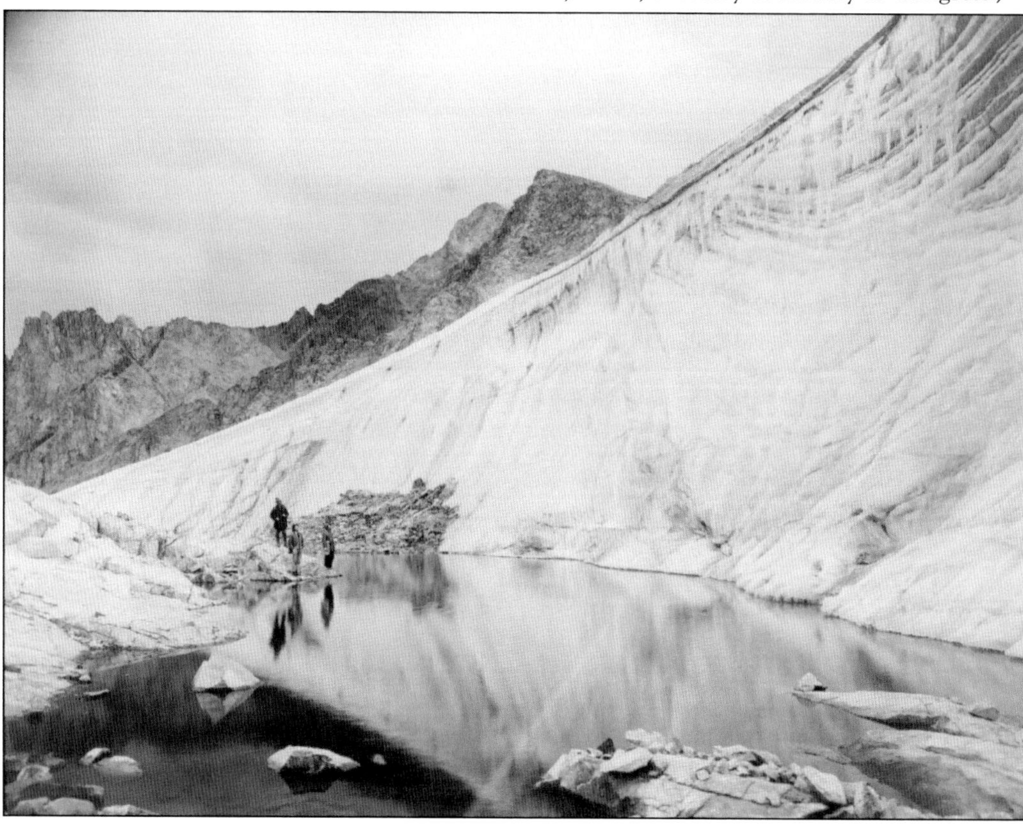

Andres Wilse and A.B. Wood, the topographer for the expedition, "set out footloose, in light marching order" with 10 days' provisions and a wool blanket from Goose Lake to examine the Stillwater canyon. En route, on September 11, 1898, the pair climbed the second-highest peak in Montana. Kimball named the peak Mount Wood after A.B. Wood, "who took its elevation and whose aid" contributed greatly to the survey. (Courtesy of Museum of the Beartooths.)

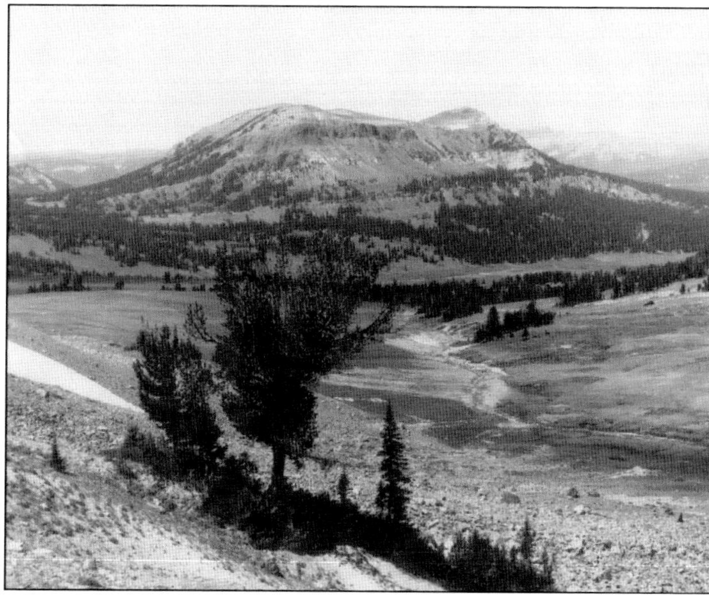

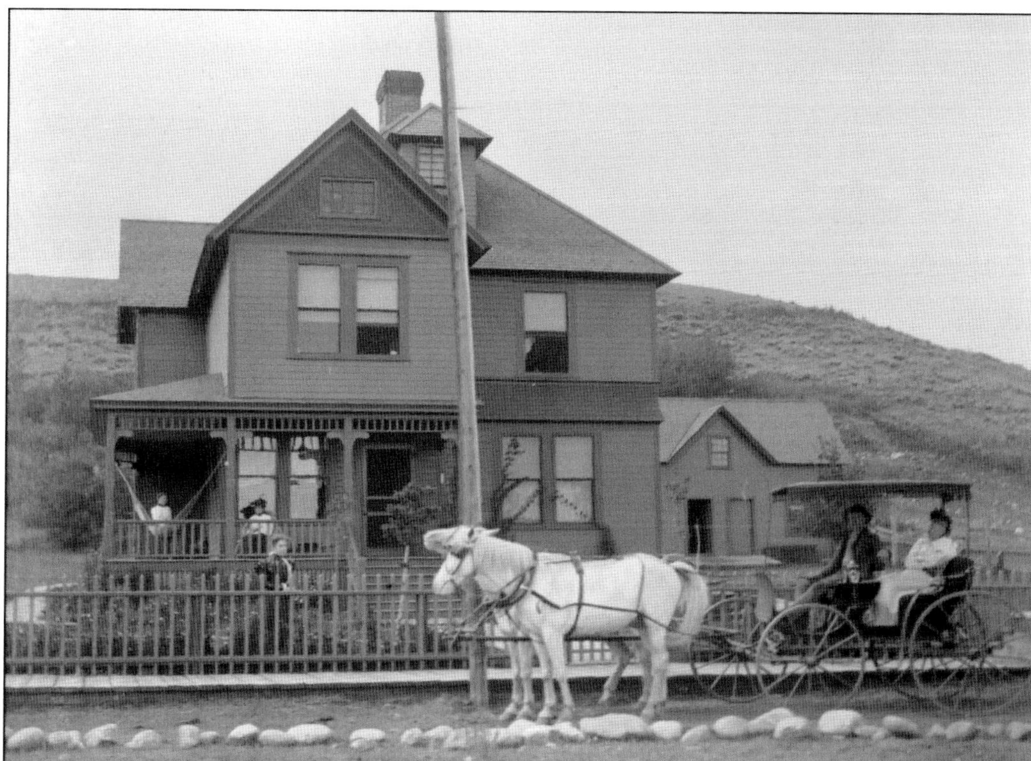

Wilse and Wood climbed several mountains and named them after contemporaries, including Mount Villard for Henry Villard, early president of the Northern Pacific Railroad; Mount Spofford—now Glacier Peak—for Charles Spofford, private secretary of Villards; Mount Fox for Dr. J. Maurice Fox, pictured here, of Red Lodge, the manager of the Rocky Fork Coal Company; and Mount Hague for geologist Arnold Hague. Wilse marveled at the wild mountain landscape and "glittering glaciers" of the Beartooths. (Courtesy of Carbon County Historical Society & Museum.)

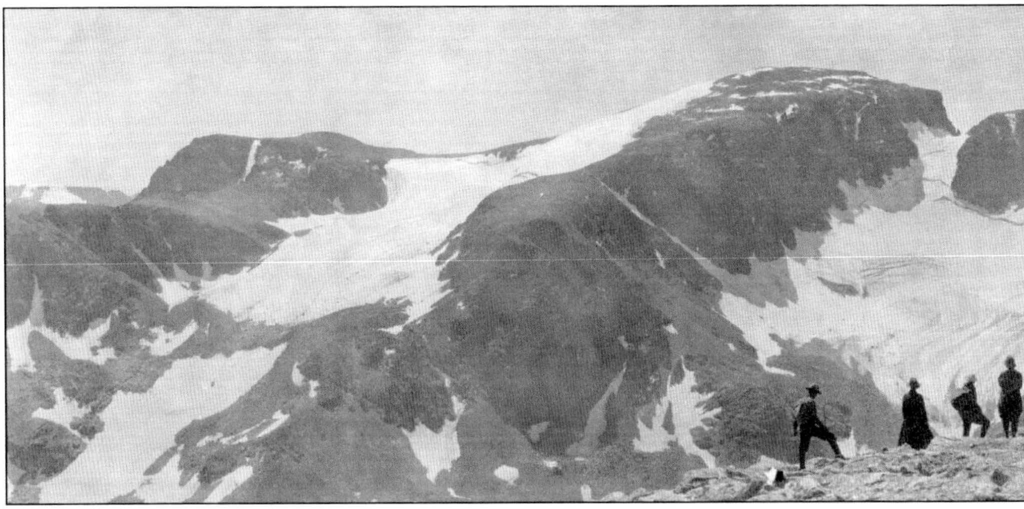

The Kimball survey disbanded in October after 102 days in the field. In 1899, Kimball published a map and article describing the high mountain adventure. He described the range as "the most picturesque alpine scenery to be found in accessible parts of the United States. As a haunt for tourists of the more adventurous sort . . . except for their picturesque value they are worthless." He died in Cody, Wyoming, in 1913. (Courtesy of Special Collections, Montana State University Library, Bozeman.)

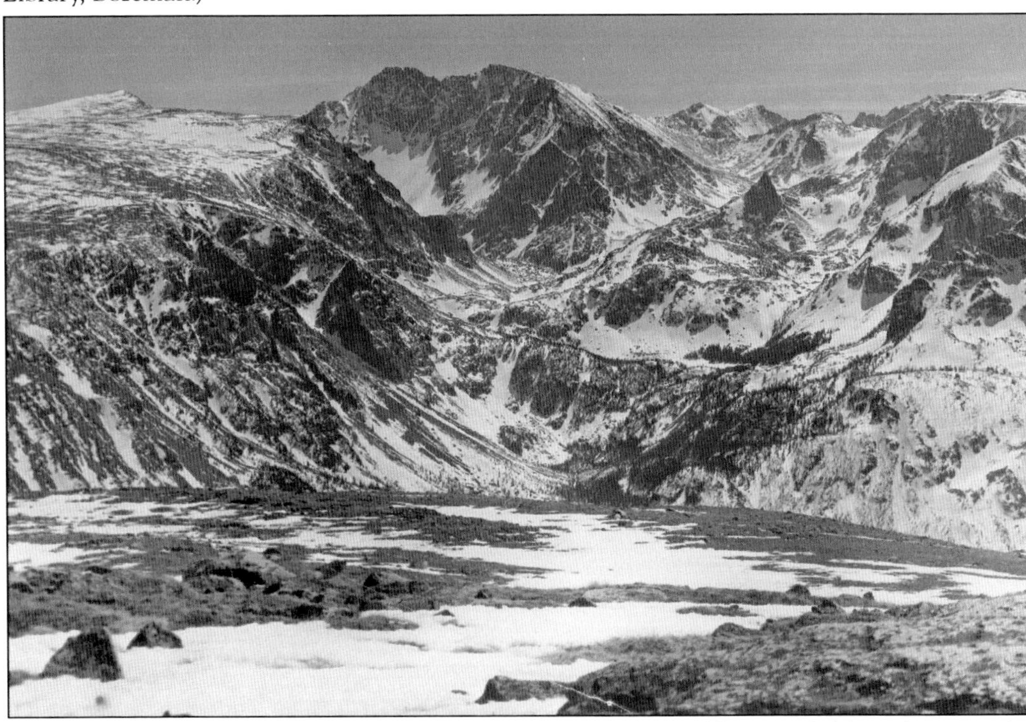

At 12,799 feet, Granite Peak is Montana's highest peak. Flanked by snowfields and surrounded by other rugged peaks, it has long attracted sightseers, hikers, and climbers. The source of the name remains a mystery, but early prospectors or hunters may have noticed the peak's metallic sheen from a distance. Arnold Hague was most likely the first to record the name in print, in the mid-1880s. (Courtesy of Museum of the Beartooths.)

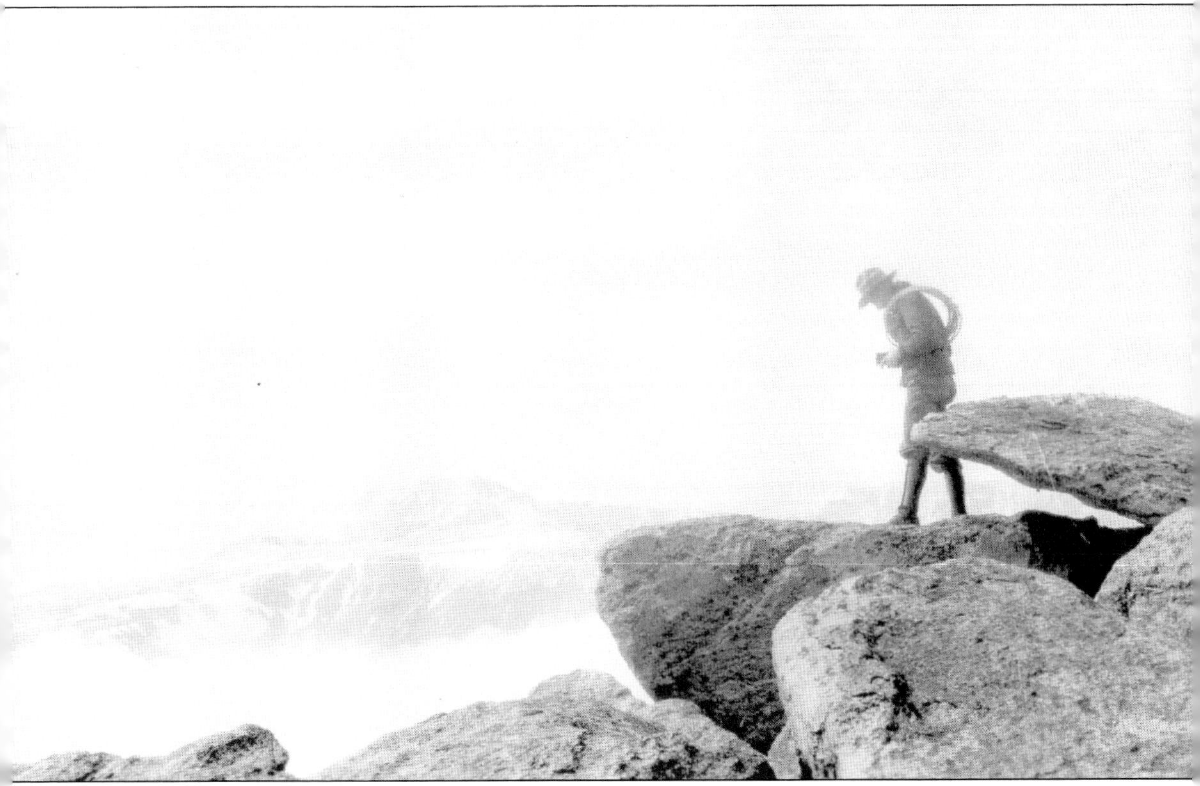

House-sized boulders were just one of the many challenges when climbing Granite Peak. A US Geological Survey party headed by Edward M. Douglas in September 1889 was the first organized effort to climb it; they were unsuccessful because of vertical cliffs and foul weather. An 1894 attempt by members of Kimball's party also fell short of the Granite Peak summit. Bad weather halted an endeavor by Fred Inabnit of Billings in 1910. In 1914, James Campbell "J.C." Whitham and party were forced to burn their walking sticks and spend an uncomfortable night at 12,200 feet near Mount Tempest, and they abandoned the climb. In August 1922, a party of five climbers led by Fred Inabnit approached Granite Peak after a two-week foray in the backcountry. Only 300 feet from the top, they encountered vertical cliffs. After several hours of trying to find a route to the top, they were forced to give up. (Courtesy of Special Collections, Montana State University Library, Bozeman.)

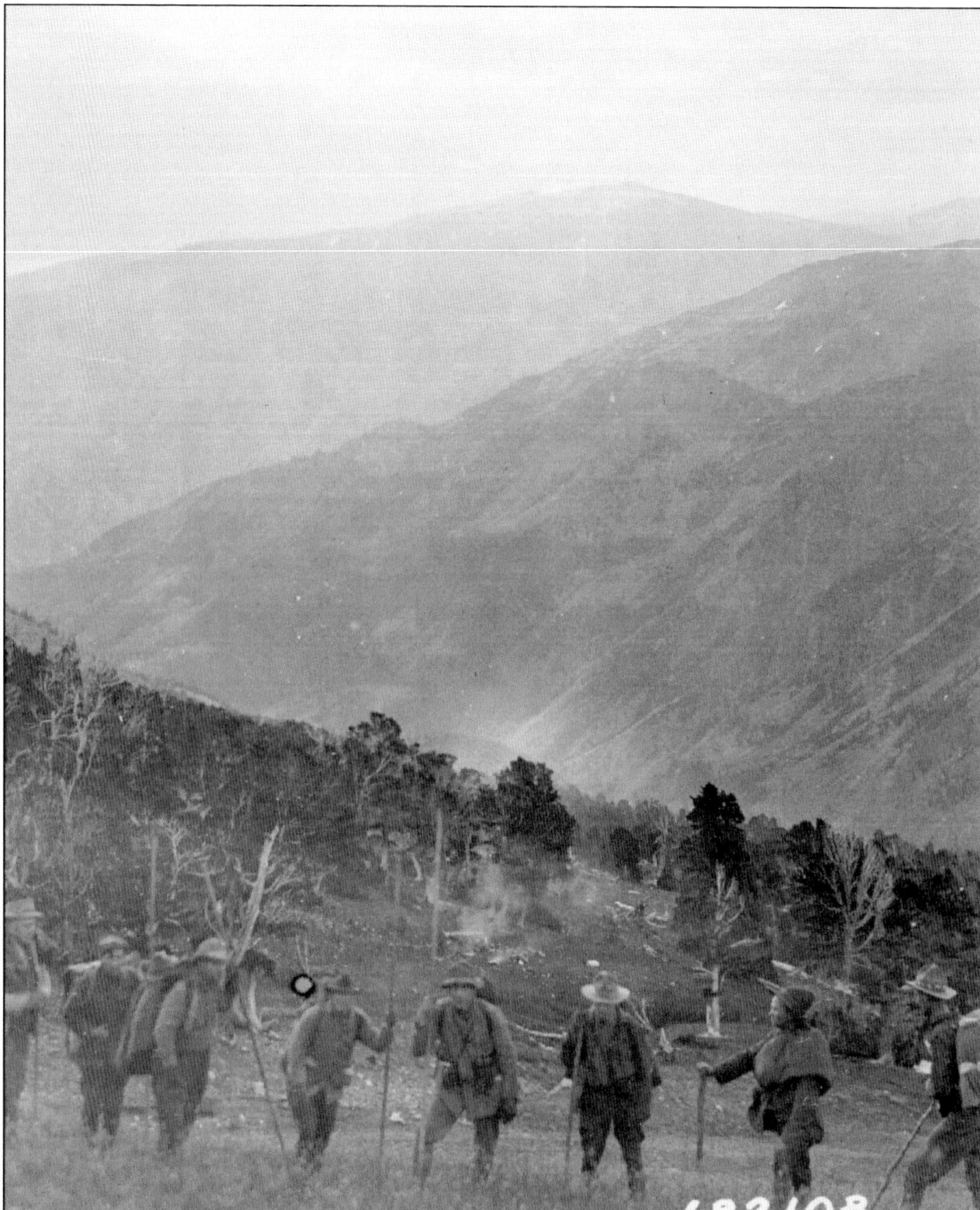

The first successful climb of Granite Peak was supposed to began on August 25, 1923. After a two-day delay to double check equipment and wait for a clearing in the weather, the group departed on August 27 from the lodge at East Rosebud Lake. The party included Elers Koch, assistant district forester; Robert T. Ferguson, supervisor of Beartooth National Forest; J.C. Whitham, supervisor of the Custer-Sioux National Forest; Guy O'Neil, Rosebud district ranger; forest guard Alvia Shiver; and a group from Billings including Harold Rixon, William Banfill, George Osten, Verne Johnson, and Fred Inabnit, all experienced climbers. The climbers left East Rosebud Lake, ascended Slough Creek to Phantom Creek, and set up base camp on the Froze to Death Plateau with three packhorses. (Courtesy of Special Collections, Montana State University Library, Bozeman.)

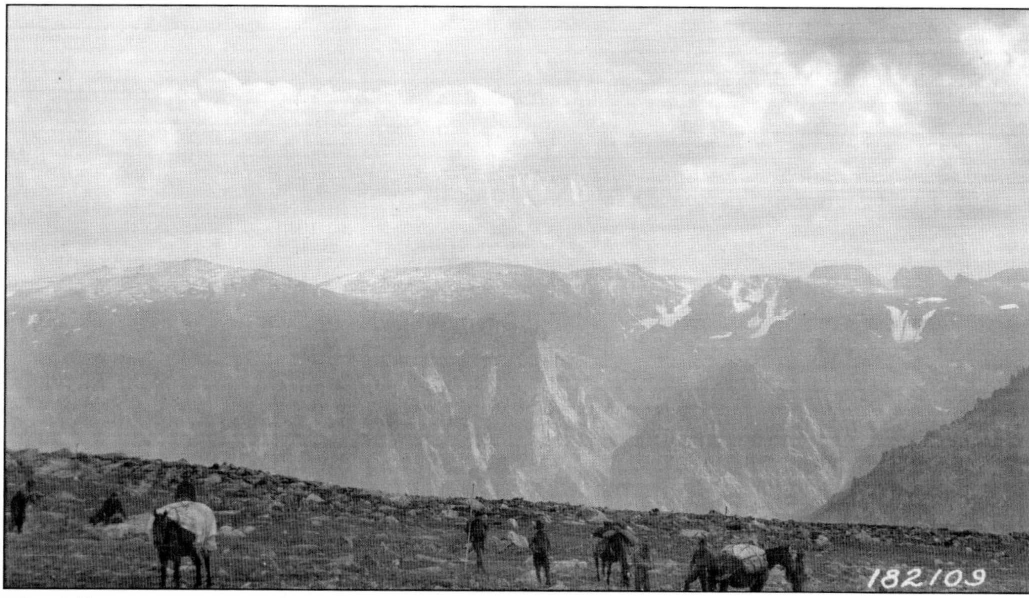

The following morning, the men said goodbye to their packhorses and loaded their backpacks to about 30 pounds, with blankets and four days of rations. (Courtesy of Special Collections, Montana State University Library, Bozeman.)

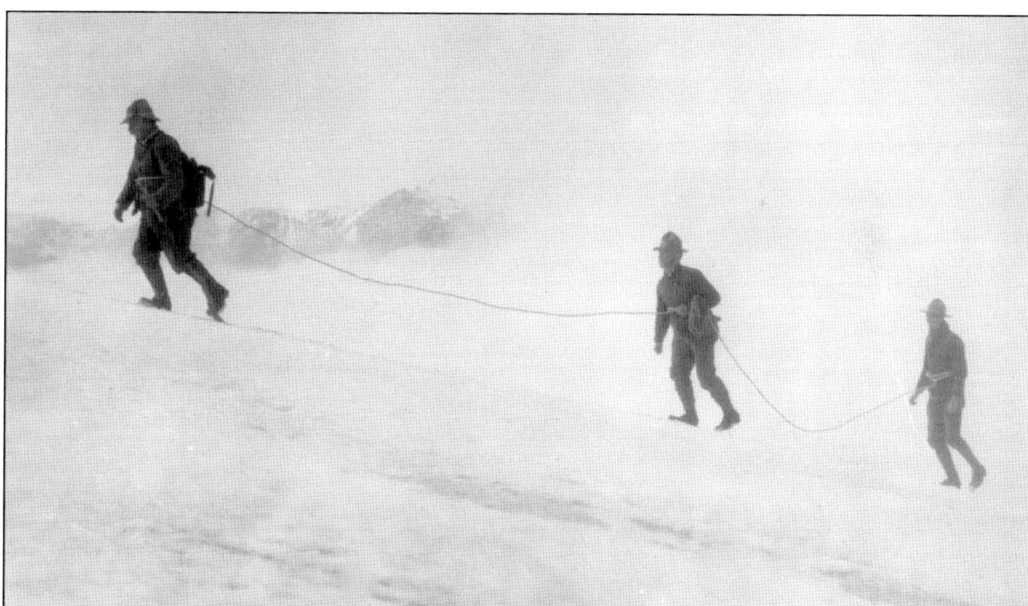

Leading the park are, from left to right, Fred Inabnit, Harold Rixen, and Elers Koch. Above Granite Glacier, Rixon was forced to turn back for base camp when his indigestion did not improve. The rest of the group reached Avalanche Lake—now Granite Creek Lakes—by 4:00 p.m. A camp was made, and Robert T. Ferguson wrote, "The night was long and cold, with no warming fire . . . none of us got much sleep." (Courtesy of Special Collections, Montana State University Library, Bozeman.)

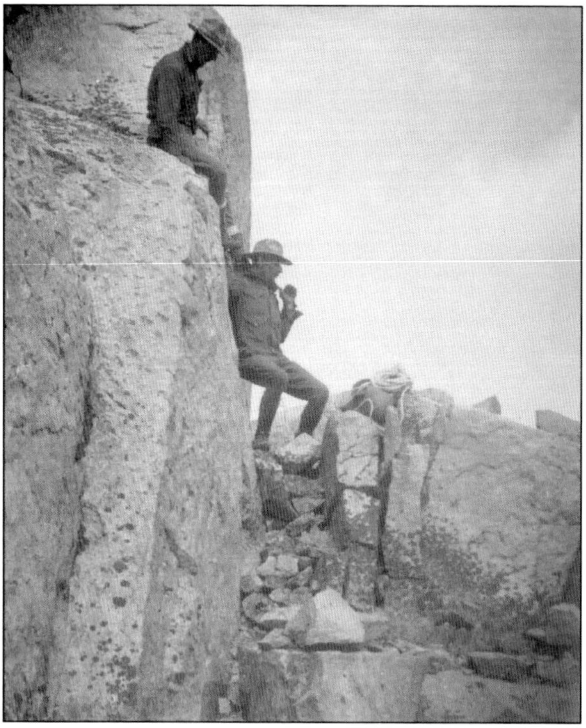

After an amicable disagreement on which approach to take, the climbers agreed to divide into two parties for the ascent. The first group, with Koch, Ferguson, and Whitham, decided to approach from the northeast ridge, while Inabnit, O'Neil, and the others climbed the southwestern slope. Here, Ferguson (above) helps Koch in a tough spot. (Courtesy of Special Collections, Montana State University Library, Bozeman.)

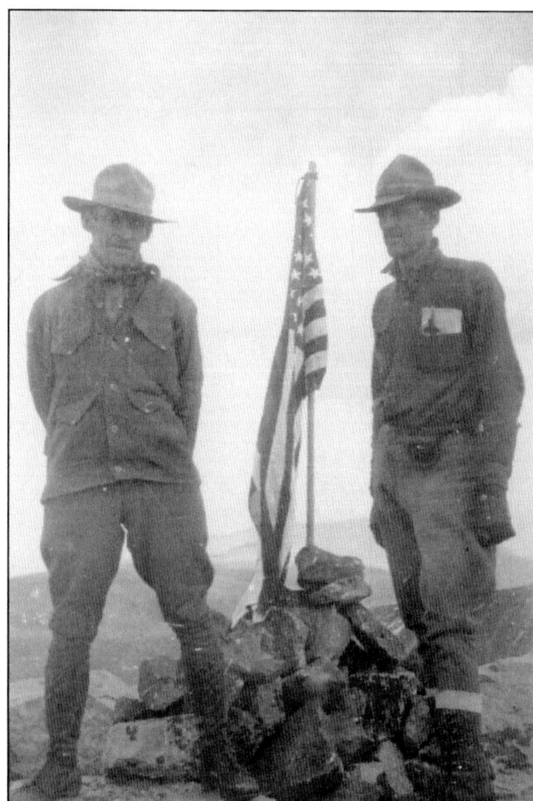

At 11:10 a.m. on August 29, 1923, Koch, Whitham, and Ferguson made it to the top of Granite Peak and remained there for two hours. Koch (left) and Ferguson placed this American flag in a rock monument they built. The pair also carved their names in the granite. Koch later reminisced, "It seems a small thing, but of all the accomplishments and achievements I may have had in my long life as a forester, the first ascent of Granite Peak is the one that I look back on with the greatest satisfaction . . . it is well to go all out sometimes." (Courtesy of Special Collections, Montana State University Library, Bozeman.)

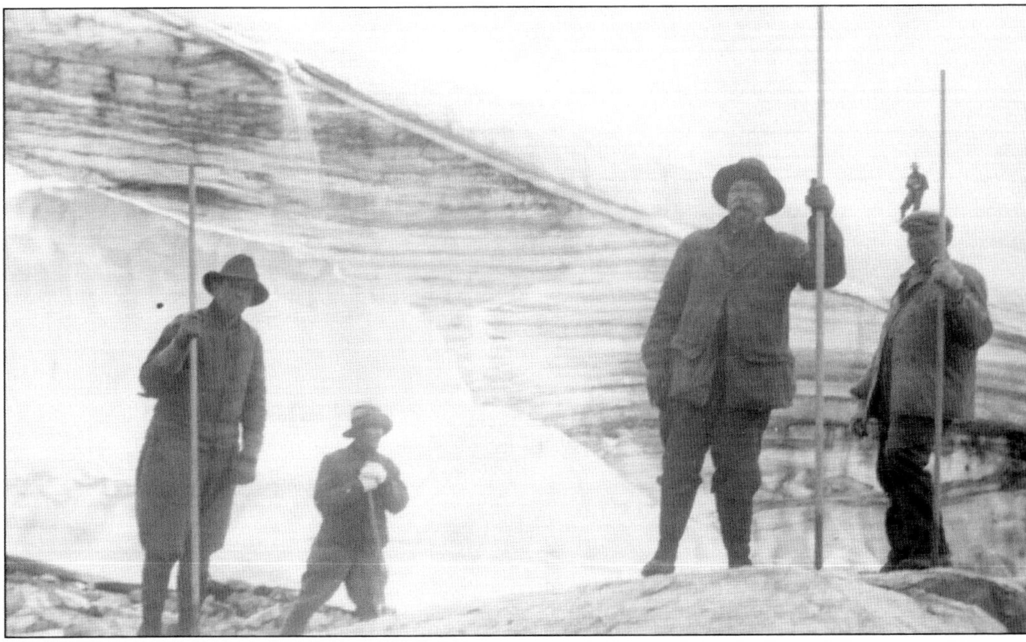

On a July trip in 1924, Inabnit (front center), along with Ernest Vogel, Harold Rixon, and George Osten were fogbound for several days along their way from the East Rosebud to Cooke City. Upon reaching the plateau, they found this storm had coated the area with snow, making it too dangerous to attempt a climb to the peak. (Courtesy of Special Collections, Montana State University Library, Bozeman.)

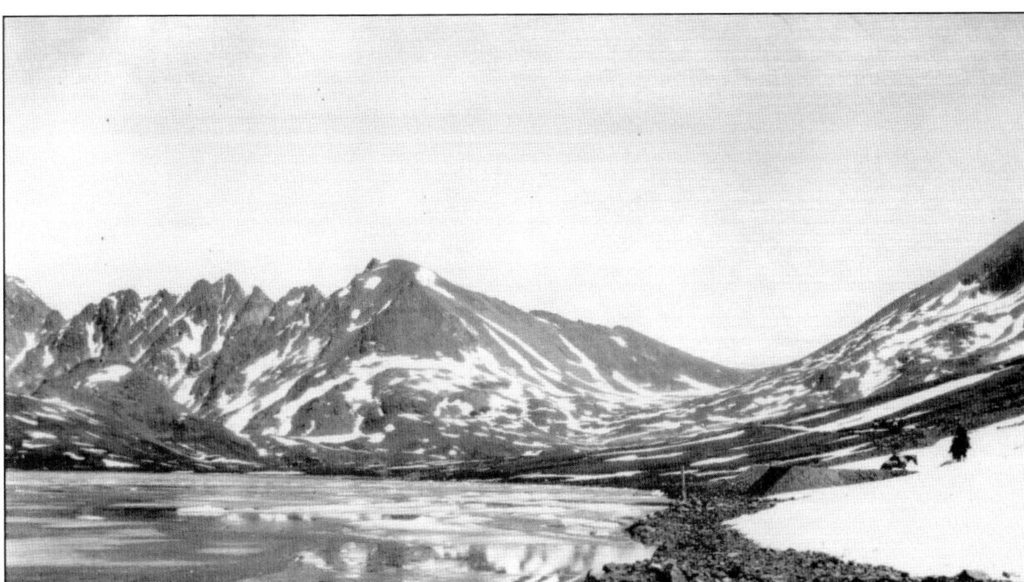

Near beautiful Goose Lake, on his annual summer trip with Harold Rixon and Ernest Vogel in 1926, Fred Inabnit coincidentally met Sierra Club mountaineer Norman Clyde, who was intrigued by Granite Peak. Inabnit offered his services to act as a guide, but Clyde advanced ahead with Vogel and they collaborated to make the second ascent. Inabnit never reached the peak, dying two years later. (Courtesy of Special Collections, Montana State University Library, Bozeman.)

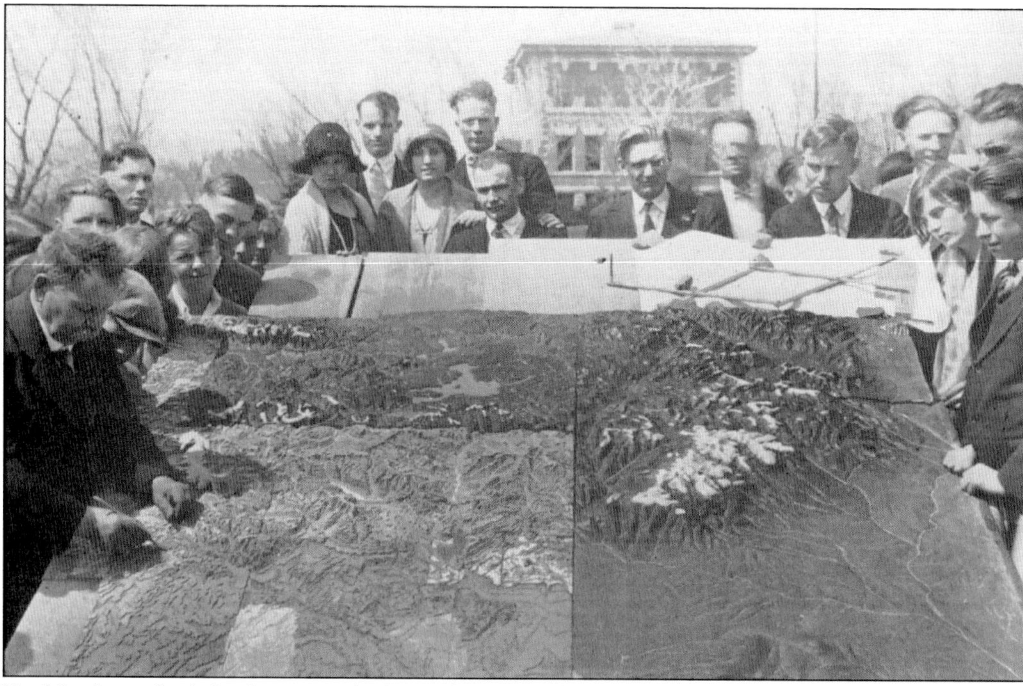

Fred Inabnit, far left, shares a relief map he created of his beloved Beartooth Mountains with students at Billings Polytechnic Institute during American forestry week in April 1926. A tireless hiker, Inabnit regularly charted circuitous trips up and over the Beartooths from Red Lodge to Cooke City and back. One route of Inabnit's that Ralph Saunders mapped covered an astounding 200 miles and 30,000 feet in just two weeks. This map is now on display at the Museum of the Beartooths in Columbus, Montana. (Courtesy of Museum of the Beartooths.)

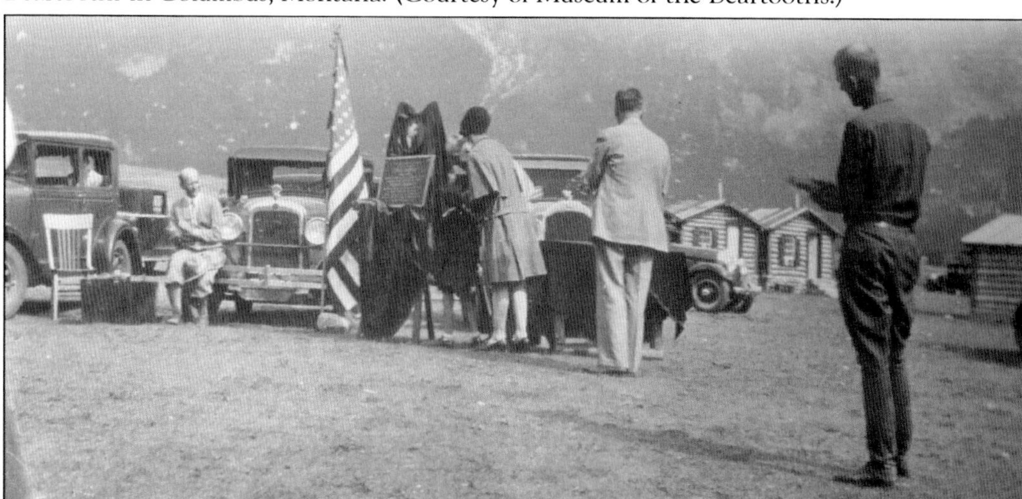

On August 25, 1929, a ceremony was held for Fred Inabnit at East Rosebud Lake and a memorial was dedicated with a plaque that read, "This tablet was placed here by the friends of Fred Inabnit, 1866–1928. A faithful official of Yellowstone County in whose honor this peak was named Mount Inabnit in recognition of his successful efforts to inspire others with his love and enthusiasm for these mountains whose silent depths and glorious heights he explored for many years." (Courtesy of Museum of the Beartooths.)

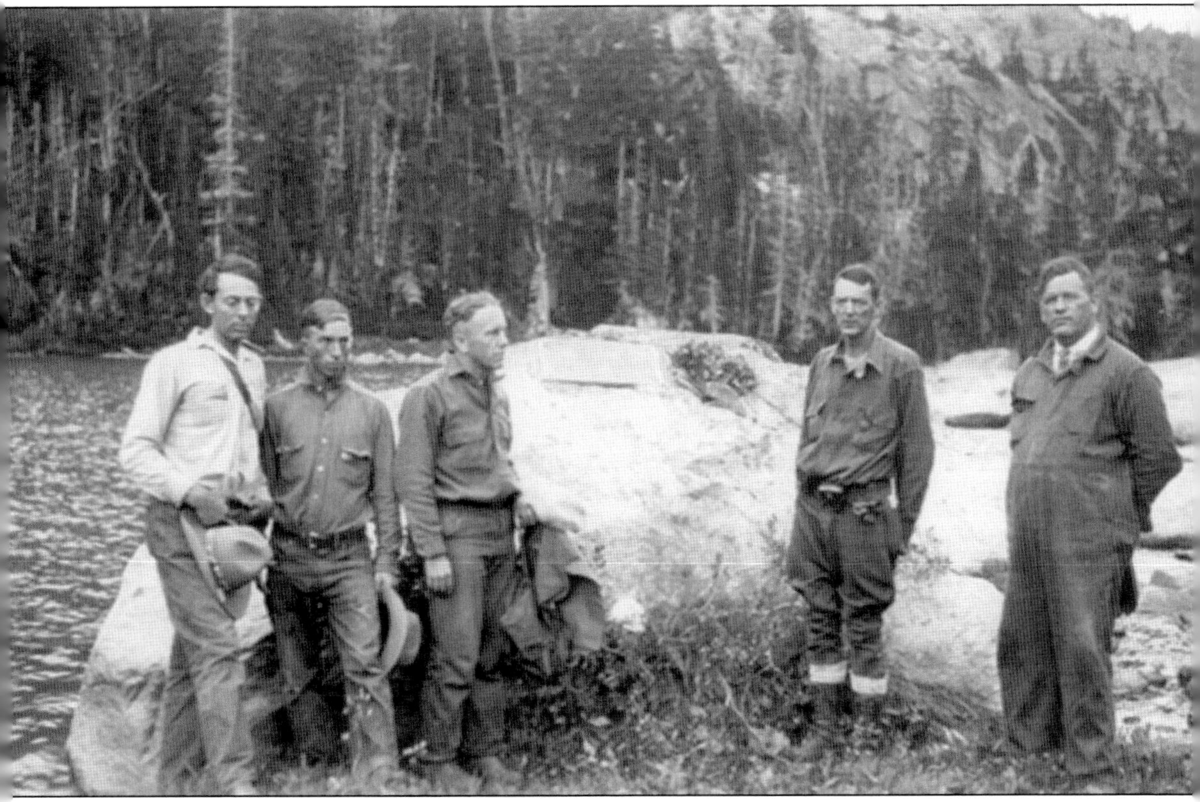

Around the bronze plaque dedicated to Inabnit in this photograph taken by George Osten are, from left to right, David Branger, Charles Umland, Harold Rixon, Robert Ferguson, and Carl Eden. This crew packed the plaque three steep miles to Snow Lakes, just below the peak that now bears Inabnit's name, and bolted it to a boulder. The plaque became dislodged from the boulder through the years and was carried down the trail in 2009 by Wayne McClane. Ralph Saunders, a map specialist, historian, and liaison for the Museum of the Beartooths, and Jeff Gildehaus of the Beartooth Ranger District, spearheaded a rededication ceremony on August 22, 2010. Roman Gillitzer handcrafted new bolts with heads that resemble small pine trees, and the refurbished plaque was placed near the East Rosebud trailhead. A historical interpretive panel is in the works to be placed near the trailhead. (Courtesy of USFS, Beartooth Ranger District.)

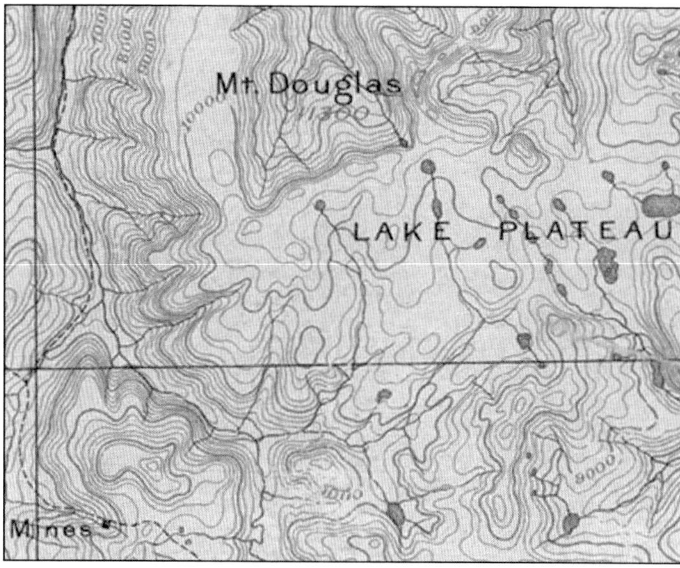

This portion of the map made by Edward Douglas, the geographer in charge of the US Geological Survey of Montana, between 1886 and 1888 features his namesake, Mount Douglas. Survey team members Frank Tweedy and W.H. Leffingwell left no record but may have been the first to climb the mountain. Douglas made the first recorded attempt to climb Granite Peak in 1889, nearly 35 years before it was successfully done. (Courtesy of the University of Texas Libraries, the University of Texas at Austin.)

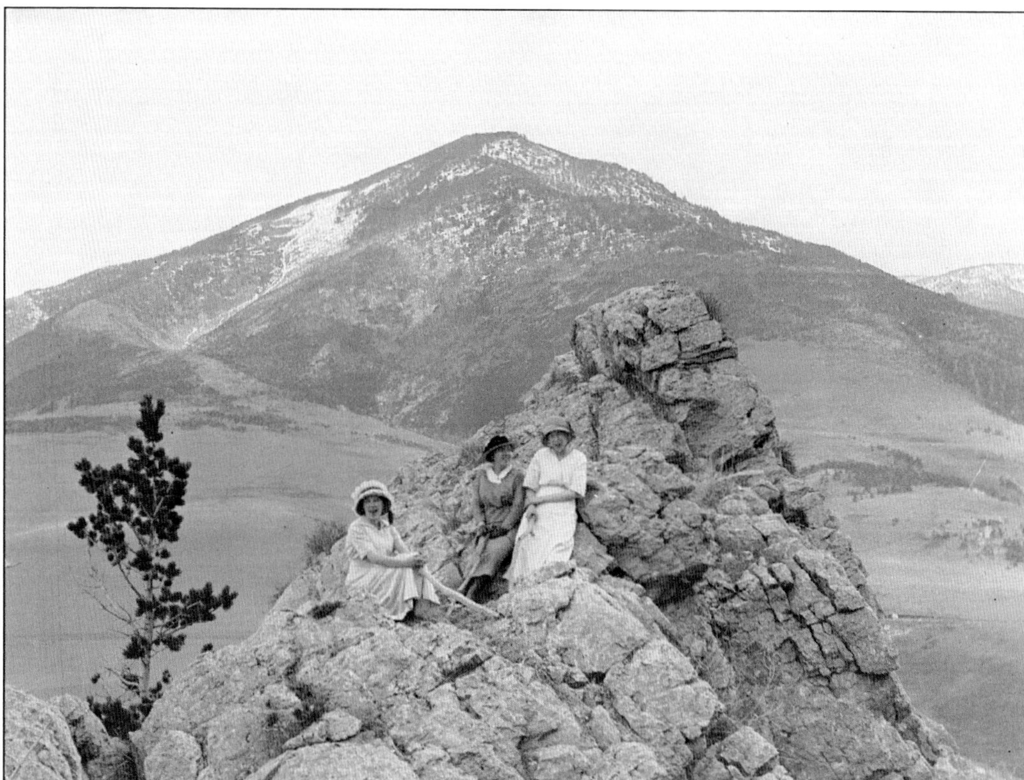

Towering behind the girls to the south of Red Lodge is Mount Maurice, named after Dr. J. Maurice Fox by his daughters Nellie, Lockey, and Lillie. In 1901, the Fox sisters climbed the mountain, placed their names in a bottle of champagne, and left it at the summit. It is thought they were the first to have registered a climb to this peak. Fox was an early superintendent of the Rocky Fork coal mines. (Courtesy of Carbon County Historical Society and Museum.)

Four

"GOLD IN THEM HILLS"

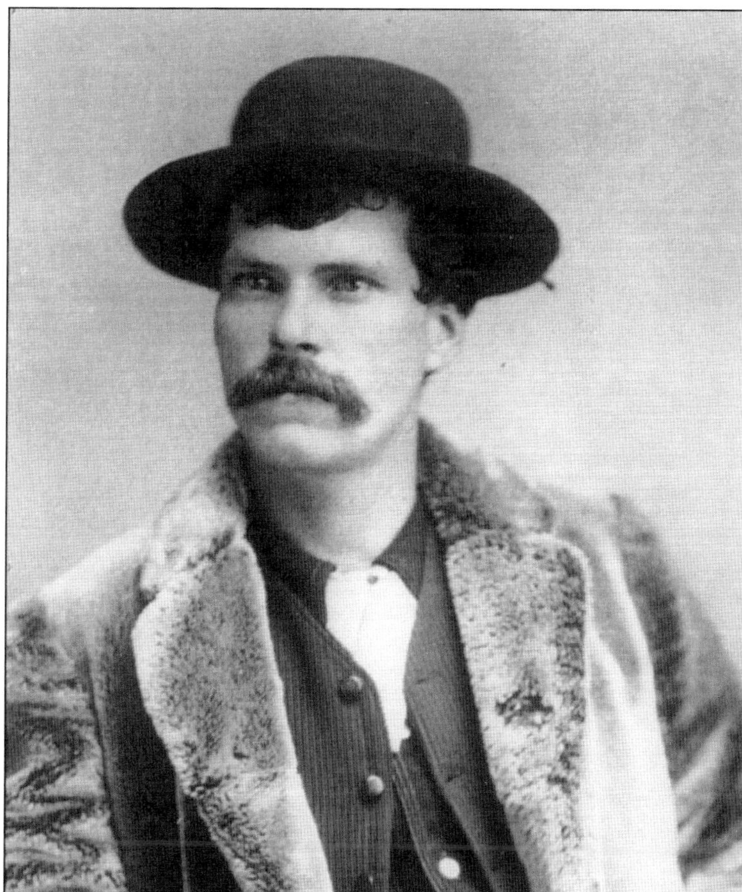

Gold was first discovered on the 10,246-foot Baboon Mountain in the Main Boulder River drainage by John Allen and Barney Hughes in 1864. However, it was Joe Keeney, pictured here, who in 1879 recorded the first claims, the "Big Spirit" and the "Little Spirit," at a site he named "Independence," located on Basin Creek three miles from the Boulder River. He also located claims nearby at what would become Solomon City. (Courtesy of Crazy Mountain Museum.)

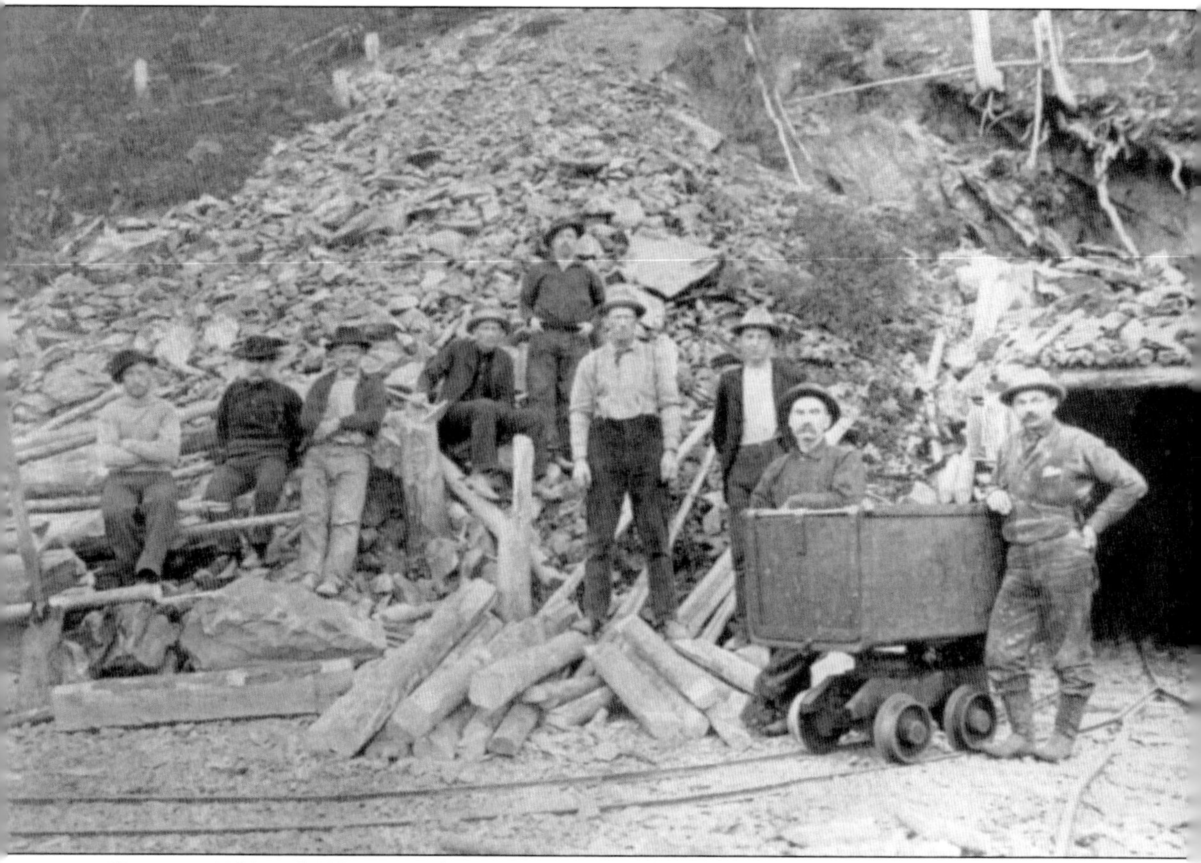

Between 1889 and 1891, several mines were opened in the Boulder mining district, including the Poorman, Hidden Treasure, Daisy, King Solomon, and Independence. In 1890, Harry E. Leveaux purchased the Independence mine and claimed to own the first piece of gold jewelry from it. During the peak mining period, seven stamp mills—rock crushers—were running, and the Independence mill produced $42,000 worth of gold bullion between 1890 and 1893. However, the mining boom ended with the Depression of 1893, the exhaustion of easily accessed ore, difficult transportation, and poor management of the operations. The Independence mine closed, but in August 1894, it was leased out and reopened. From 1890 to 1905, the district reportedly produced gold and silver ore valued at about $120,000. (Courtesy of Crazy Mountain Museum.)

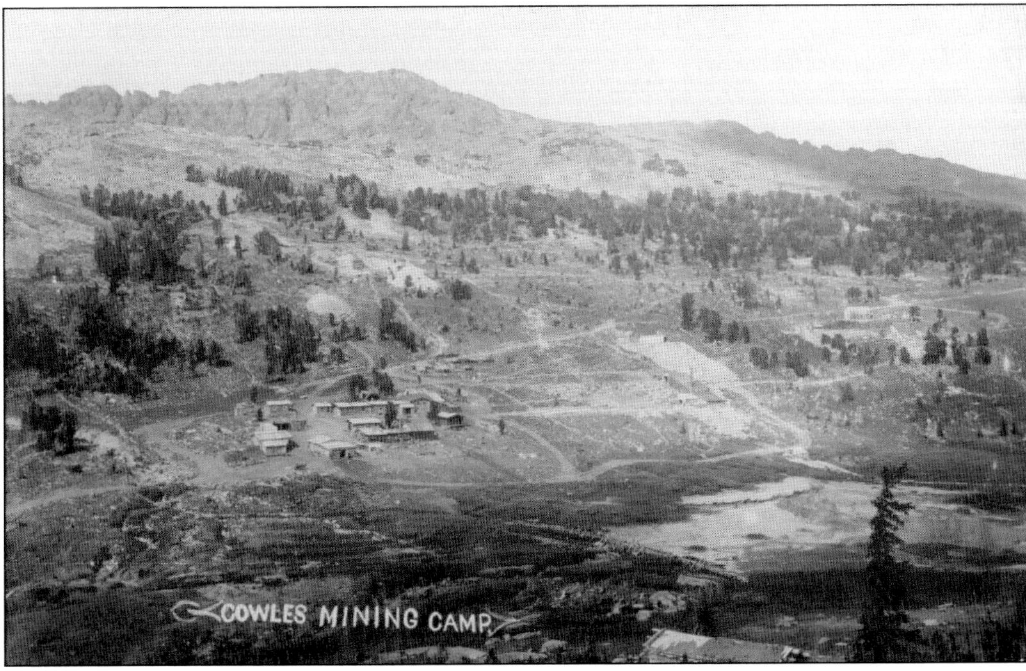

In 1897, Ethan Cowles of Boston reopened the Independence, Hidden Treasure, and Poorman mines and built Cowles Mining Camp, pictured here, complete with a 10-stamp steam mill. By 1900, a total of 30 men were employed at Hidden Treasure, operating the stamp mill 24 hours a day. Cowles sold out in 1900 to investors but managed the operations until the Hidden Treasure mill burned down in 1904. Workings were again reopened in the early-to-mid-1930s on the Daisy and Independence mines, but the ore was rapidly mined out. In 1934, Dr. Yeager of Big Timber leased property from the Cowles Mining Company and reopened the mine, but two workmen were killed and work was given up shortly after. (Above, courtesy of Crazy Mountain Museum; below, courtesy of USFS, Big Timber Ranger District.)

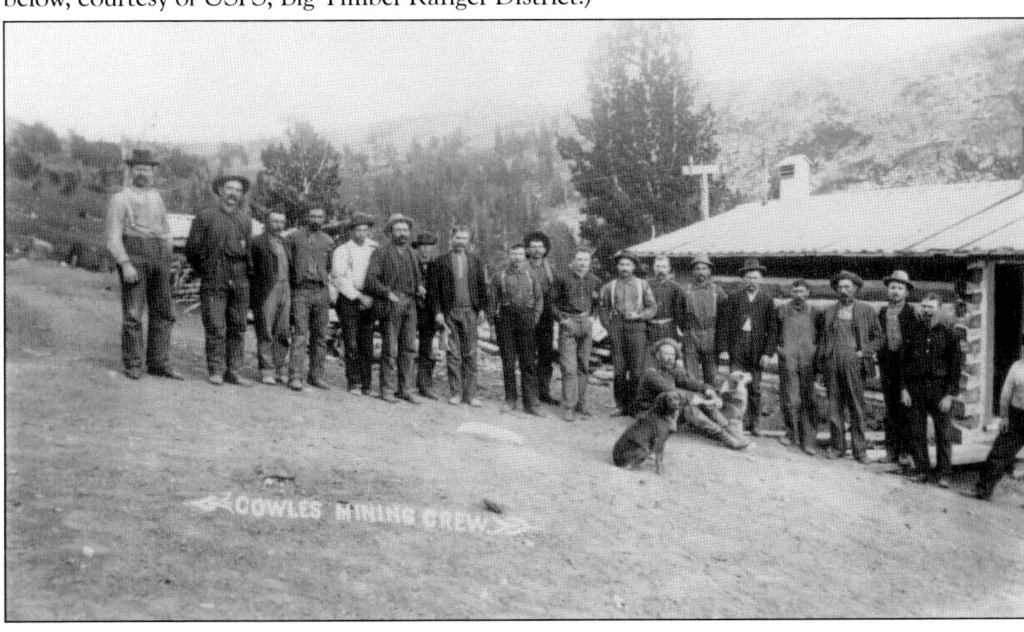

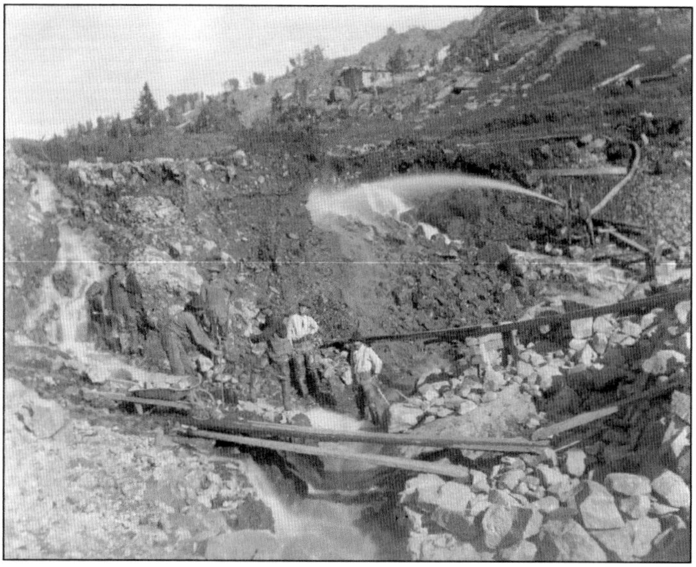

High-pressure water directed against the banks allowed thousands of yards of gravel to be washed down and recovered. The most active mining period was from 1888 to 1893, when the mining camps of Independence and the auxiliary camps of Solomon City and Horseshoe Basin employed around 500 men. Hidden Treasure, Independence, and Daisy mines were the main producers of gold, silver, copper, and lead in the area. (Courtesy of USFS, Big Timber Ranger District.)

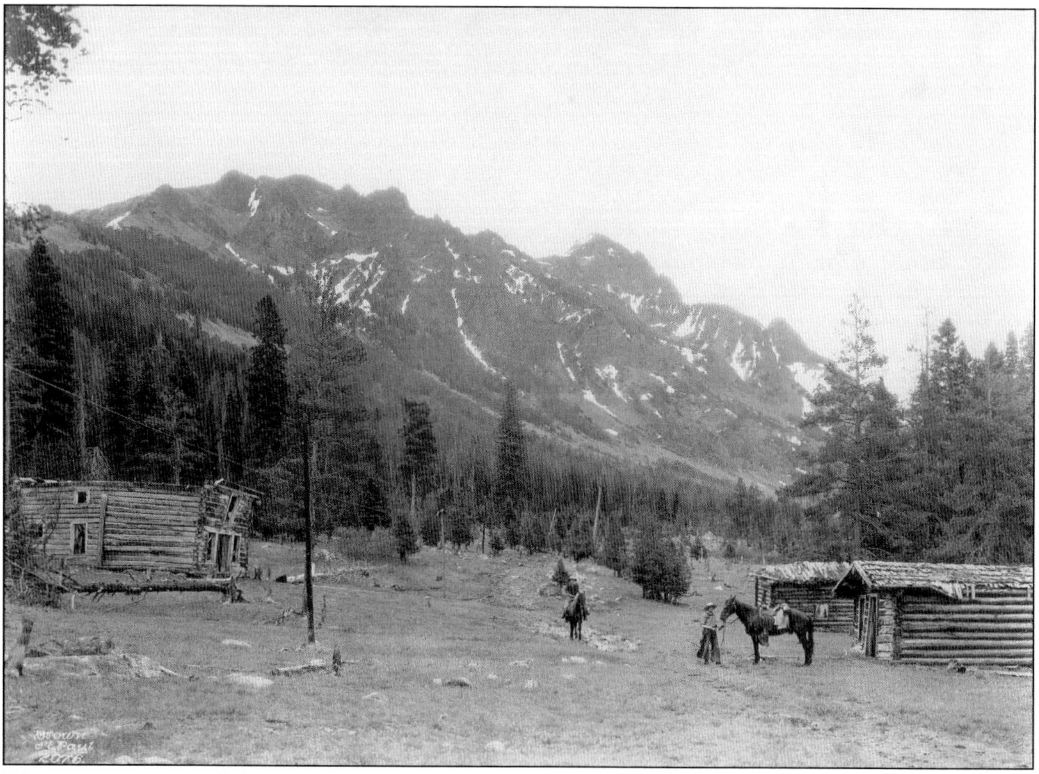

These remains are all that is left of Independence, once the service center for the Boulder mining district. The town offered a sawmill, two general stores, a restaurant, a blacksmith, a stable, two gambling establishments, and a house of prostitution, which was the only building made of sawn lumber boards. By 1893, a triweekly stage was operating the 52-mile run from Big Timber to Independence. That same year, a waterwheel-driven hydroelectric power plant was constructed, bringing electricity to Independence. A post office was established in 1892 but closed in 1895. (Courtesy of Parmly Billings Library.)

Thomas Leforge had mining interests in the Poorman mine, but he sold out because of frustrations and the inaccessibility of the mine in winter and spring. He is best known for his memoirs, published as told to Thomas Marquis in the book *Memoirs of a White Crow Indian*, which chronicled his life at the Crow agencies as well as his marriage and ties to the Crow peoples. (Courtesy of Crazy Mountain Museum.)

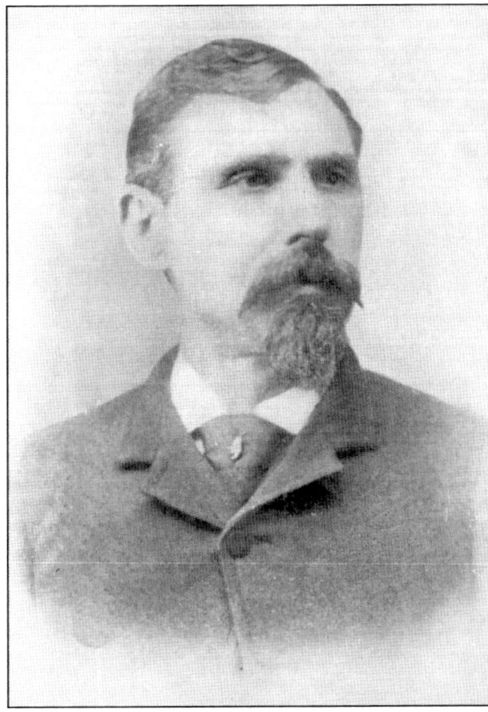

The mining settlement of Contact was located near the base of Contact Mountain, a 10,056-foot peak named for two mineral deposits, limestone and quartz, that were clearly defined on the mountain. The area became a flurry of activity in 1893 when Antonio Drago and Hector McRae found a vein of quartz "fairly glistening with native gold" in their Minnie mine on Slate Mountain. (Courtesy of Crazy Mountain Museum.)

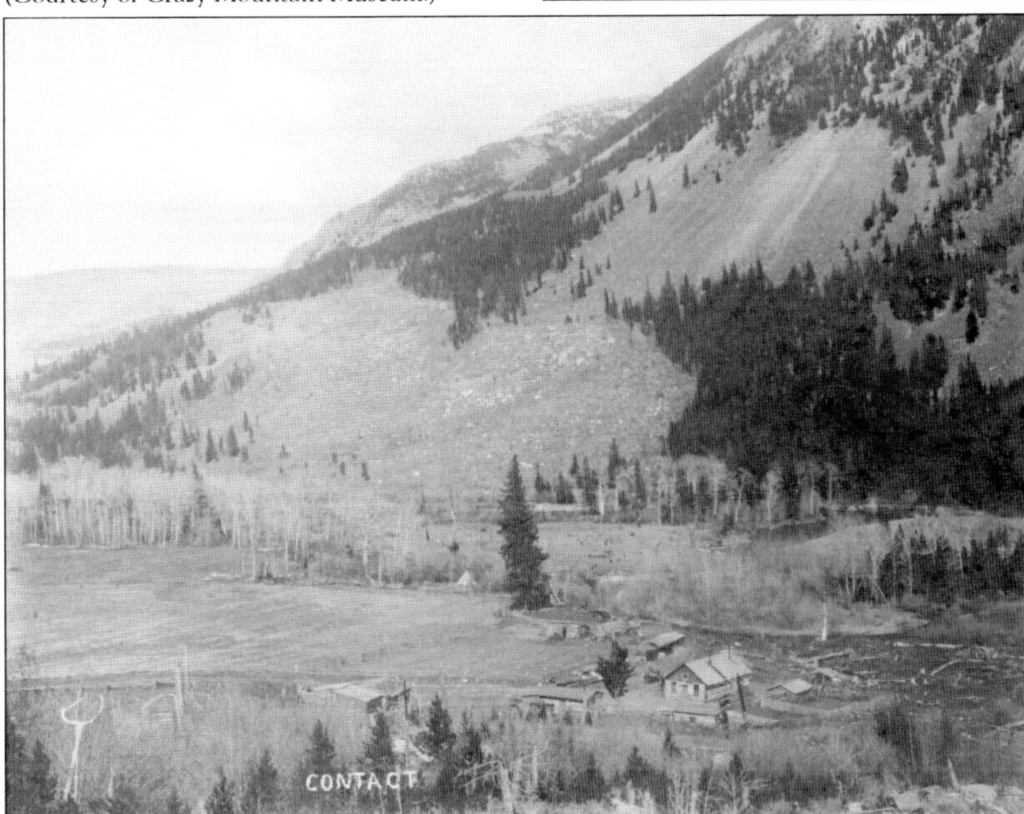

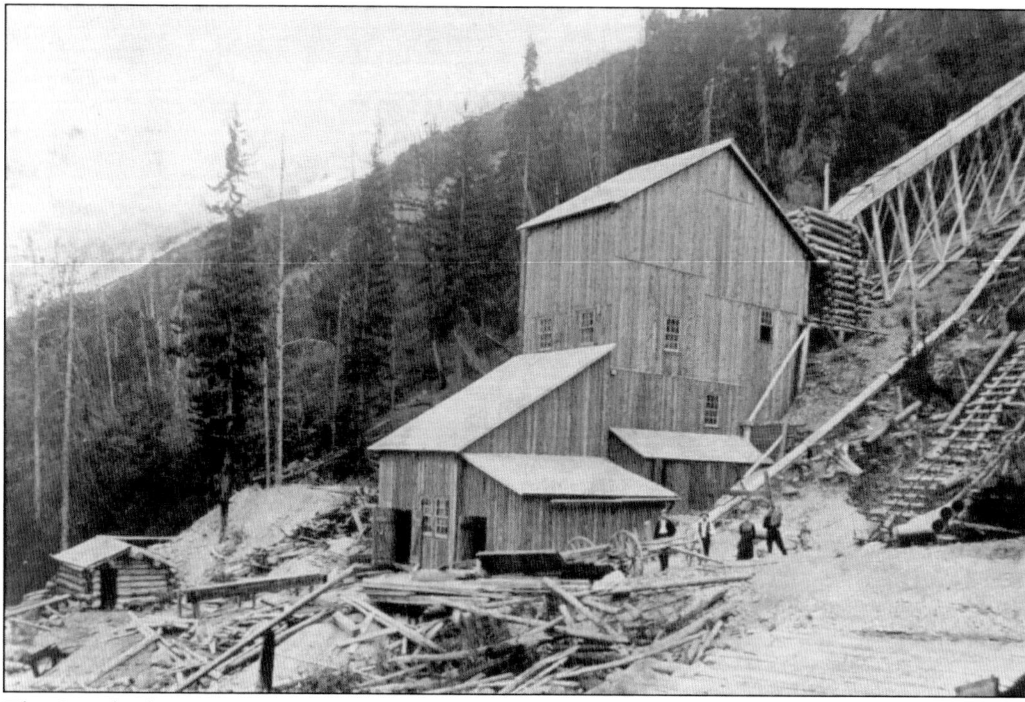

The Standard Mining Company of Montana owned this mill and several others in the Contact area, including Minnie, Calumet, and other small claims. The Milwaukee-Montana Natural Bridge Gold and Copper Company was its major competitor. (Courtesy of Crazy Mountain Museum.)

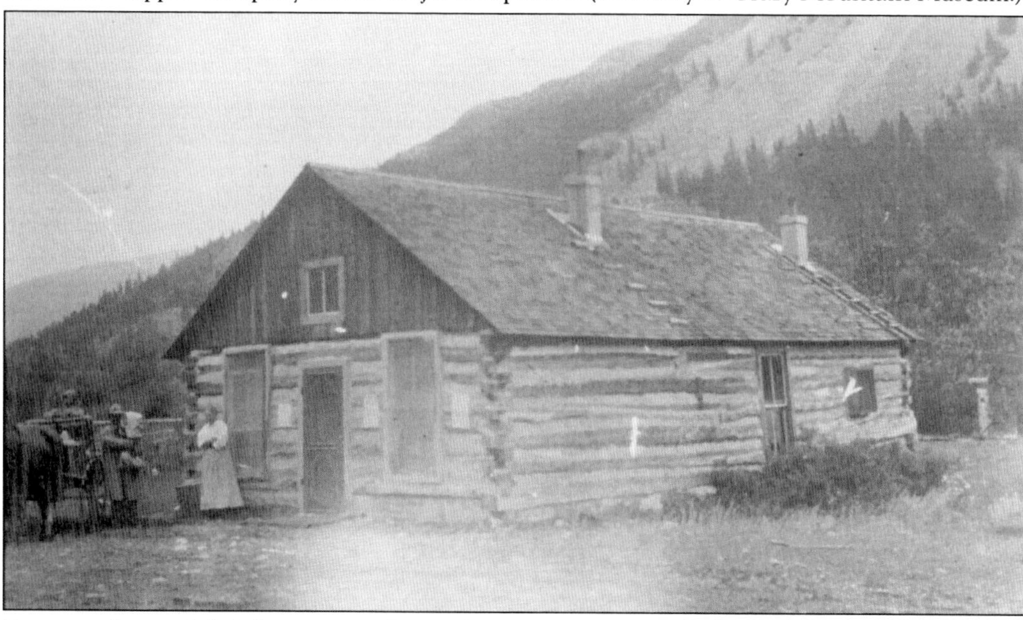

Stagecoaches and freight wagons changed teams en route to Independence at this "Halfway House" in Contact. Operated by A.B. Gould, it met travelers' needs and served as the post office. The Bucket of Blood Saloon, a gambling establishment owned by Joe Keeney, a livery, and a school—which held class only in spring and summer—made up the rest of the town. (Courtesy of Crazy Mountain Museum.)

In 1870, gold seekers Adam "Horn" Miller, James Gourley, Ed Hibbard, and Bart Henderson set out from the Yellowstone River to explore the upper Soda Butte Creek region. Miller found some galena ore, but they quickly cached their supplies in what is now Cache Creek after a group of Indians ran off with their horses. A larger return expedition located the discovery, and the New World mining district was formed on July 19, 1872. (Courtesy of Special Collections, Montana State University Library, Bozeman.)

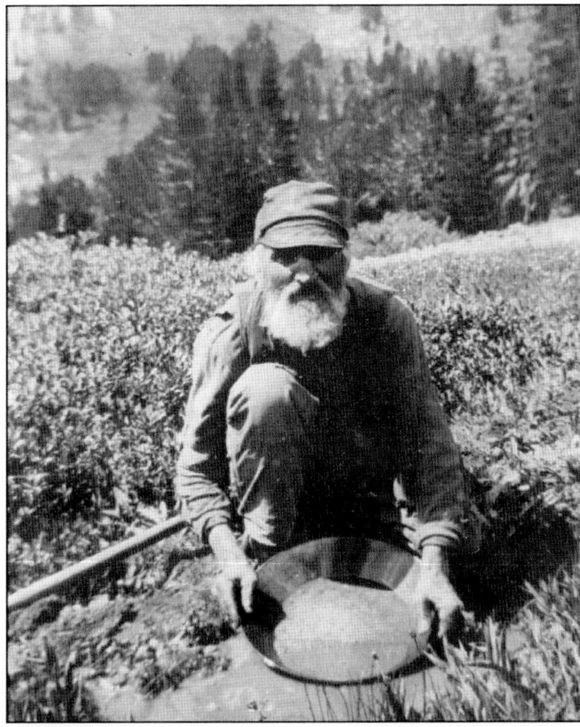

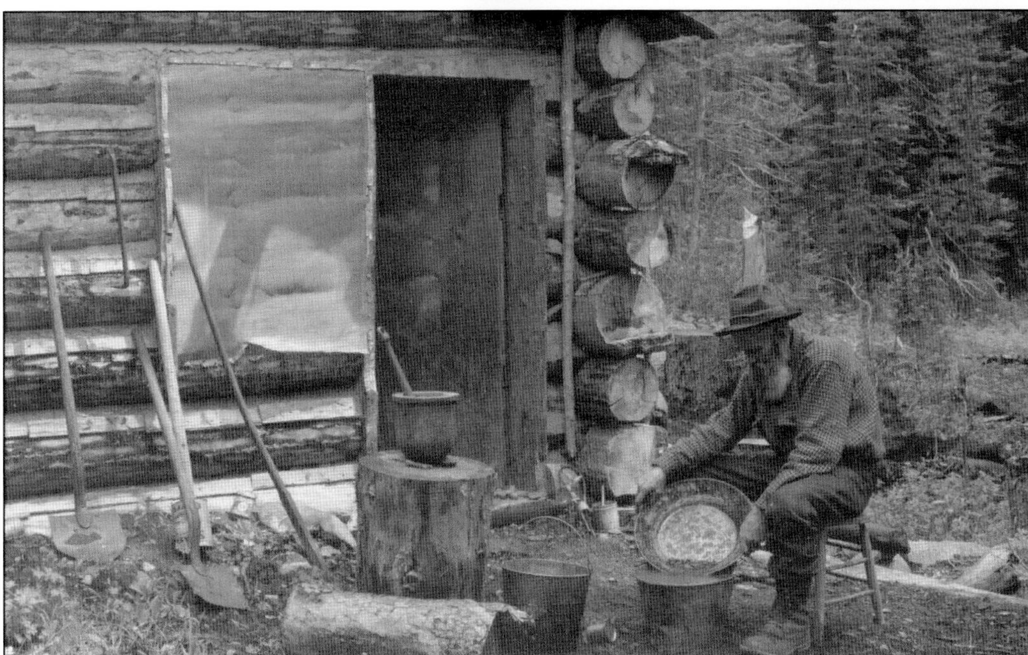

In 1875, a small Mexican-style roasting furnace was built to treat lead-silver ore near the small settlement that had been established near Cache Creek. However, development was minimal, because the New World district was on Crow land and prospecting and mining were not allowed. Although there was some lode development, it was speculative and marginal, since there was no legal basis for ownership of claims. (Courtesy of Carbon County Historical Society & Museum.)

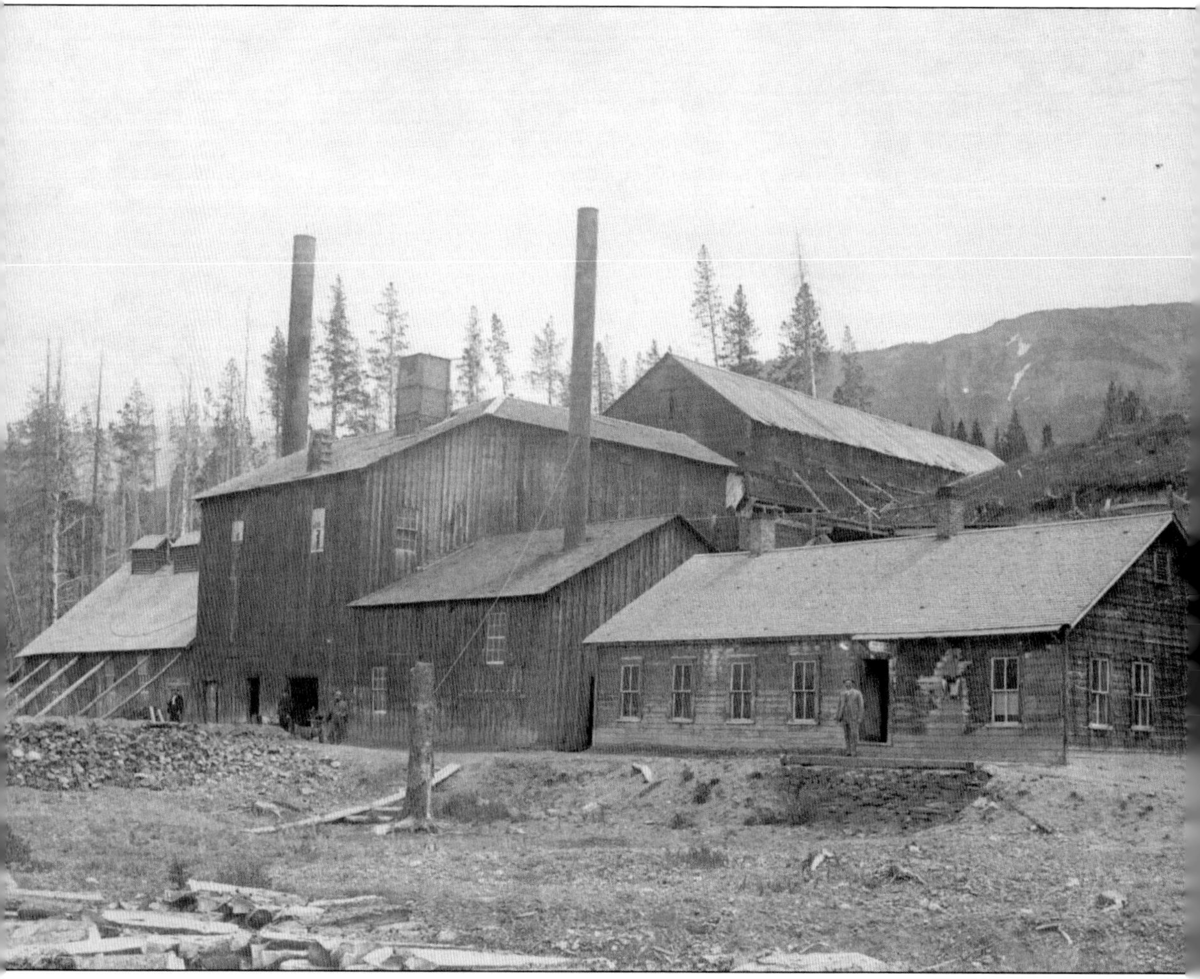

In 1882, a great portion of the Crow reservation was ceded to the government, paving the way for mine development. By late 1882, miners had recorded over 1,450 locations in the New World district. Republic mine, pictured here, was one of the first major mines developed in the district. George O. Eaton bought it, as well as the Greely, Houston, and New World mining claims, and organized the Republic Mining Company. By 1883, the company had spent $300,000 developing the Republic mine. Two years later, 440 tons of silver-lead bullion were produced and sold for $95,000. However, the profits were eaten up by difficulties in smelting and freighting costs. A de-silvering plant was proposed, but capital could not be raised, and the mine was closed. In 1885, mining shifted in another direction when Sam Mathers filed the Homestake claim on Henderson Mountain, which proved to be rich in gold, silver, and lead ore. The Daisy and Alice E mines were also located on Henderson Mountain. (Courtesy of Yellowstone National Park, No. 7139.)

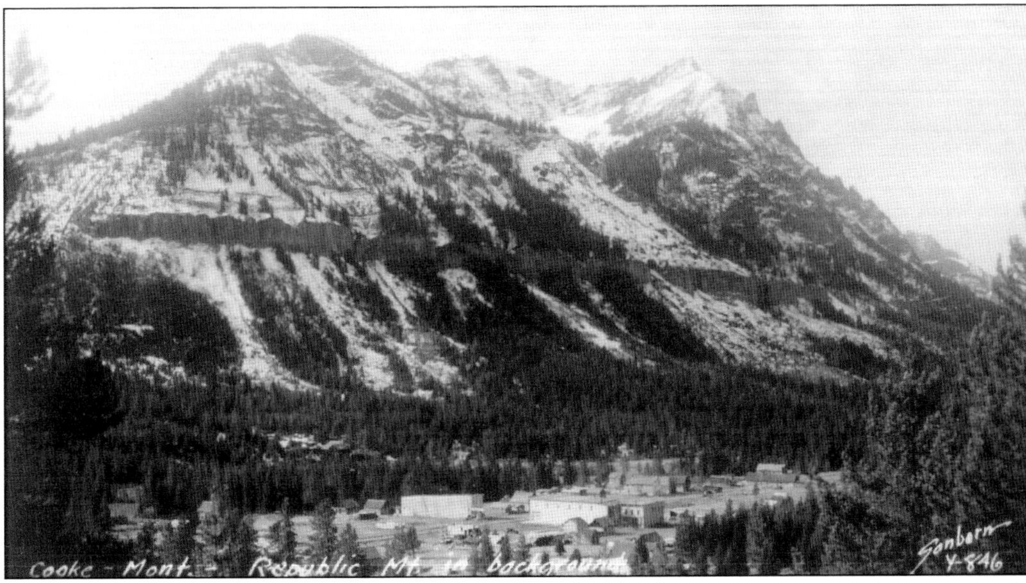

Having been previously known as Miner's Camp, Clark Fork City, and even Edelweiss, Cooke City, Montana Territory was officially named on February 1, 1882, in honor of Jay Cooke Jr., the son of a wealthy eastern financier who came to visit the mining area. Cooke estimated that the ore at the Republic mine was worth $100 a ton, but his operation would require massive outlays of money, much of which he funded. (Courtesy of Parmly Billings Library.)

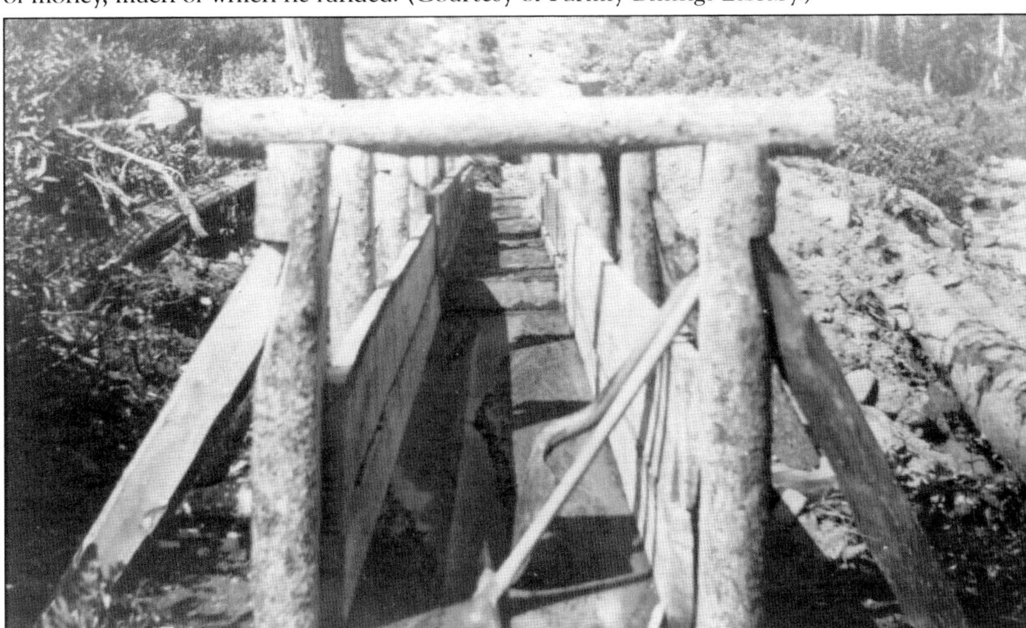

This sluice box was just a small example of the flurry of activity in the New World mining district. By 1890, three hundred additional claims had been filed. By the mid-1890s, about $50,000 of gold ore was shipped from the district. In 1894, in the wake of the national depression and the repeal of the Silver Act of 1890, which required the US Treasury to purchase silver, the Homestake, Daisy, and Alice E mines ceased operations. By 1905, several companies had reopened properties and developed new ones. (Courtesy of Carbon County Historical Society & Museum.)

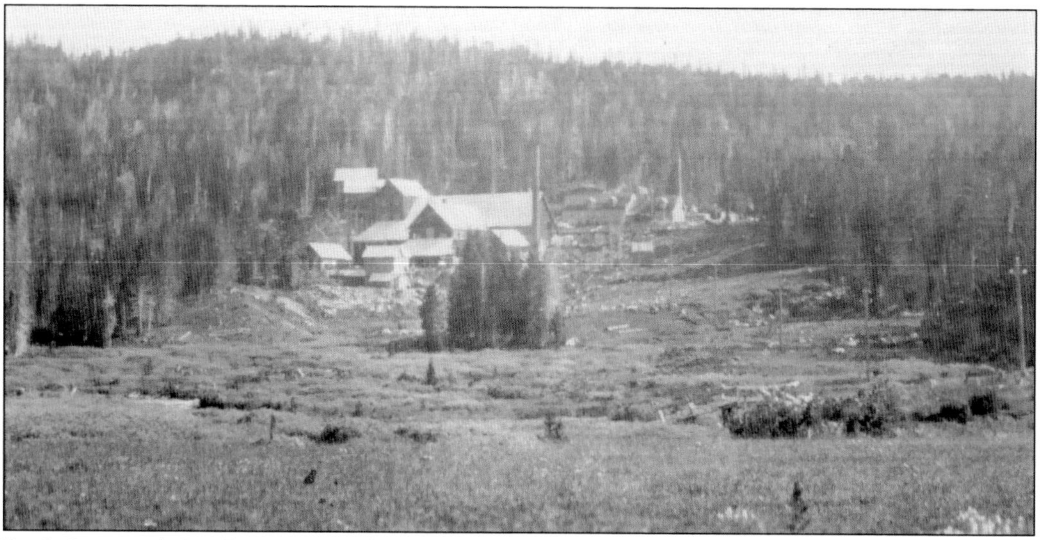

Prof. Gottwerth L. "Doc" Tanzer formed the Western Smelting and Power Company (WS&P), pictured here, in 1904. Tanzer began purchasing mining claims and raising capital for a large-scale mining venture with financial sources from throughout the United States and Europe, and by the 1910s, WS&P began development along the Fisher Creek area. The ambitious plan included a flume and 250-kilowatt hydroelectric generating plant located on the Clarks Fork River, a transmission line, sawmills, and a copper and gold smelter. The smelter was connected to the Gold Dust and Homestake mines by a 2,500-foot-long aerial tram. With the possible exception of the Homestake mine, none of the WS&P mines ever produced significant amounts of ore. The stock market crash of 1929 curtailed any investing and effectively ended mining development in the district. (Above, courtesy of Museum of the Beartooths; below, courtesy of USFS.)

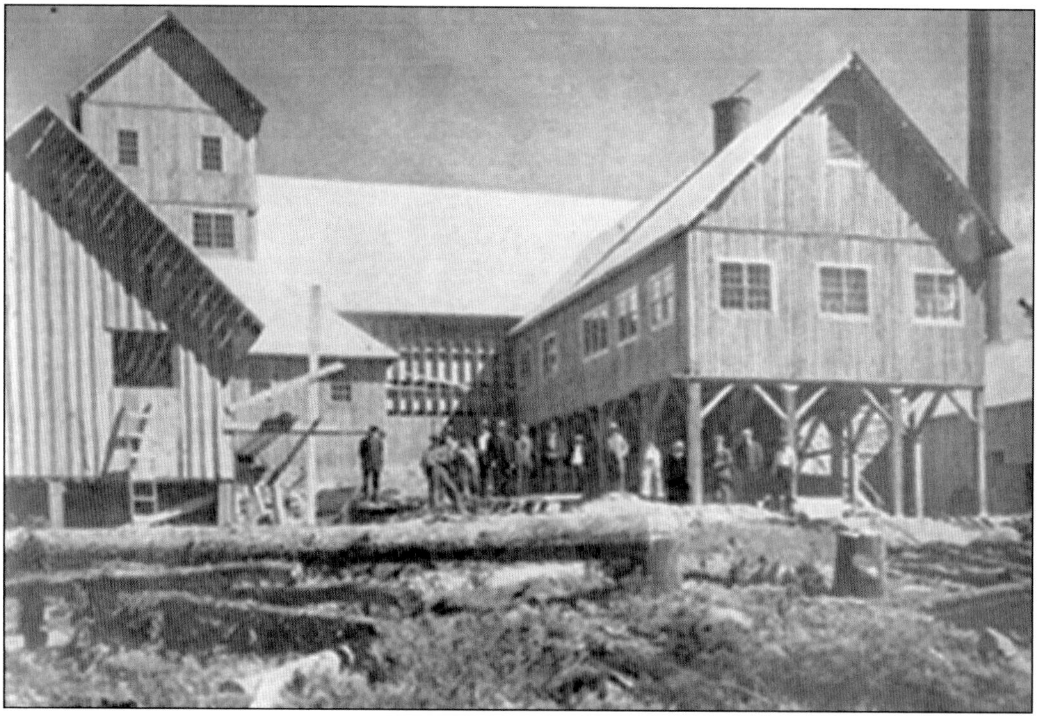

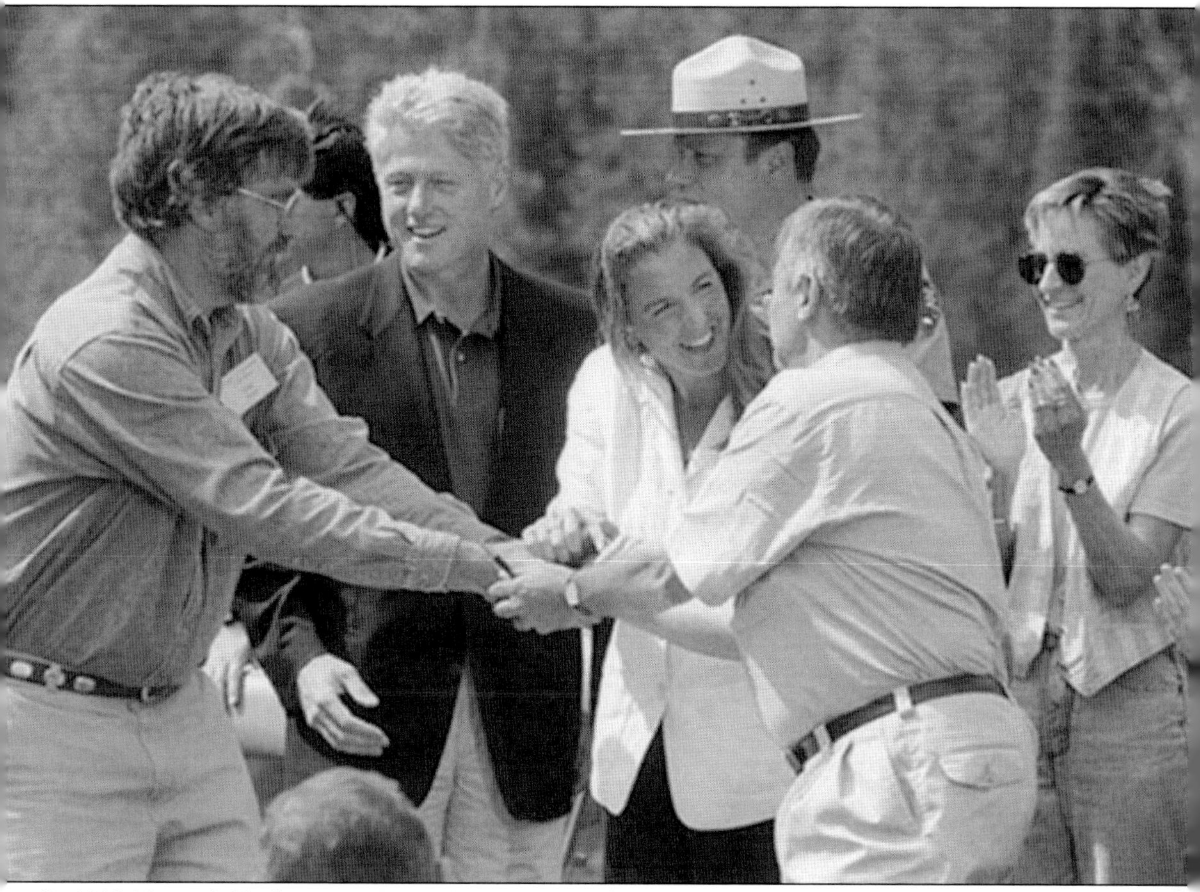

In 1990, Noranda Exploration–Crown Butte Mines submitted a hard rock permit application to the Montana Department of State Lands and the US Forest Service. The plan included underground mining near Henderson Mountain. From 1993 through 1997, a massive Draft Environmental Impact Statement was prepared. On August 25, 1995, Pres. Bill Clinton expressed concern that the proposed mine could endanger the Yellowstone ecosystem and ordered government officials to negotiate with Crown Butte Resources for a buyout or swap. A year later, President Clinton announced that an arrangement had been negotiated, the land and mineral rights were to become the property of the US government, and Crown Butte Mines would receive $65 million for its claims and mineral rights, with $22.5 million set aside for reclamation in the district. After surviving two attempts to develop a mine, one in the 1920s and one in the 1990s, gold-silver-copper deposits remain intact inside Henderson Mountain, under the protection of Gallatin National Forest. Additionally, a large portion of privately owned mining claims were purchased in 2010 and transferred to the Custer and Gallatin Forests. (Courtesy of *Bozeman Daily Chronicle.*)

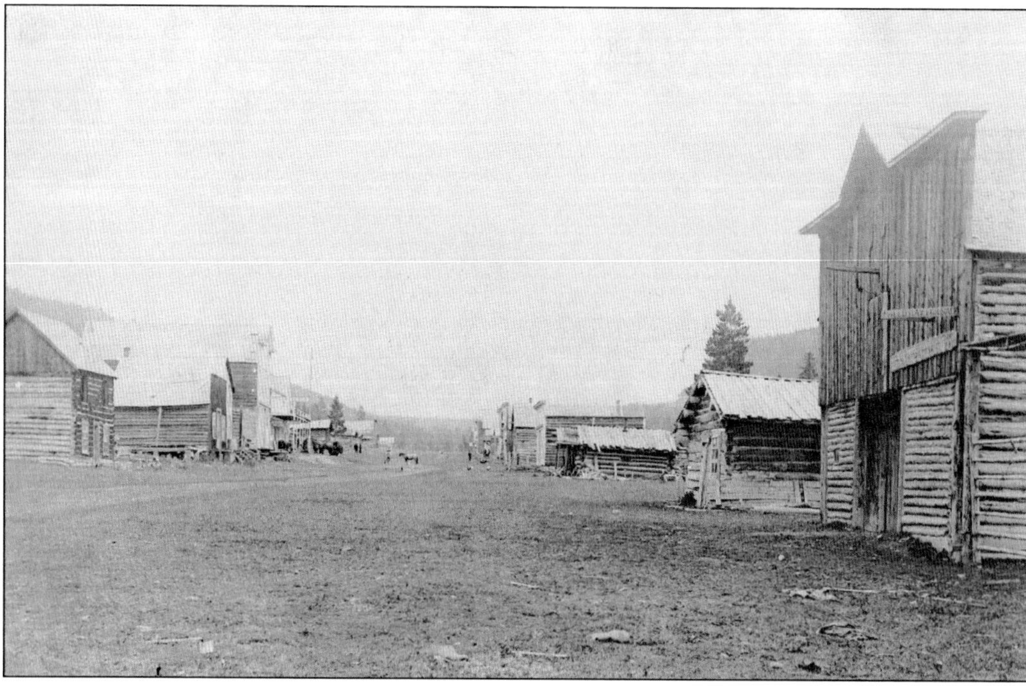

By late 1882, a total of 135 log cabins were scattered in the Cooke City area, along with two smelters, two sawmills, three general stores, two hotels, two livery stables, and a meat market. Town platting began in 1883. (Courtesy of Carbon County Historical Society & Museum.)

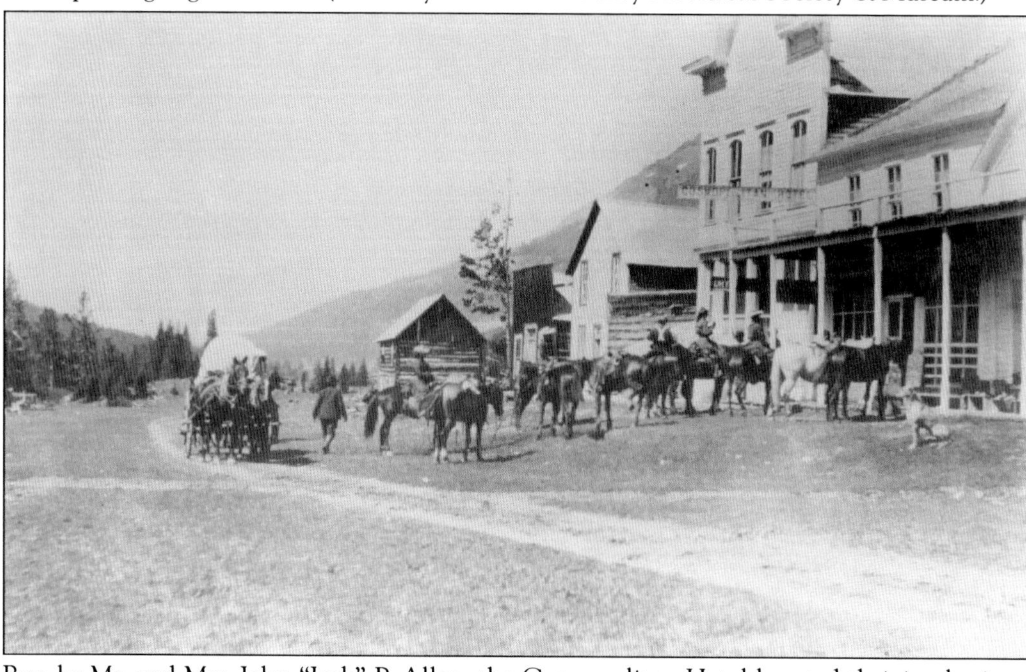

Run by Mr. and Mrs. John "Jack" P. Allen, the Cosmopolitan Hotel boasted thriving business and was home to many bachelor miners. Fred Koch, with the Hague expedition, stayed in Cooke City in 1893, paying $1.80 for one day of board and lodging and the same for stabling and feed for his horse. (Courtesy of Carbon County Historical Society & Museum.)

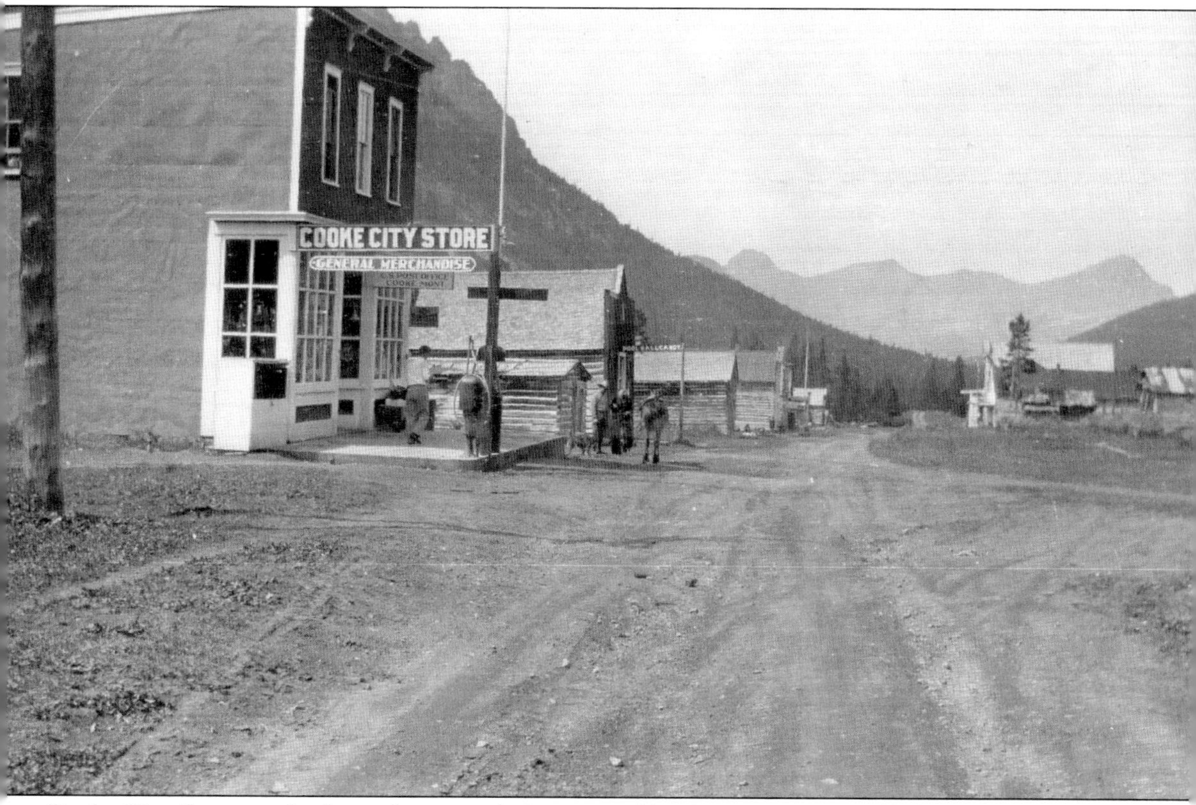

Cooke City Store was built on the grounds first owned by George Huston called the "Cache of Ore" Mill site. The spring of 1886 found John Savage and John Elder beginning construction of their general merchandise store here. By the late 1880s, they were supplying the community and area miners but had competition from the Bause and French general store. In the summer of 1893, when the national economy was experiencing a major depression, Cooke City Store, which had changed hands several times, was used for storage. In 1905, with a boost in the mining operations in part due to more efficient ore processing, several mining companies reopened. The Cooke City Smelter began leasing the store but only did it for a few years. In 1908, Nels and Elizabeth Soderholm bought the store. A nephew of the Soderholms, Sam Brady, took control until 1977, when Ralph and Sue Glidden purchased the store. Today, the store is owned and operated by Troy and Beth Wilson. (Courtesy of Museum of the Beartooths.)

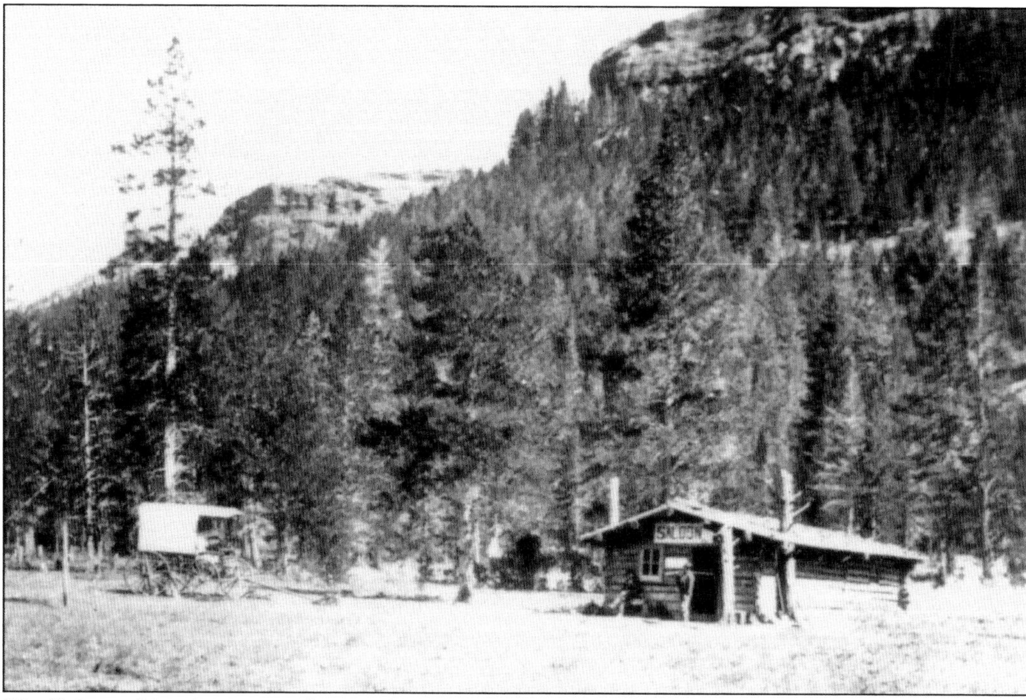

“Red” Sowash’s saloon near the Cooke City road, seen here in 1884, served miners traveling from Cooke City to Mammoth Hot Springs in Yellowstone Park. It was discovered in 1886 that the saloon was within the park boundary, and it was removed a year later. (Courtesy of Yellowstone National Park, No. 36522.)

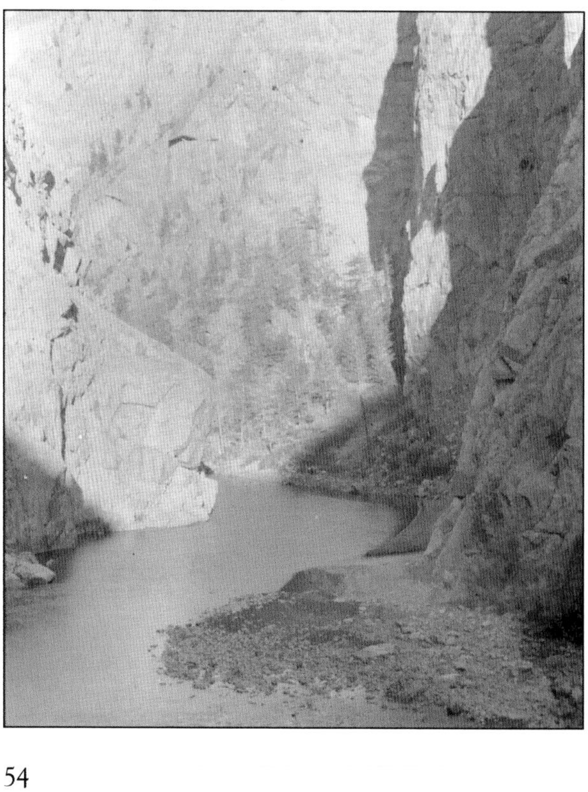

As early as the 1890s, gold seekers found the Clarks Fork River and canyon areas. One local newspaper account from 1893 mentioned that two men working about four miles above the mouth of Bennett Creek were getting paid $1.50 a day for eight and a half hours of work. It was also noted that the Chapman families filed a claim on the Mascot mine and the Sirrine family filed claims on the Nugget Queen and the Lookout. (Courtesy of Carbon County Historical Society & Museum.)

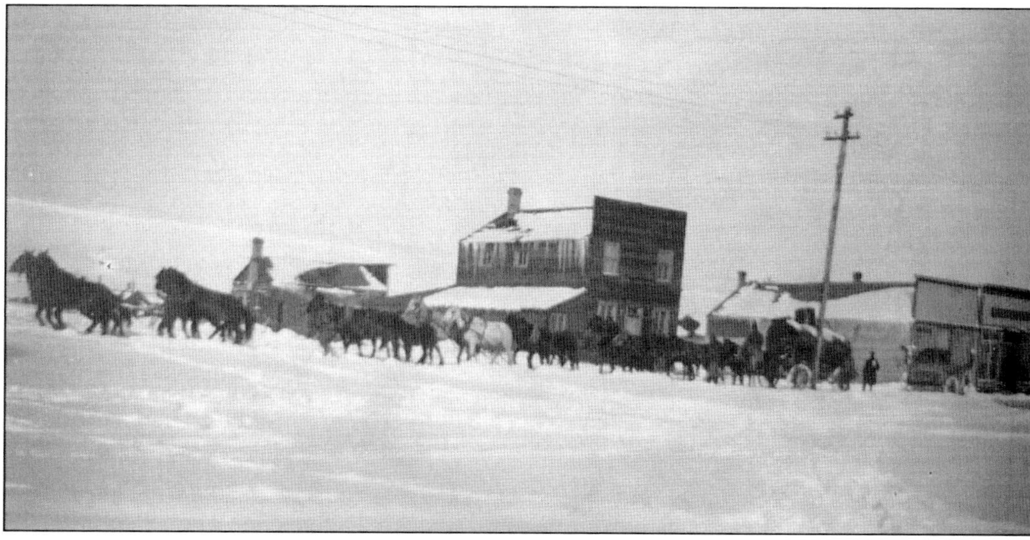

By 1914, gold-mining procedures along the Clarks Fork changed from using simple flume and sluice boxes to using dredging equipment. These dredges, made with excavating cranes, could pull in yards of material at one time. This eight-horse team hauls a 60-horsepower boiler to be used in an electric plant at a Clarks Fork mining camp, lending visibility for night shifts. (Courtesy of Carbon County Historical Society & Museum.)

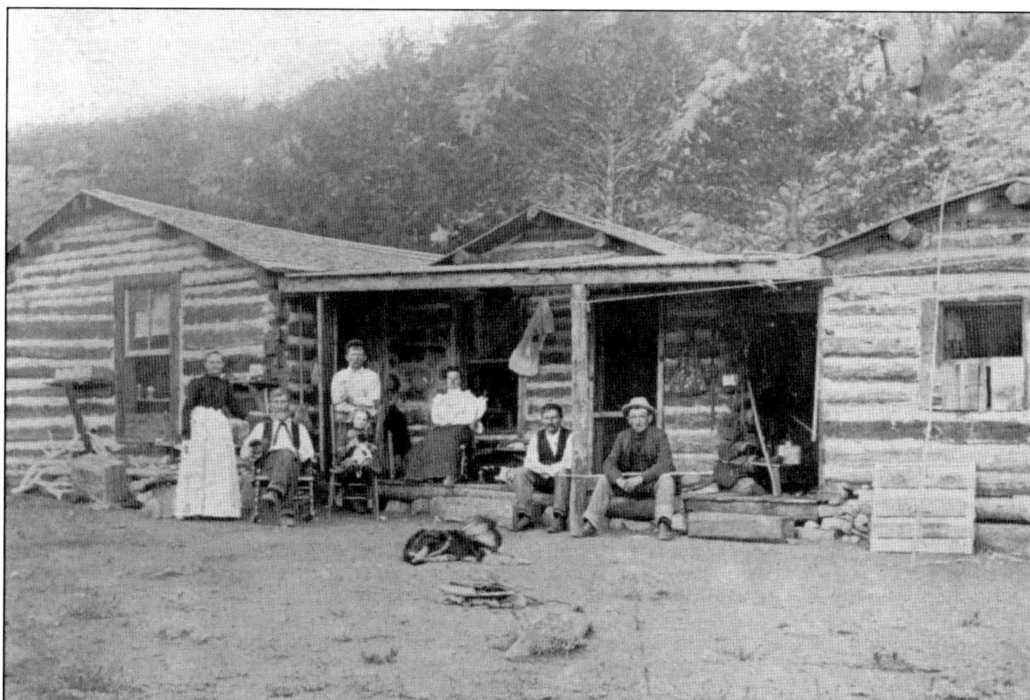

The J.P. Hughes homestead was located near Nye City. Hughes was a seasoned prospector from the Cripple Creek, Colorado, and Old Mexico mines. In 1901, six miles from the Nye post office at Camp Hugheston, he found what was thought to be the largest mother lode in the district. The assay showed large amounts of gold and silver, but Hughes sold his claims the following year. (Courtesy of Museum of the Beartooths.)

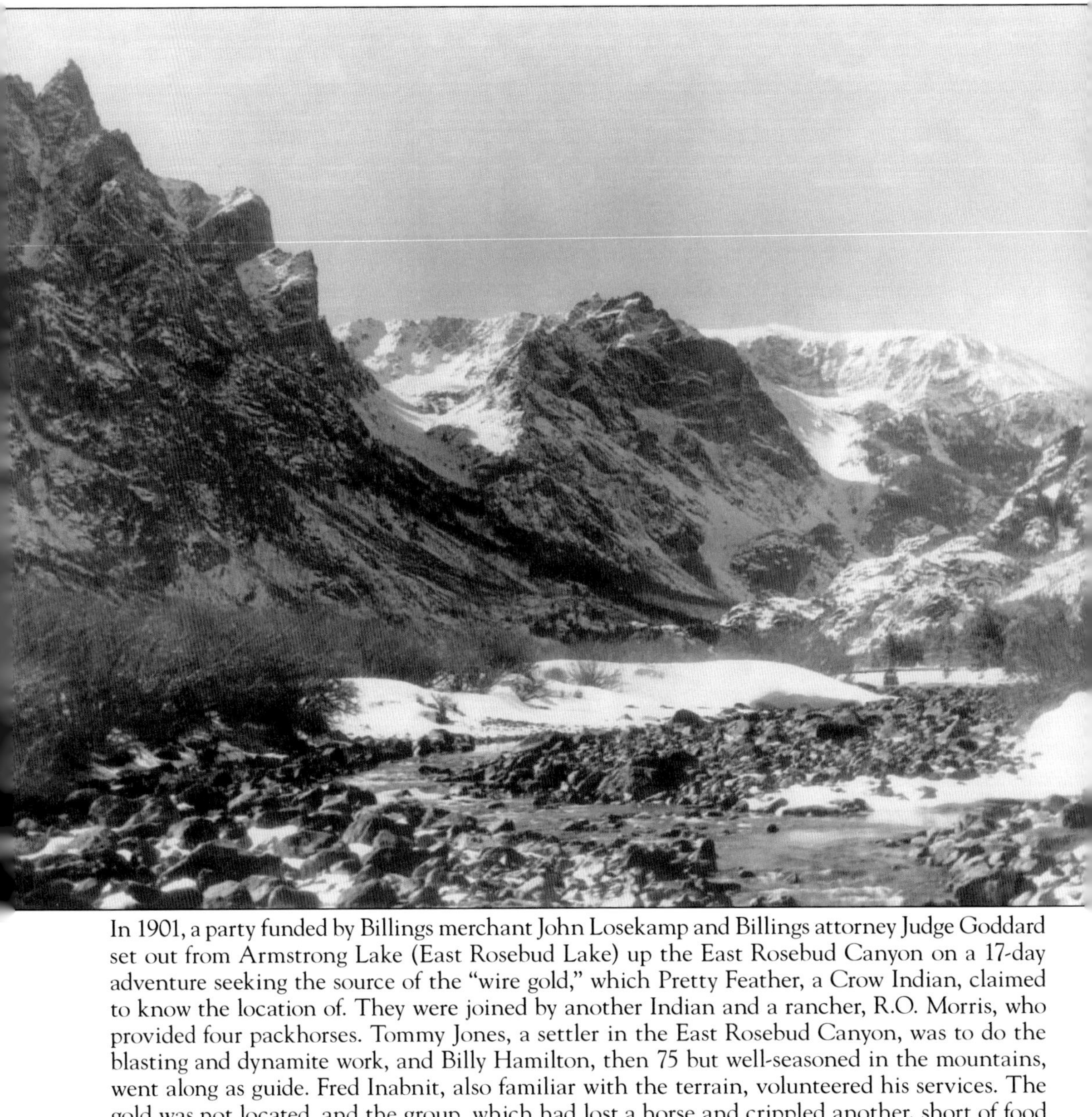

In 1901, a party funded by Billings merchant John Losekamp and Billings attorney Judge Goddard set out from Armstrong Lake (East Rosebud Lake) up the East Rosebud Canyon on a 17-day adventure seeking the source of the "wire gold," which Pretty Feather, a Crow Indian, claimed to know the location of. They were joined by another Indian and a rancher, R.O. Morris, who provided four packhorses. Tommy Jones, a settler in the East Rosebud Canyon, was to do the blasting and dynamite work, and Billy Hamilton, then 75 but well-seasoned in the mountains, went along as guide. Fred Inabnit, also familiar with the terrain, volunteered his services. The gold was not located, and the group, which had lost a horse and crippled another, short of food and wet from three days of rain, returned discouraged and disgruntled. (Courtesy of Museum of the Beartooths.)

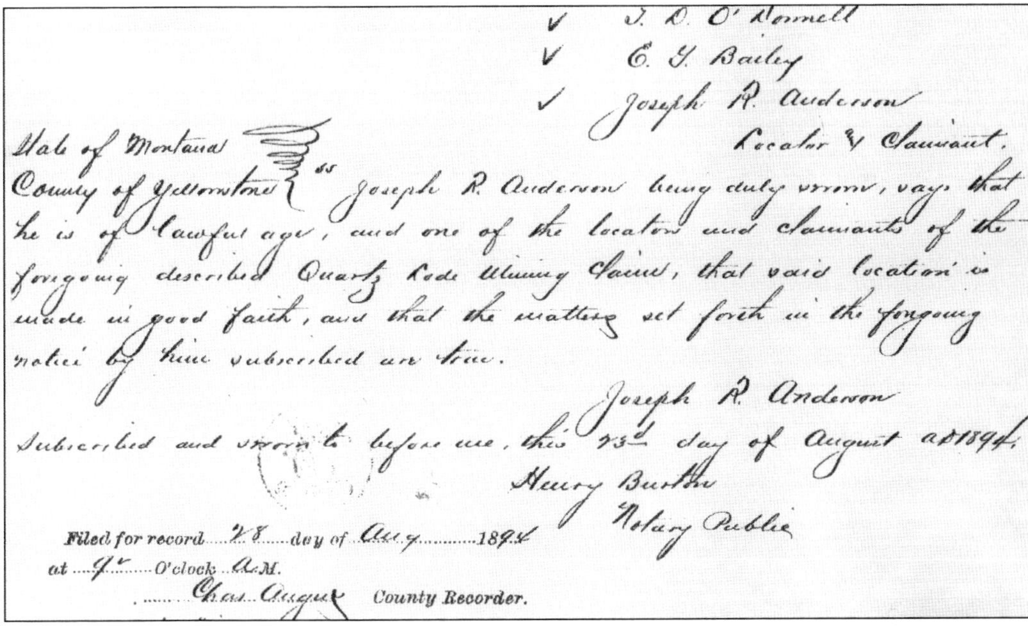

I. D. O'Donnell
E. G. Bailey
Joseph R. Anderson
Locator & Claimant.

State of Montana
County of Yellowstone } ss

Joseph R. Anderson being duly sworn, says that he is of lawful age, and one of the locators and claimants of the foregoing described Quartz Lode Mining Claim, that said location is made in good faith, and that the matters set forth in the foregoing notice by him subscribed are true.

Joseph R. Anderson

Subscribed and sworn to before me, this 23rd day of August AD 1894.

Henry Burth
Notary Public

Filed for record 28 day of Aug 1894
at 9 O'clock A.M.
Chas. August County Recorder.

Joseph Anderson, known as "Skookum Joe," came to Montana from Oregon in the 1860s. In his diaries, he mentions being in the Natural Bridge area on the Boulder River in 1870. By the late 1880s, he was opening mines in the Nye area. With financial backing from Edward Bailey, George Griggs, and Ignatius Daniel "I.D." O'Donnell, Skookum Joe filed many claims in the Stillwater and East Boulder basins, including the 1894 quartz claim in the East Boulder (above). In 1892, he built a road to the Picket Pin Canyon (below), which he reportedly named for "an iron picket pin in a tree" near the camp and the general abundance of pickets, used to stake horses, found around the first camp he set up in 1887. Shortly before his death, Skookum Joe claimed to have found several large gold nuggets. (Above, courtesy of Museum of the Beartooths; below, courtesy of Crazy Mountain Museum.)

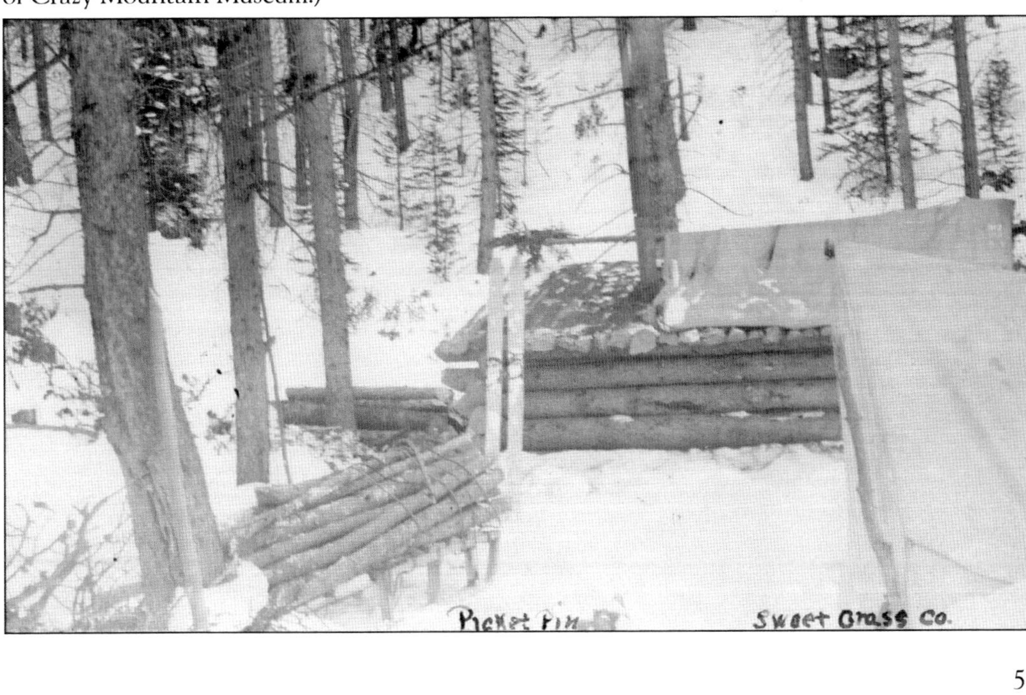

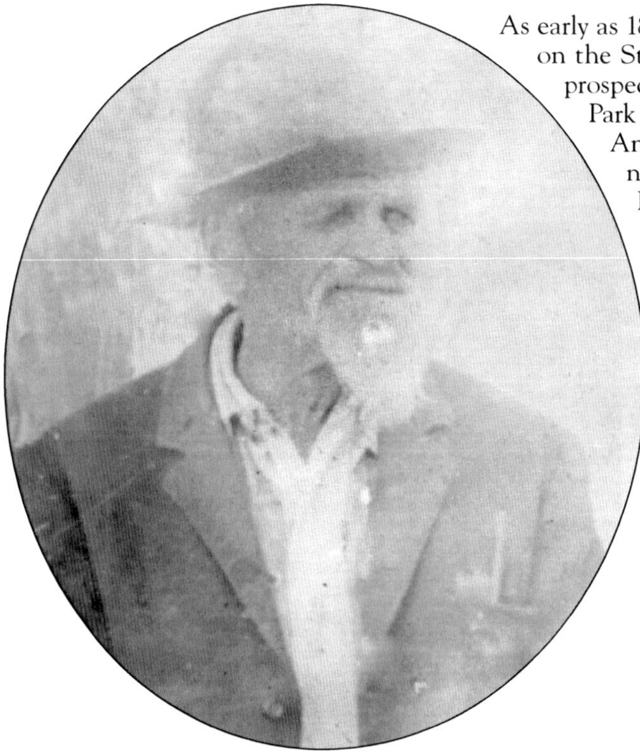

As early as 1864, Ansel Hubble was trapping furs on the Stillwater River, when an eye out for prospects directed him to the Yellowstone Park region. Prospecting here with the Lou Anderson party in 1867, he named several natural features, such as Crevice Creek, Hell Roaring Creek, and Slough Creek. Near the East Boulder River, he filed a claim in 1893 on Iron Creek, and the following year, he filed claims near the Dry Fork, in what is now known as Hubble Gulch. The mines produced some gold and nickel but mostly copper. (Courtesy of Museum of the Beartooths.)

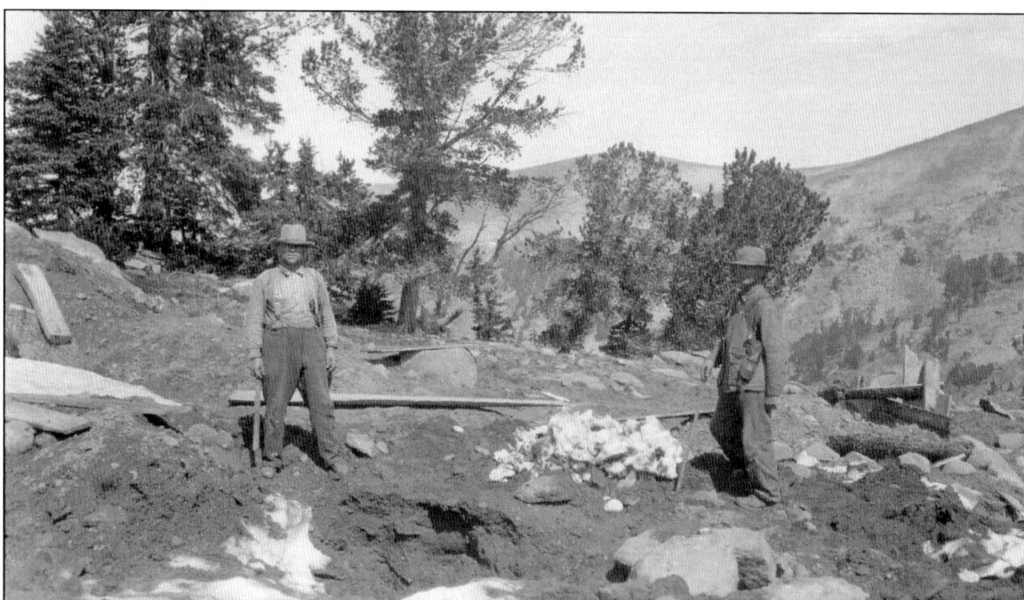

In September 1924, sheriff Ed Brannin (left) of Sweet Grass County started out on a search reported by area forest ranger Harry Kaufman, who suspected Henry Hughson missing when he passed near the prospector's cabin at Independence, where Hughson owned a mining claim. A trail found leading to a nearby lake made it look like a drowning, but it was a decoy, and Hughson's murdered body was found nine months later in an old tunnel. The suspect, Frank Lewis, escaped from jail and was never found. (Courtesy of Crazy Mountain Museum.)

Five

RESOURCE DEVELOPMENT

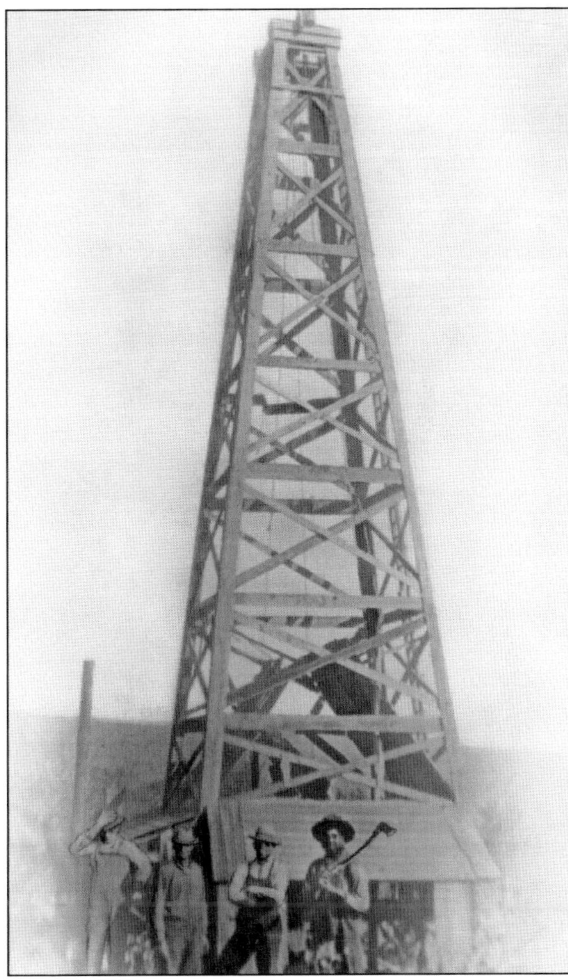

This oil well in the Butcher Creek district, west of Red Lodge, had six holes ranging in depth from 400 feet to 750 feet and producing heavy petroleum. First discovered by the White brothers, the wells were filed upon by Sam Taggart and George Taff in 1892. Dividing their ownership with a new partner, Thomas Cruse, the newly named Butcher Creek Oil Company included 1,120 acres of patented oil land. (Courtesy of Carbon County Historical Society & Museum.)

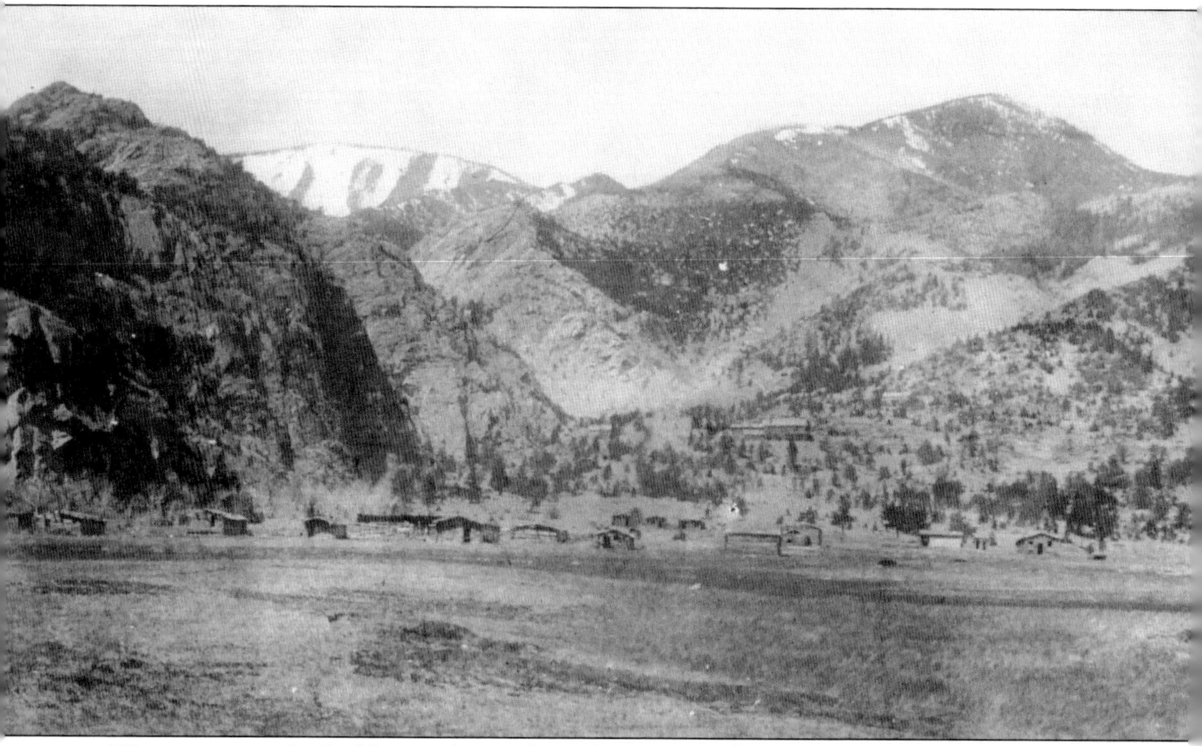

The existence of valuable metal ores along the upper Stillwater River drainage was discovered in the late 1860s by Ansel Hubble and Joseph "Skookum Joe" Anderson. In 1883, Jack Nye, with Jimmy and Jonas Hedges, located copper and nickel deposits nearby. Jack Nye then formed the Stillwater Mining Company in 1884 and sold their claims to Minneapolis Mining the following year. Serious development of the mining properties began when the Stillwater Mining Company, Minneapolis Mining, and the Nicollet and Hennepin Company moved into the area. By 1886, a small smelter had been assembled, and Nye City, pictured here, grew to a peak population of 300 to 400 people, with six saloons, a store, a commissary, a boardinghouse, and an assay office. However, a government survey of the Stillwater basin revealed that Nye City was actually on Crow reservation lands. Since government laws prohibited exploitation of tribal lands, the mining operations had to be removed. By 1889, Nye City was abandoned. However, in 1892, Congress ratified the Crow cession of 1,800,000 acres of the reservation, opening homesteading, claim staking, and mining in the area. (Courtesy of Museum of the Beartooths.)

This mining complex and mill camp, with housing for the workers in the foreground, came directly from the efforts of William Mouat. In 1913, while employed as a geologist with Prairie Oil Company, Mouat became intrigued with the mining potential of the Nye area. And in the mid-1930s, he persuaded Princeton University to study for chromite in the locale. By 1941, the property was incorporated as Mouat Nickel Mines. (Courtesy of USFS, Custer National Forest.)

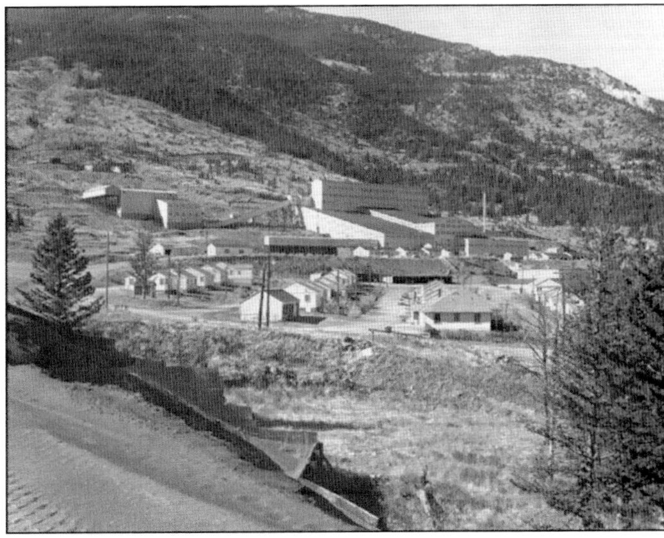

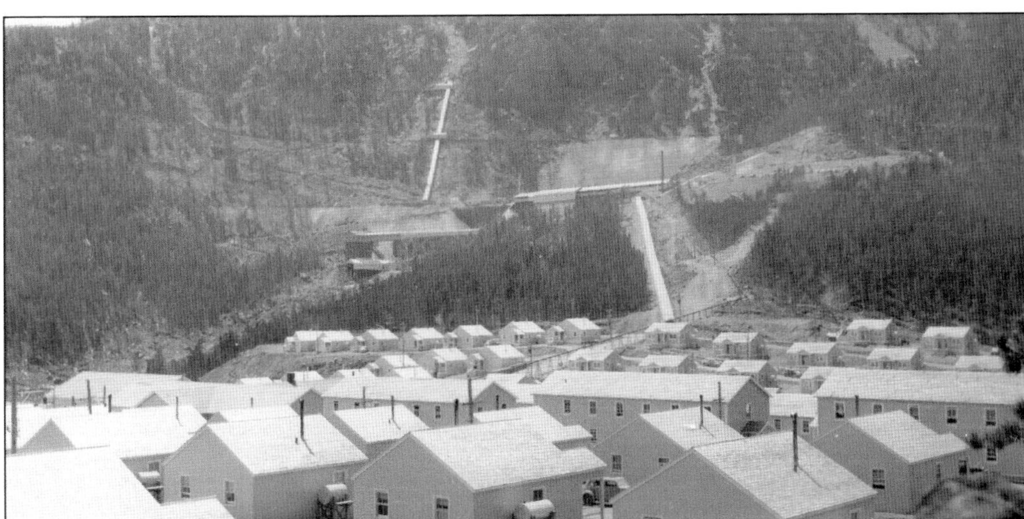

As World War II broke out, foreign supplies of chromite ore were cut off and the federal government deemed it imperative that ore be obtained for strengthening alloy steels so they did not rust or corrode. The Anaconda Minerals Company, acting as supervisor for the federal government's Metals Reserve Corporation, opened this mine. The workers' camp in the foreground was known as "Lake Camp" because of the adjacent lake. (Courtesy of Museum of the Beartooths.)

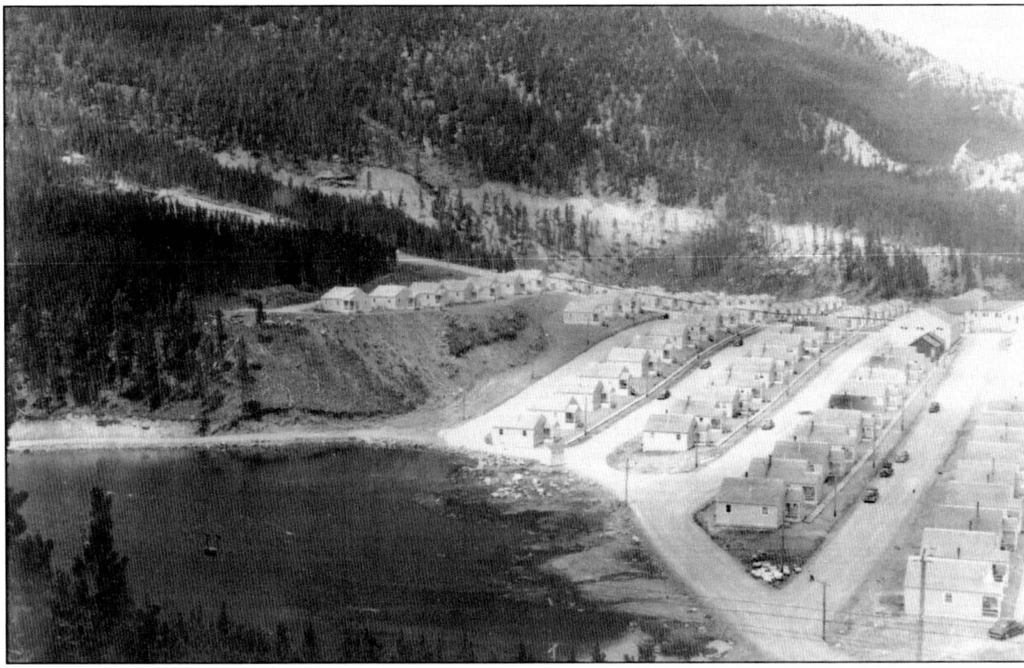

Lake Camp, with the lake in the foreground, included 100 homes, eight dormitories, and a mess hall and recreation center with a bowling alley. Over $8.4 million was spent building the plant, the ore treatment plant, and the two housing complexes for workers. Mining was halted in 1943, as foreign supplies of chromite ore were available once again, but the mine was kept on standby until the end of the war. (Courtesy of Museum of the Beartooths.)

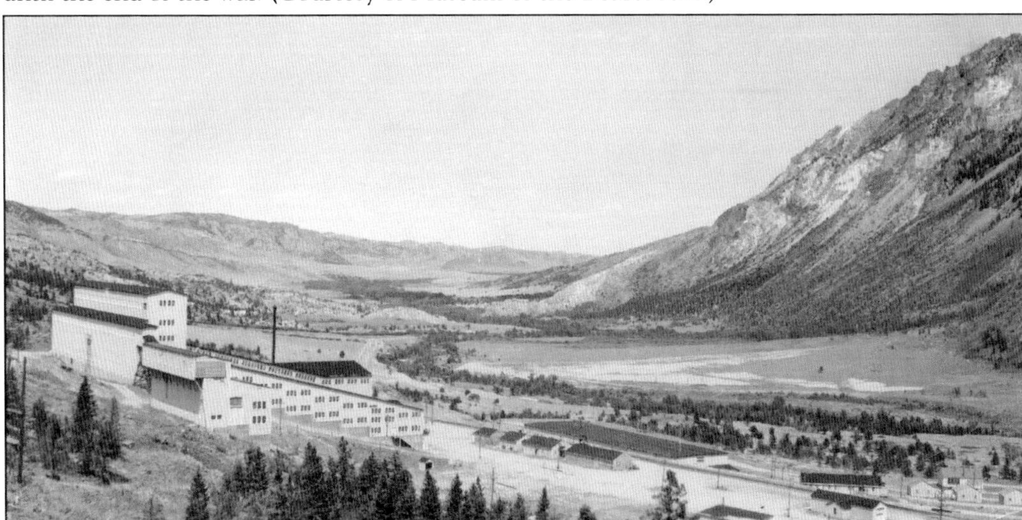

By the mid-1940s, most of the remaining housing had been sold and removed. In 1952, during the Korean War, the federal government awarded an eight-year contract to American Chrome Company to stockpile chromite. The Mouat mine was renamed the American mine, with updated equipment and rebuilt housing. By 1962, the mine closed, and the company sold all the assets, and abandoning the area once again. Today, the site is owned by Stillwater Mining Company. (Courtesy of Museum of the Beartooths.)

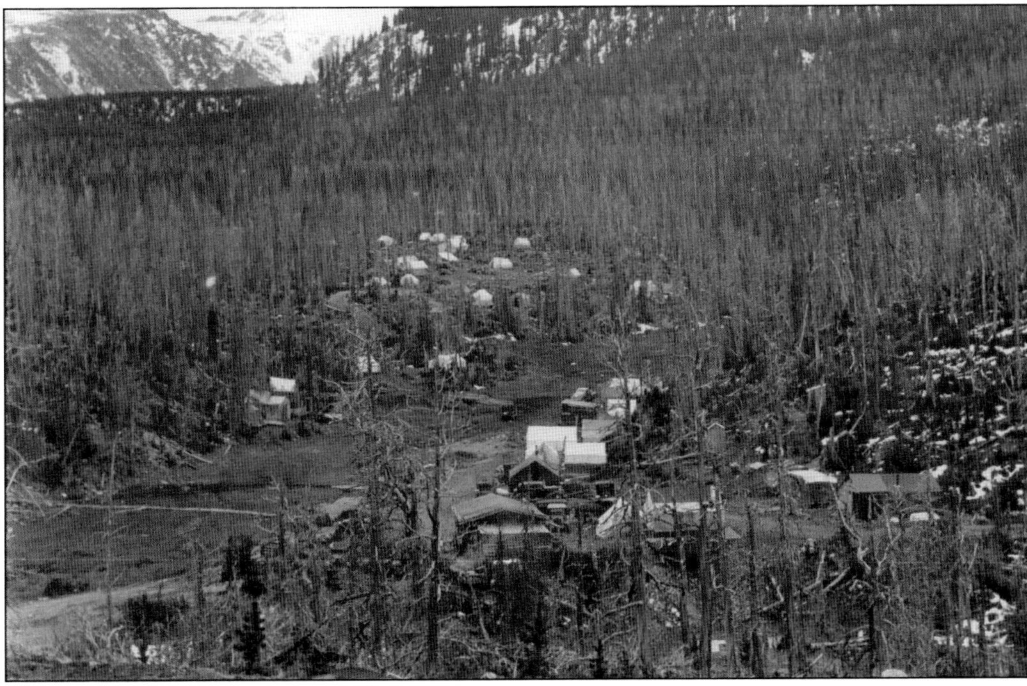

Thomas Chalkey Benbow was the first to develop a chromite mine along Little Rocky Creek near Dean in 1905. This early mining camp at Benbow did not develop in earnest until 1929, when a road and cabins were built and three adits were dug, one over 500 feet long. This horse, struggling in a 1929 spring snowstorm at Benbow, shows that conditions were harsh, with some of the mines located as high as 8,500 feet. This same year, due to financial uncertainties, further mining activity was halted. Thomas Benbow never lived to see his dreams of a productive mine come true, dying on December 17, 1932. His claims were sold but remained dormant. (Both, courtesy of Museum of the Beartooths.)

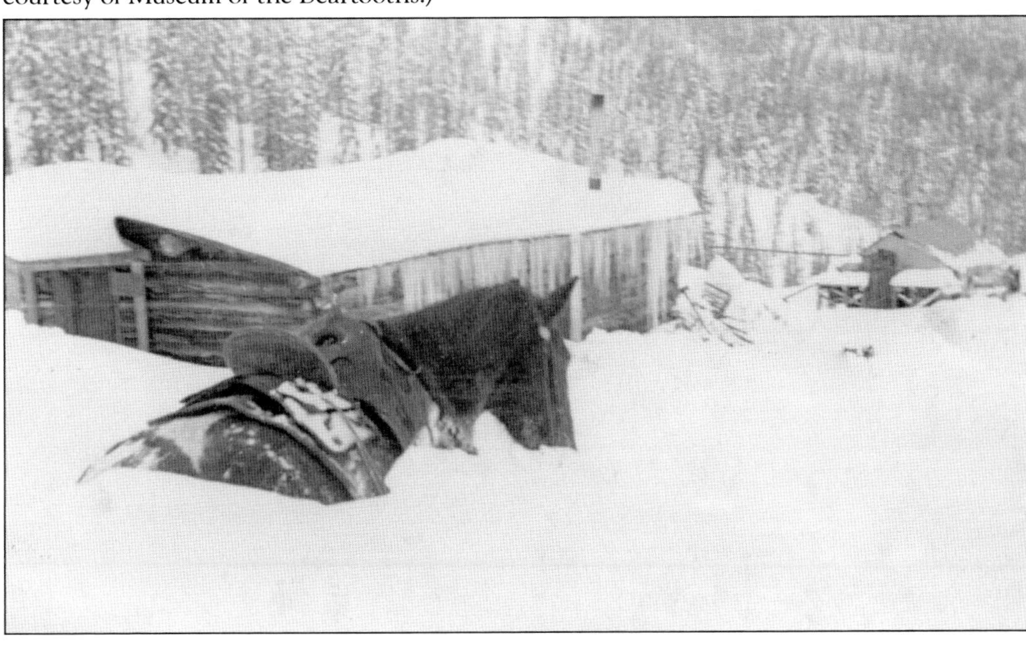

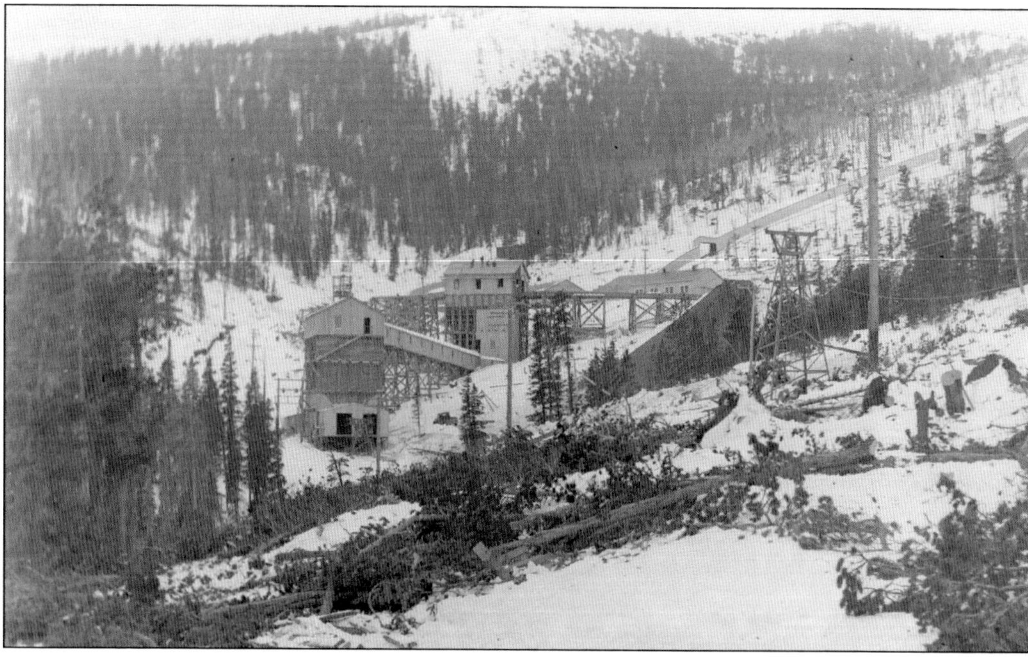

In 1941, the Anaconda Minerals Company, in cooperation with the federal government, took over the mining properties in the Stillwater area, including the Benbow and Mouat mines and the Gish mine area on the Boulder River. During this period of World War II, chromite ore was on the strategic list of minerals essential to the war. A 10-year lease led to expansion of the Benbow mining area pictured here. A warehouse, shop, garage, and 30 cabins for miners were built at the camp. A 3.5-mile aerial tram and a 1,400-foot-long incline tram, covered by a shed, ran to the upper adits. In 1943, the US government halted the mining, as higher-grade foreign ore was once again available. The leases at Benbow were canceled in 1946, and the surface facilities at the mine and mill were removed. (Both, courtesy of Museum of the Beartooths.)

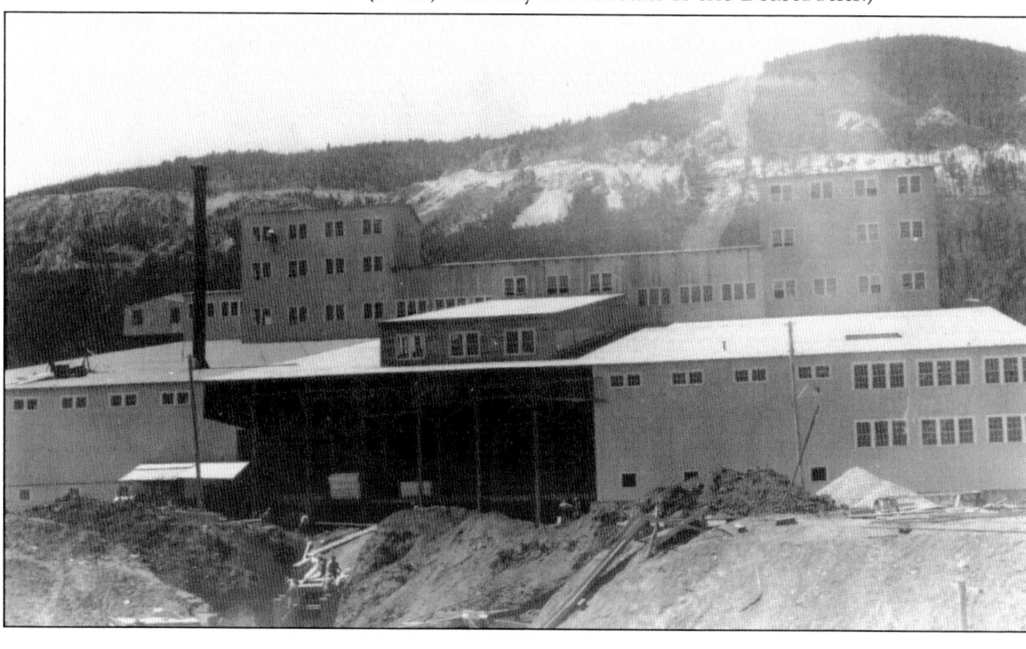

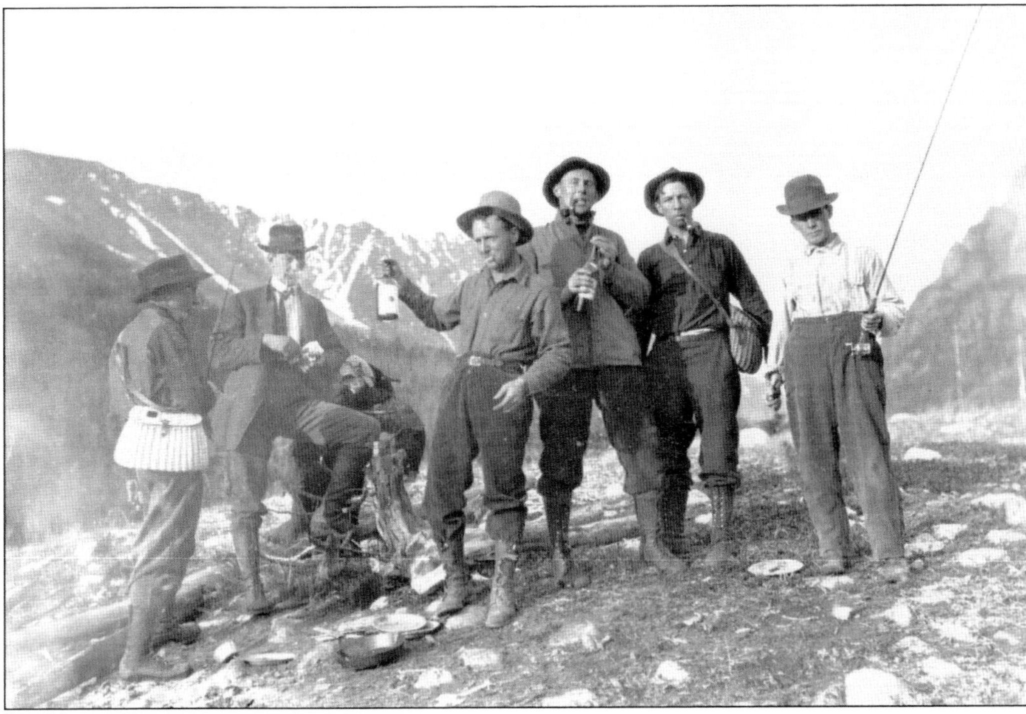

While this group was living it up on Hellroaring Plateau, serious development was also taking place there. Chrome deposits were filed up in 1920 by Melvin E. Martin. In 1933, Montana Chrome, Inc., organized to develop the mines. Later, with the outbreak of World War II, the stockpiling of chromite increased, and US Vanadium Corporation contracted with the US government to mine. By 1941, an eight-mile road had been constructed to the mining camp on the Hellroaring Plateau. (Courtesy of Carbon County Historical Society & Museum.)

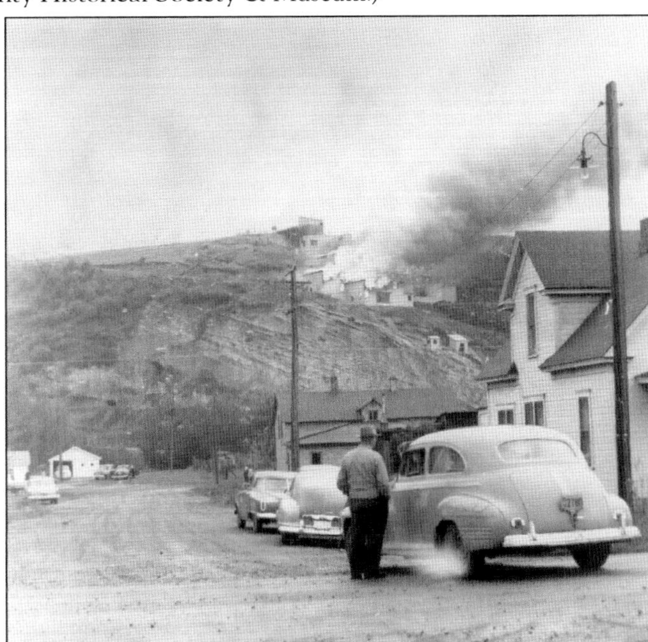

The Beartooth Highway provided the route for hauling ore to the mill on the east bench of Red Lodge. Over 7,000 tons of chromite ore were mined, hauled, and stockpiled by 1942. In the following two years, 76,000 tons were stockpiled from the Line Creek and Hellroaring operations. Red Lodge chrome mining ended in 1943, when foreign supplies became available. The Red Lodge mill burned in 1951. (Courtesy of Carbon County Historical Society & Museum.)

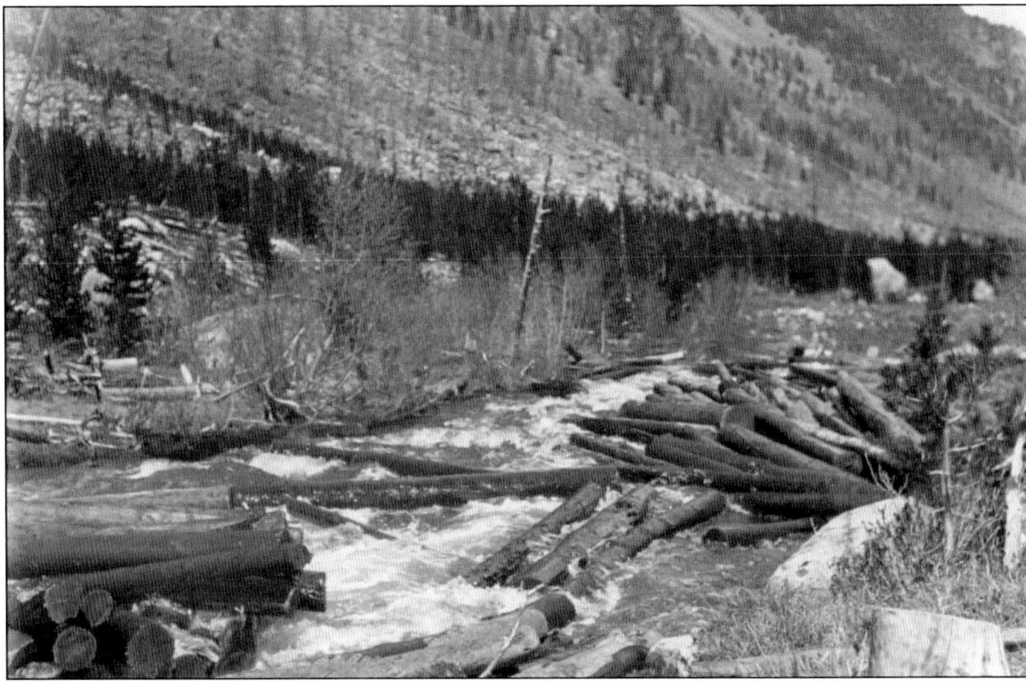

From about 1899 to 1916, Rock Creek was used annually for "spring drives" to float logs cut during the winter down to Red Lodge sawmills. A few drainages west, the Montana Lumber Company floated logs similarly down the Boulder River, piling them near the company's sawmill at Dornix below the mouth of the Boulder River for railroad ties. (Courtesy of Carbon County Historical Society & Museum.)

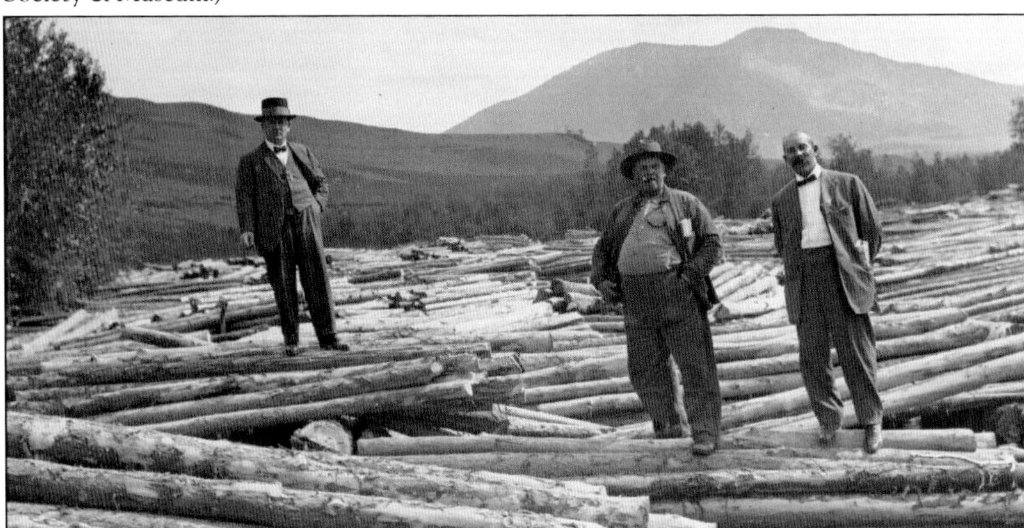

In 1889, A.S. Douglas brought the first sawmill into the area. Sawmills in the Red Lodge area produced lumber as early as 1890, bunching up logs near Red Lodge. The area was well suited for it, with the steep canyons providing "ground chutes" to skid the tree-length logs to the river's edge. Lumber was in heavy demand in this area for use in mine props and housing for miners. Great amounts of cordwood were also consumed in the lime burners. (Courtesy of Carbon County Historical Society & Museum.)

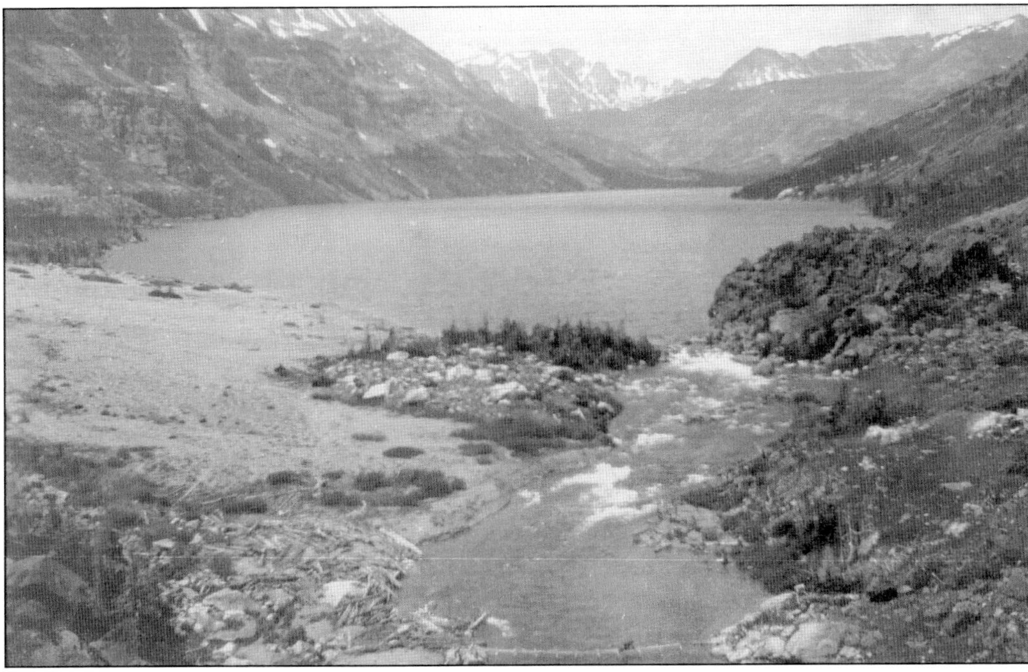

Nestled in the Beartooth Mountains at 7,560 feet along the West Rosebud drainage lays Mystic Lake, a natural reservoir that was tapped for the Mystic Lake power plant project, pictured here before the dam was constructed. After 15 miles of new road were completed in 1923, the road alone had cost $75,000, while the total project costs were around $1 million. (Courtesy of Museum of the Beartooths.)

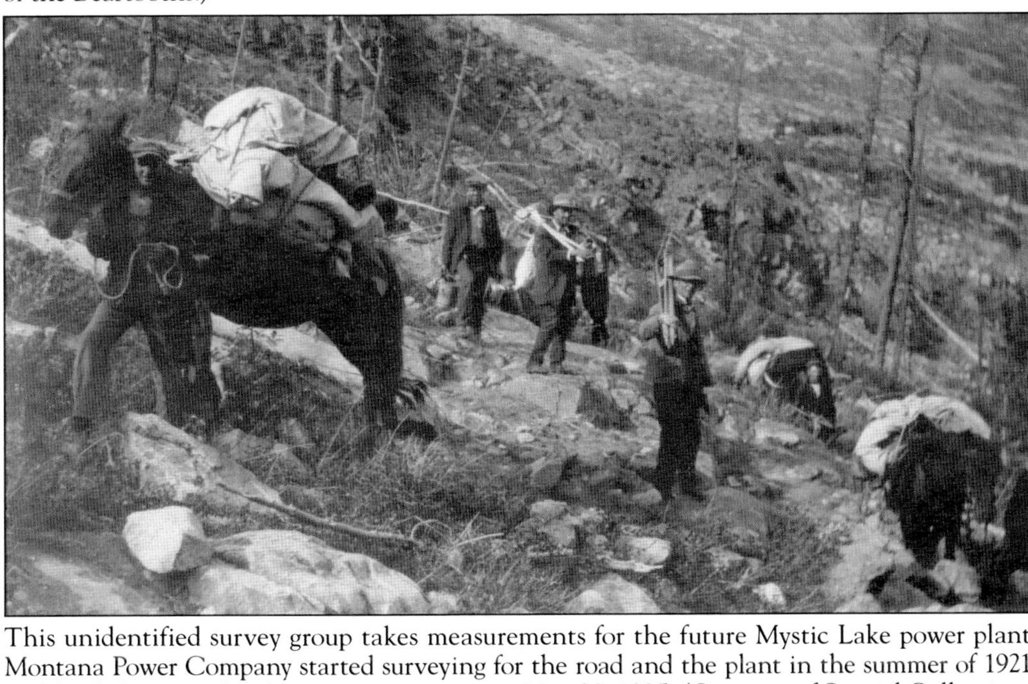

This unidentified survey group takes measurements for the future Mystic Lake power plant. Montana Power Company started surveying for the road and the plant in the summer of 1921, and final clearance for the system was given on May 20, 1925. (Courtesy of Special Collections, Montana State University Library, Bozeman.)

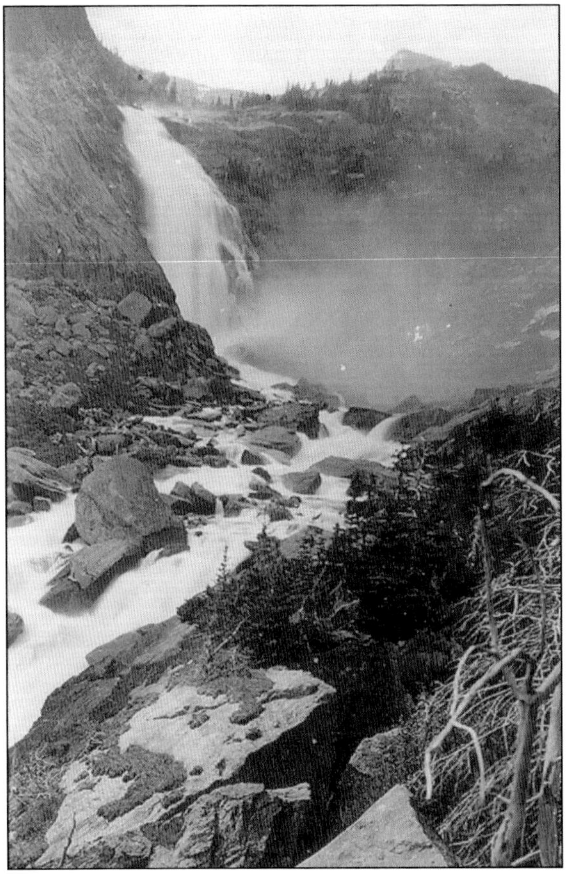

West Rosebud Falls was a popular destination for outdoor enthusiasts, but the falls were eliminated when Mystic Lake, the water source of the falls, was channeled for the Mystic Lake power project. The lake bed was shattered with dynamite, and a tunnel was bored to channel the waters into a pipeline that followed the mountainside down to the power plant. (Courtesy of Museum of the Beartooths.)

This 48-inch pipeline was constructed of cedar banded together and conducted the water from the lake bed for two miles. The water then coursed into a surge tank before entering steel penstock pipe that split the water and channeled it into the powerhouse, propelling a pair of eight-ton Pelton wheels that created 6.2 megawatts of power each. (Courtesy of Museum of the Beartooths.)

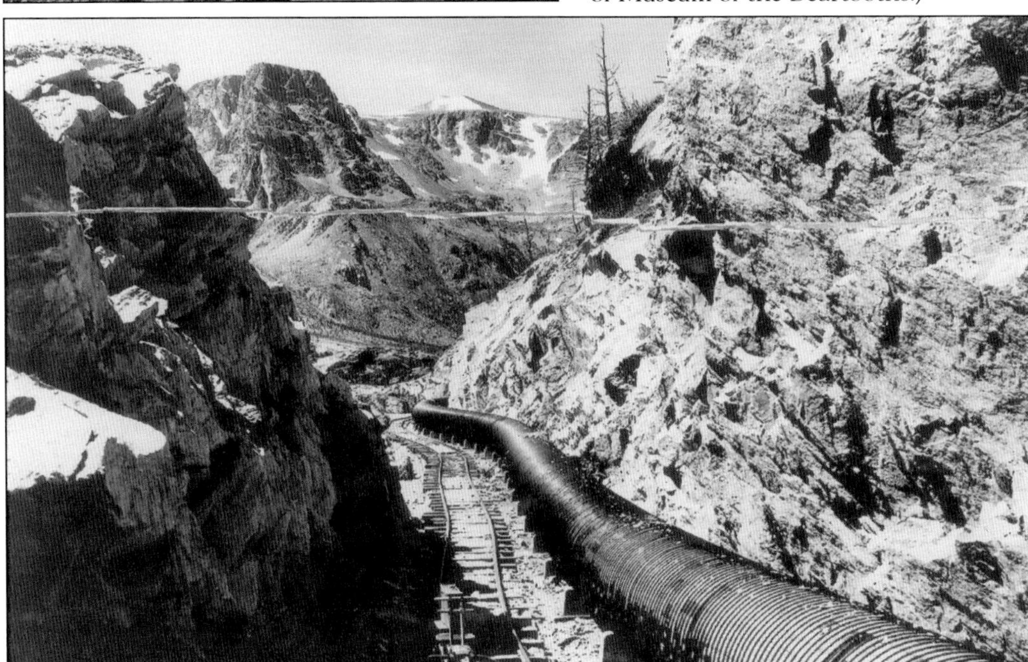

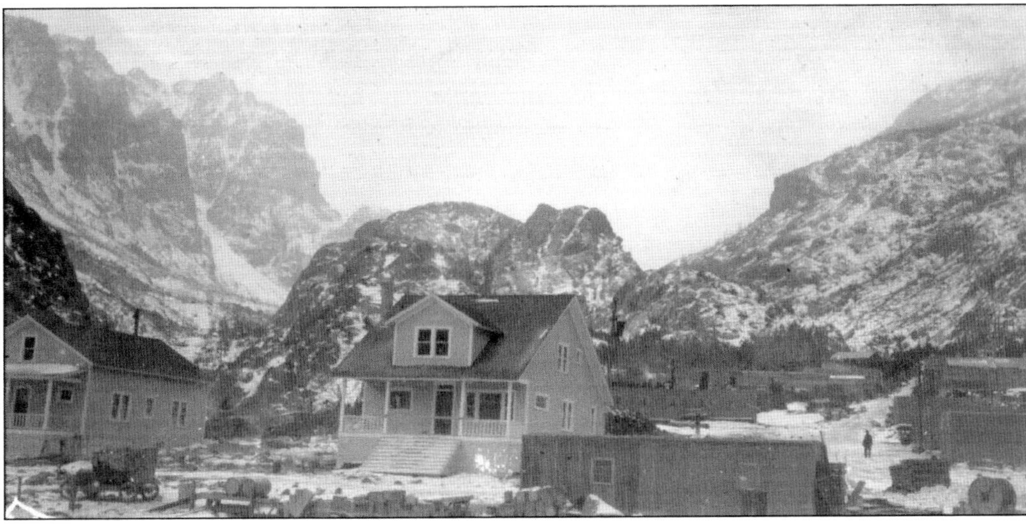

Eight homes, a community center, a school, warehouses, a stable, and storerooms were constructed near the power plant. With a few updates, the power plant still produces power today, although there are fewer homes and no school, and the path of the pipeline was modified due to a landslide. (Courtesy of Carbon County Historical Society & Museum.)

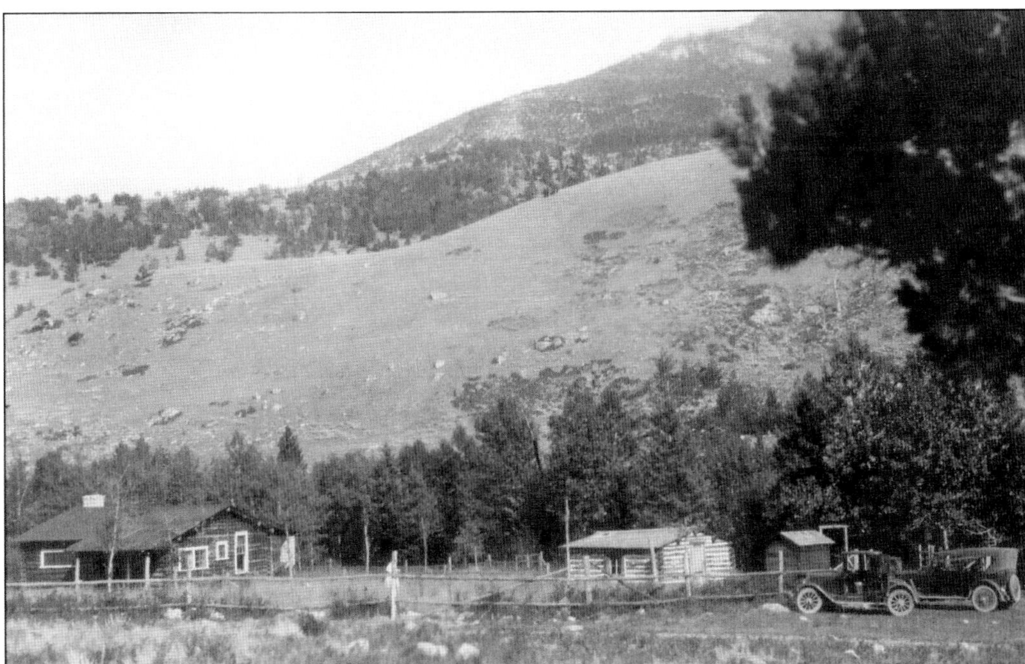

In 1930, W. Taylor Thom Jr. and Richard Field from Princeton's geology department, along with 19 participants, initiated the Red Lodge Project to conduct geologic studies and train students around Red Lodge. The Beartooth Mountains were chosen for their relatively unknown geology. Dr. Siegfriedt's camp near Piney Dell, pictured here, was the base of operations for three years. (Courtesy of Carbon County Historical Society & Museum.)

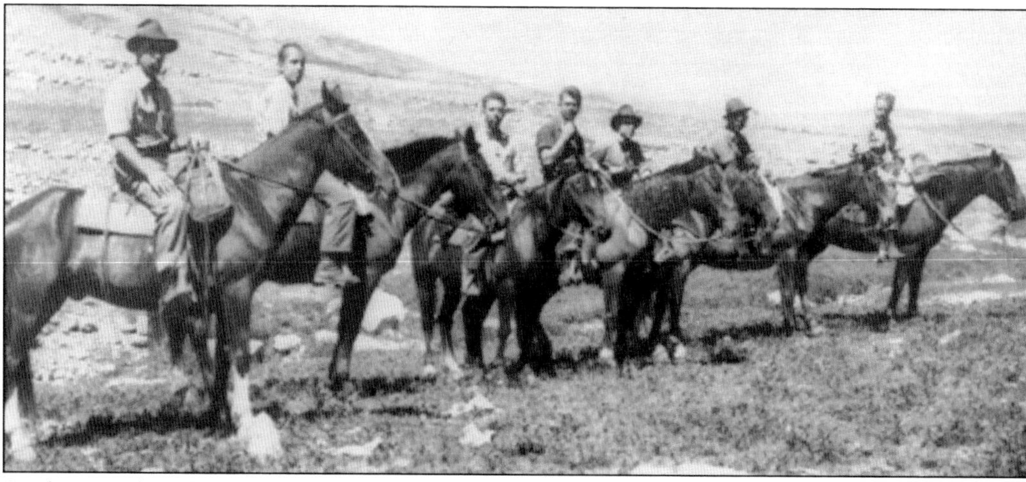

Students and professors from the Red Lodge Project ride horseback at the foot of Beartooth Butte in 1931. They are, from left to right, Ferd Roebling, Archbald Brooks, Alfred Rode Jr., Allen Whitlock, John Kemmerer Jr., Erling Dorf, and John Disbrow. Field parties led by Professor Dorf returned for a number of years. Once, a rumor spread that they were fishing without a license, but upon showing their fish fossils to the sheriff, he declared, "Doggonit, the drinks are on me back in town." (Courtesy of Yellowstone Bighorn Research Association.)

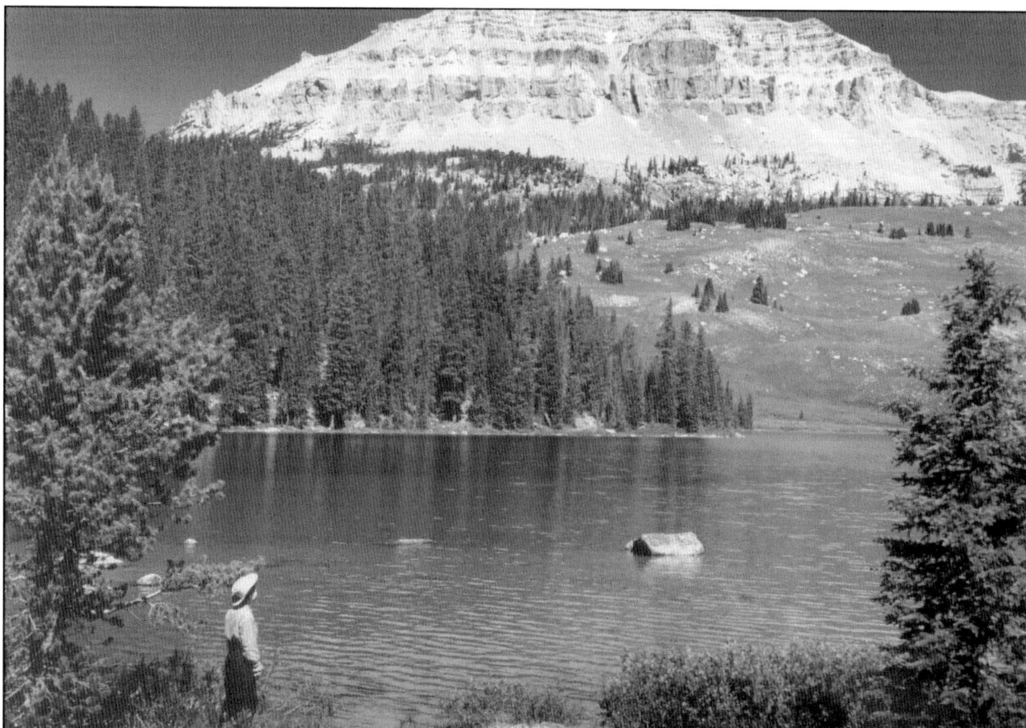

Located in the upper left center of Beartooth Butte is a red channel-shaped stream deposit named the Beartooth Butte Formation. Prof. Erling Dorf, shown here in 1930, collected 29 fossil species of bony-plated Devonian fish called ostracoderms. The project also uncovered some of the most primitive terrestrial plants that had been discovered at that time. (Courtesy of Carbon County Historical Society & Museum.)

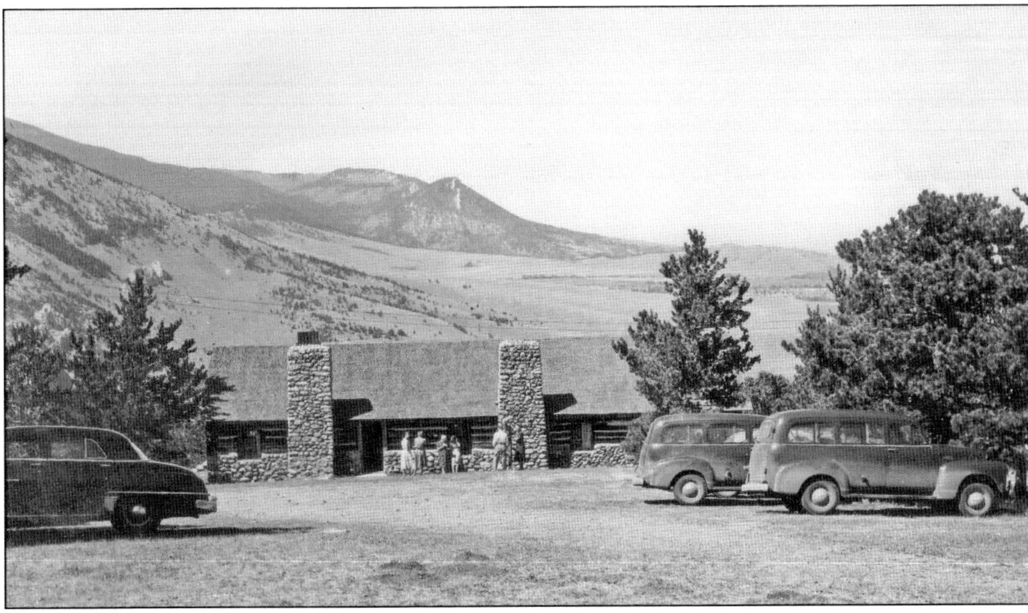

The nonprofit Princeton Geological Association purchased 120 acres of property on the slopes of Mount Maurice from the Northern Pacific Railway Company, and construction on its new camp began in 1935. By July 1, 1936, Bearcreek miner Roy Wadsworth and others finished the lodge, shower house, and 14 cabins. A reservoir was built in Howell Gulch, which was named after Prof. Benjamin Howell. (Courtesy of Yellowstone-Bighorn Research Association.)

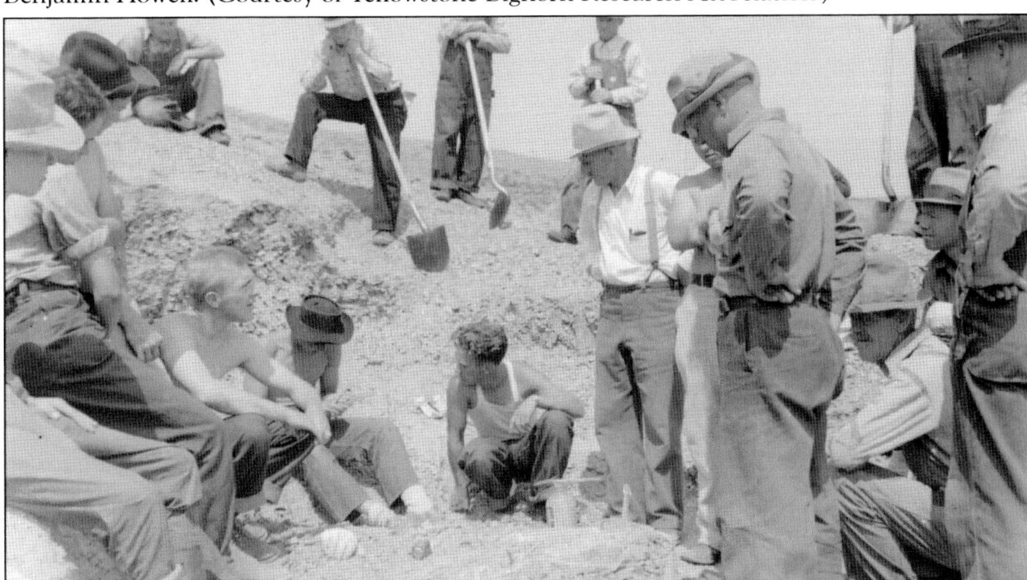

Students excavate a research site on the property, which was transferred to the Yellowstone-Bighorn Research Association (YBRA) in April 1942. The YBRA was incorporated six years earlier, on July 14, 1936. Although research has taken a secondary place to education during the last few decades, numerous graduate and faculty research programs continue to use the YBRA facilities. The association celebrated its 75th anniversary in 2011. (Courtesy of Carbon County Historical Society & Museum.)

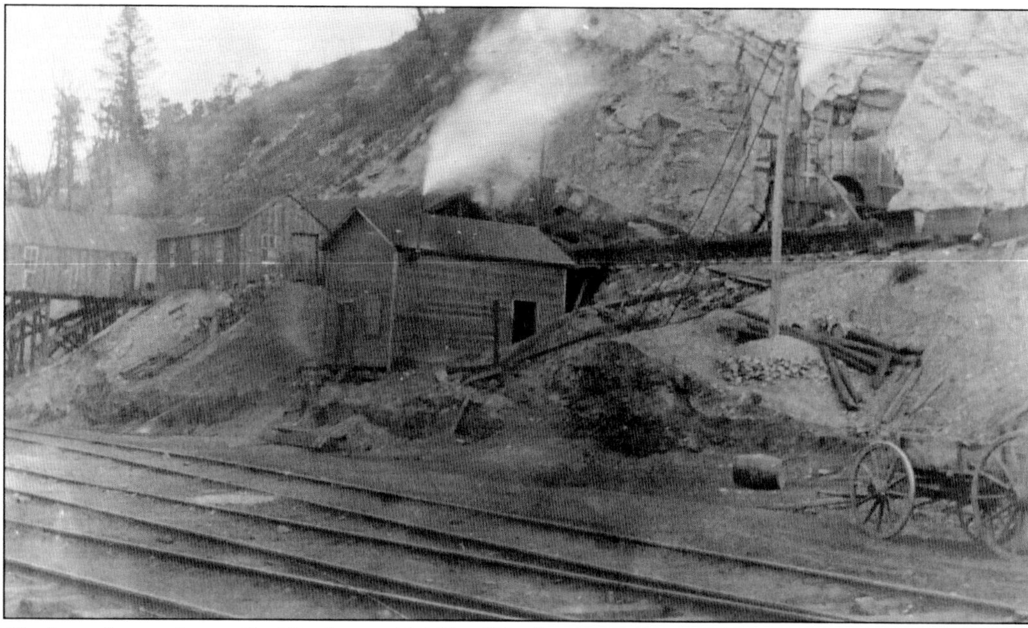

Coal was located near Red Lodge in 1866 by "Yankee Jim" George, but it was not until 1887 that the first company, Rocky Fork Coal Company, began to mine coal in Red Lodge here at the East Side "Sunrise" mine. By 1891, it employed 400 miners. Pay was 90¢ per ton, with a skilled miner taking out 10 tons a day. The mine averaged 800 total tons of coal per day. (Courtesy of Carbon County Historical Society & Museum.)

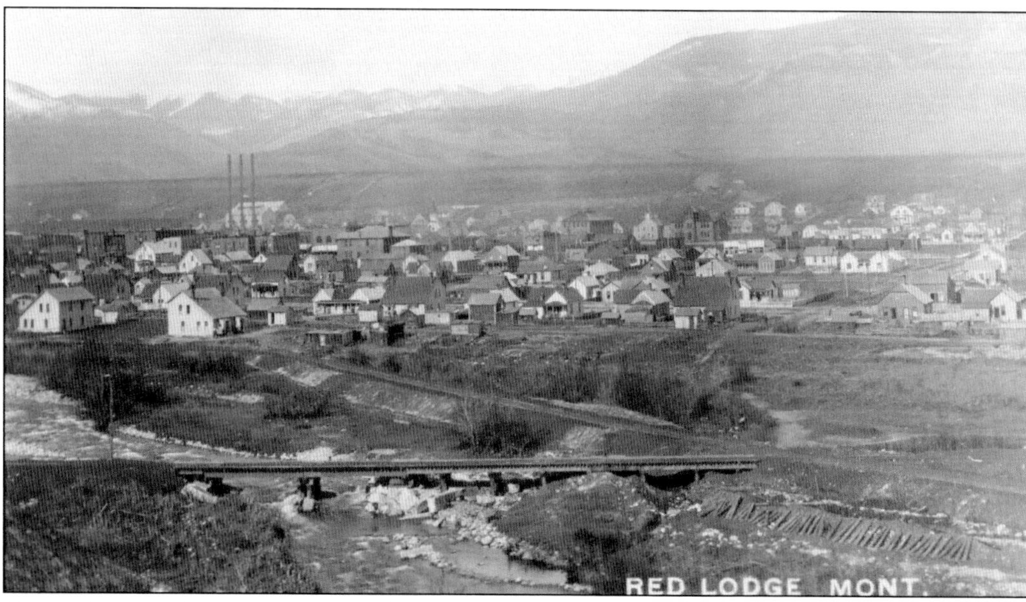

To supply a growing coal market and to ease transportation problems, the Rocky Fork & Cooke City Railway reached Red Lodge in 1889. The Northern Pacific Railroad formally acquired the line in 1890, and a subsidiary of the line, the Northwestern Improvement Company, began mining in 1898. Miners flocked to the now-bustling Red Lodge and the West Side "Sunset" mine, and three smoke stacks opened in 1907. By 1910, the population of Red Lodge rose to nearly 5,000. (Courtesy of Parmly Billings Library.)

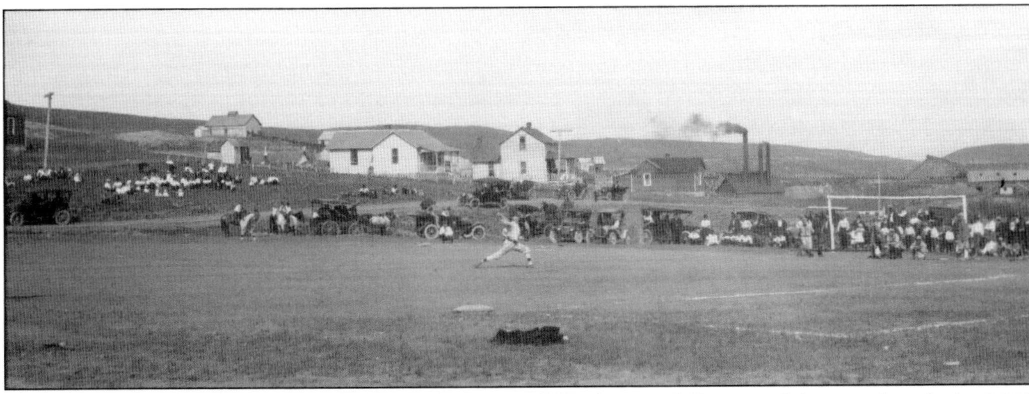

Over the hill from Red Lodge, the mining towns of Washoe and Bearcreek boomed with the 1906 completion of the Yellowstone Park Railroad. There was a steady demand for high-grade coal to power the Northern Pacific locomotives, the smelters at Anaconda, and the furnaces at the Great Western Sugar Company in Billings. By 1910, five coal companies operated in this narrow valley. Town ball games, like this one between Washoe and Klein, relieved stress. (Courtesy of Special Collections, Montana State University Library, Bozeman.)

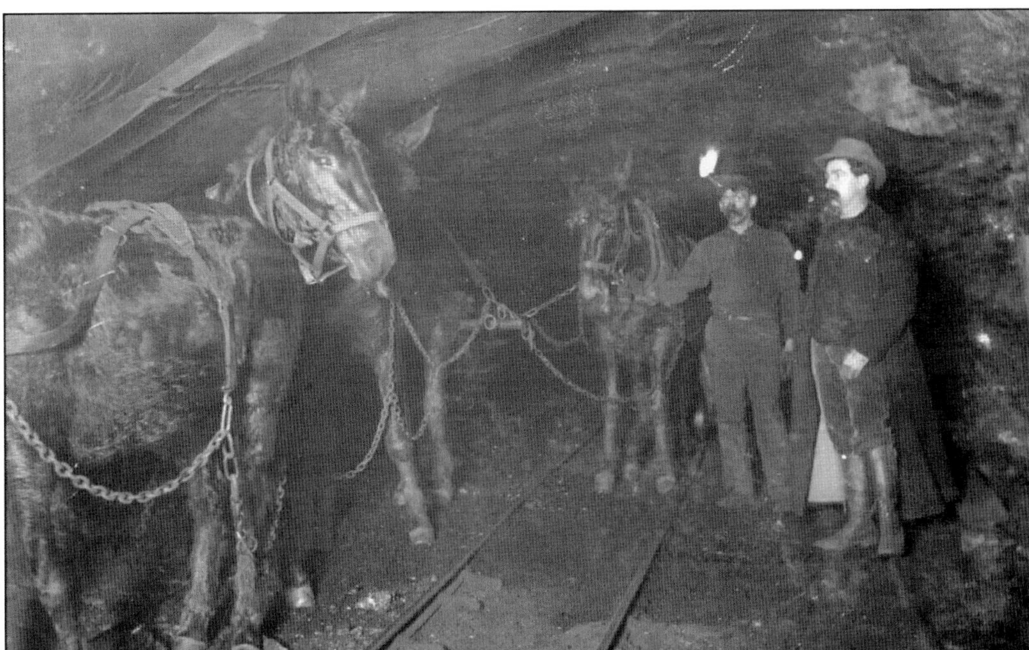

Mining brought tragedy in 1906 when Red Lodge experienced its first mine disaster, a fire that killed eight men. Jim Fleming (left), pictured here several years earlier with L.F. Johnston in a Rocky Fork mine, risked his life to save others. The largest mine disaster of the era was in Bearcreek at the Smith mine, where on February 27, 1943, a total of 74 men were killed in an explosion that devastated the county and affected many generations. (Courtesy of Carbon County Historical Society & Museum.)

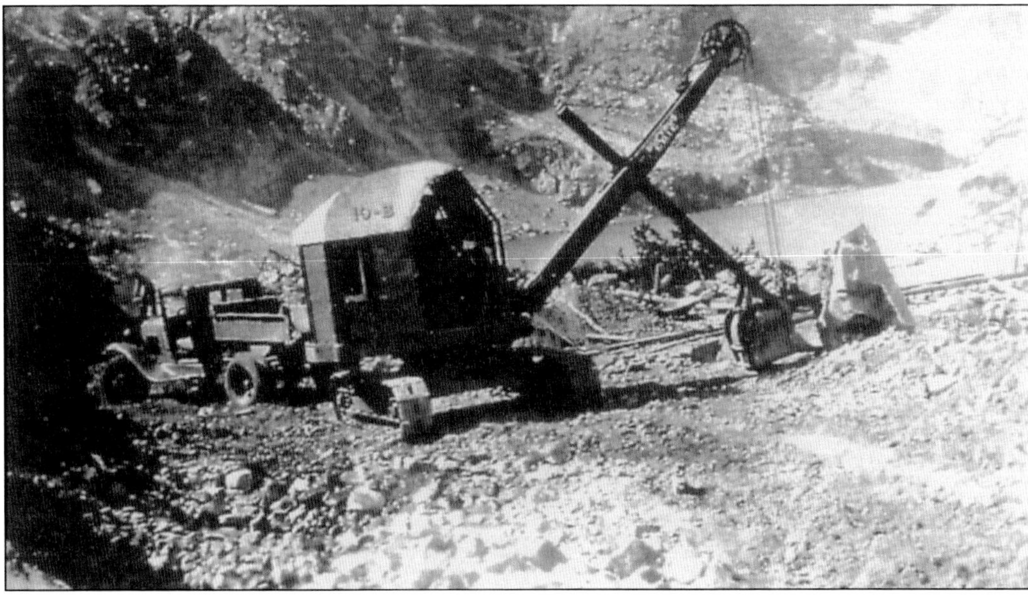

Built with funds secured by Montana governor Frank Cooney, the Glacier Lake dams are located at the headwaters of Rock Creek south of Red Lodge. Construction began in 1936 and was completed a year later. The dams are owned by the Montana Department of Natural Resources and Conservation (MT DNRC) by special permit with the Forest Service and are operated by the Rock Creek Water Users. The dams are rock fill with a concrete upstream face. The south dam controls about 2,849 acre-feet and is 20 feet high and 253 feet long. The north dam controls 4,980 acre-feet and is 65 feet high and 260 feet long. Materials, including a power shovel, compressors, three dump trucks, a rock crusher, and a 2,500-pound water gate, were transported by a one-inch high-line cable stretched across the valley. (Above, courtesy of Carbon County Historical Society & Museum; below, courtesy of Sam Johnson, MT DNRC.)

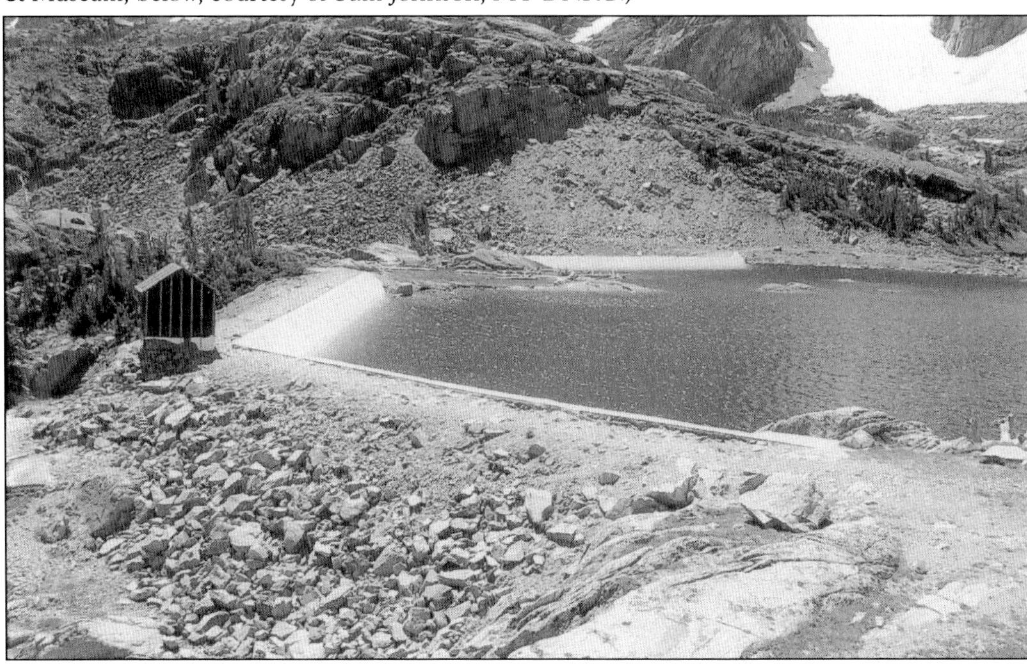

Six

SHEEP AND CATTLE

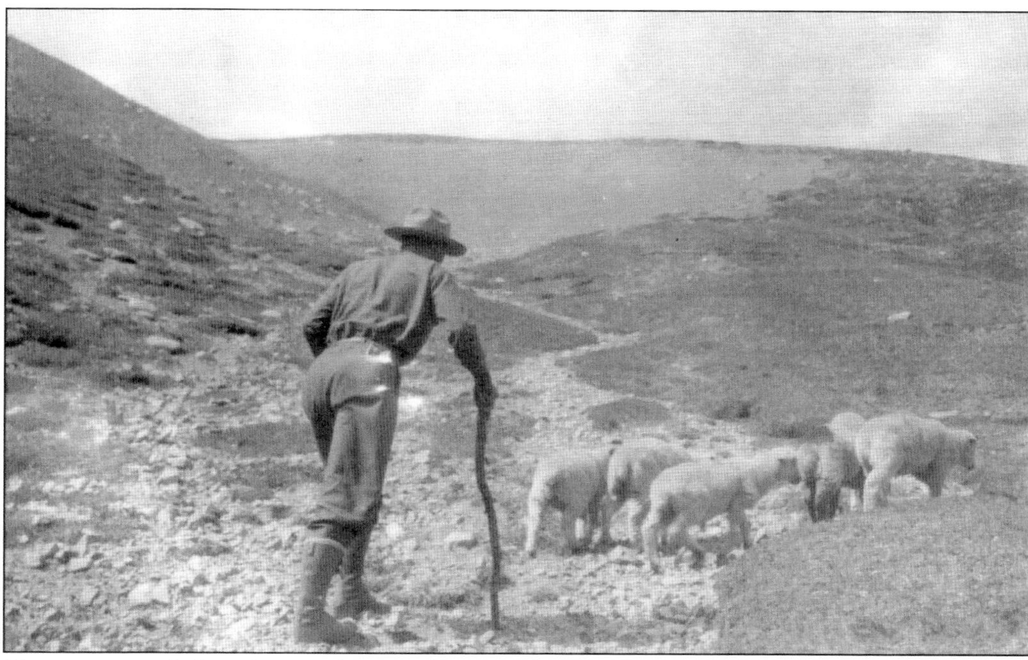

Sheep were trailed to the meadows in the many basins of the Beartooth Mountains during the mid-1900s. One such trail led past the Richel Lodge dude ranch south of Red Lodge. In exchange for food and lodging, lambs were given to the owners. By 1960, many of the last bands of sheep grazed this high country as a result of a Forest Service policy shift that reduced the number of animals allowed in order to protect the tundra areas. (Courtesy of Special Collections, Montana State University Library, Bozeman.)

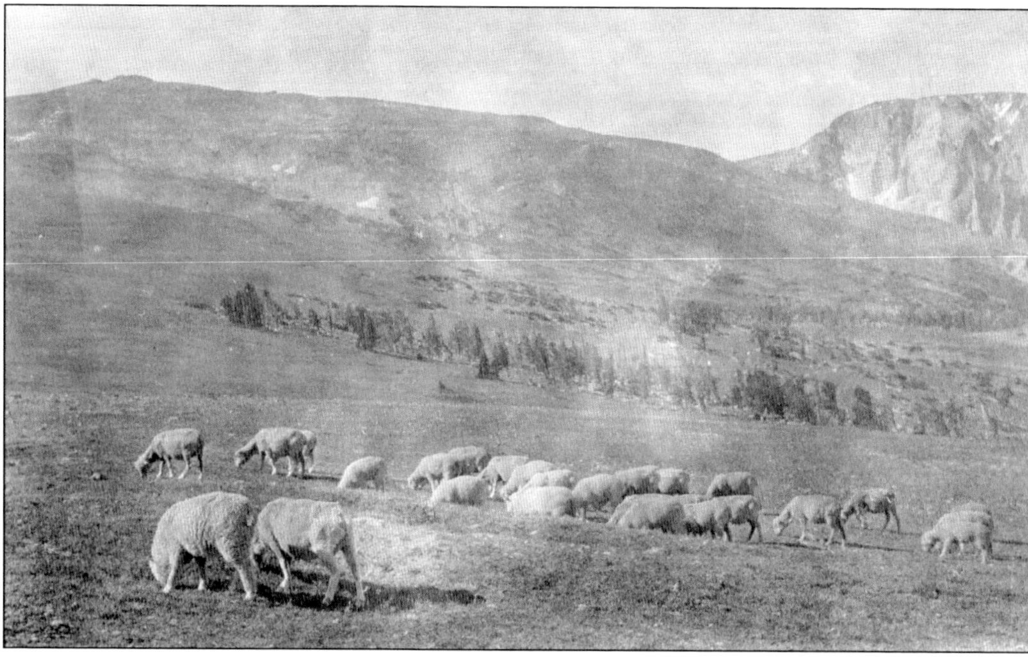

Local shepherds west of Red Lodge, including Alfred and Fred Eckle, Henry Loyning, Irvin and Martin Lofthus, Torvill and John Fiveland, and Knut Straatveit, trailed their bands across the base of the Beartooth Mountains to the rodeo grounds in Red Lodge. They camped the night before heading down the airport hill and south through town on their way to Sheep Creek—now Bear Track trailhead—to the Silver Run Plateau, seen here. (Courtesy of Special Collections, Montana State University Library, Bozeman.)

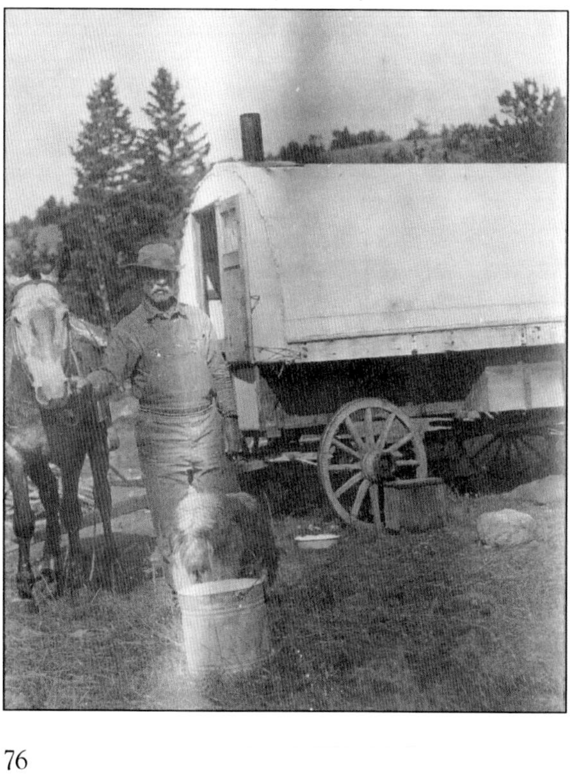

Sheepherders were an integral part of mountain grazing, warding off predators and herding sheep away from other bands. Grazing permits in 1910 allowed 90 days in the forest, but by 1915, the number of bands allowed in the forest had been reduced and a shorter grazing period was instituted. (Courtesy of Special Collections, Montana State University Library, Bozeman.)

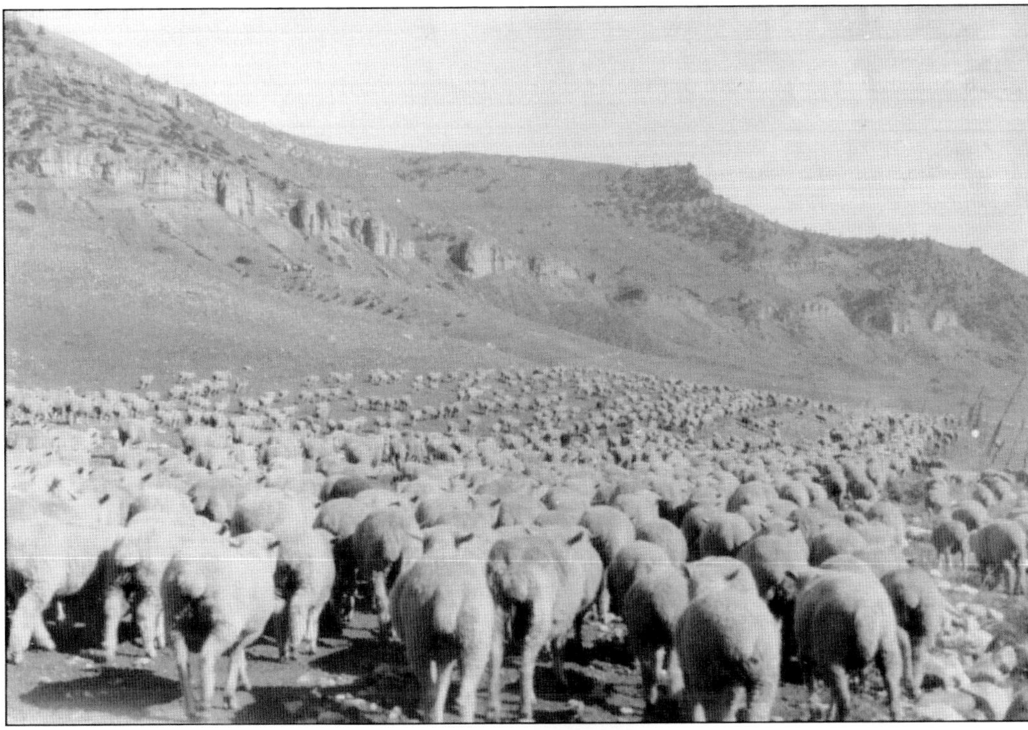

In 1941, petitions were presented to reduce grazing in the forest, claiming that overuse was increasing sagebrush and loosening surface soil, which allowed more weeds. With transportation costs increasing and the difficulties of finding a herder, sheep men found it less and less inviting or cost-effective to use the forest allotments. In 1973, the allotments near the Boulder River south of Big Timber saw only 6,000 sheep, compared to the 90,000 that grazed in 1913. (Courtesy of Crazy Mountain Museum.)

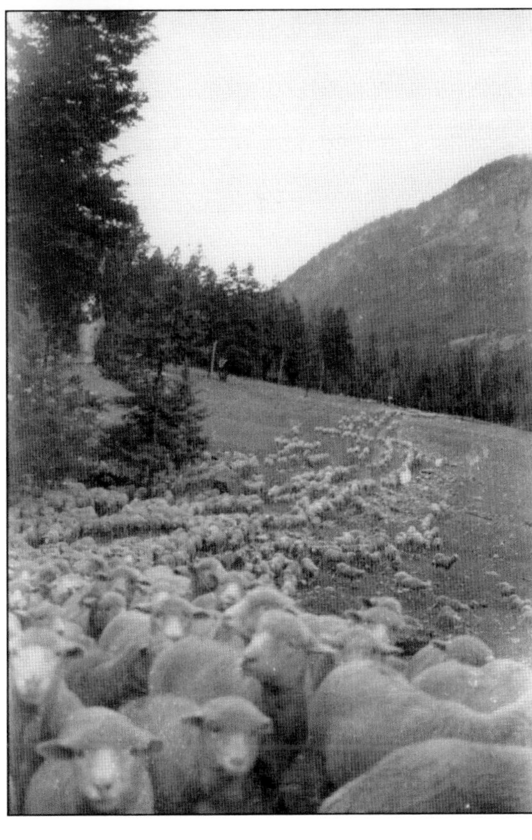

Trailing along Chippy Creek, a tributary of the Boulder River, these sheep did not realize that the creek was also a national forest campground. Chippy Park was named after a group of women who set up temporary accommodations for miners passing through to Independence. The Absaroka Forest district tried to change the names to Bobcat Creek and Bobcat Park, but they never caught on. (Courtesy of Crazy Mountain Museum.)

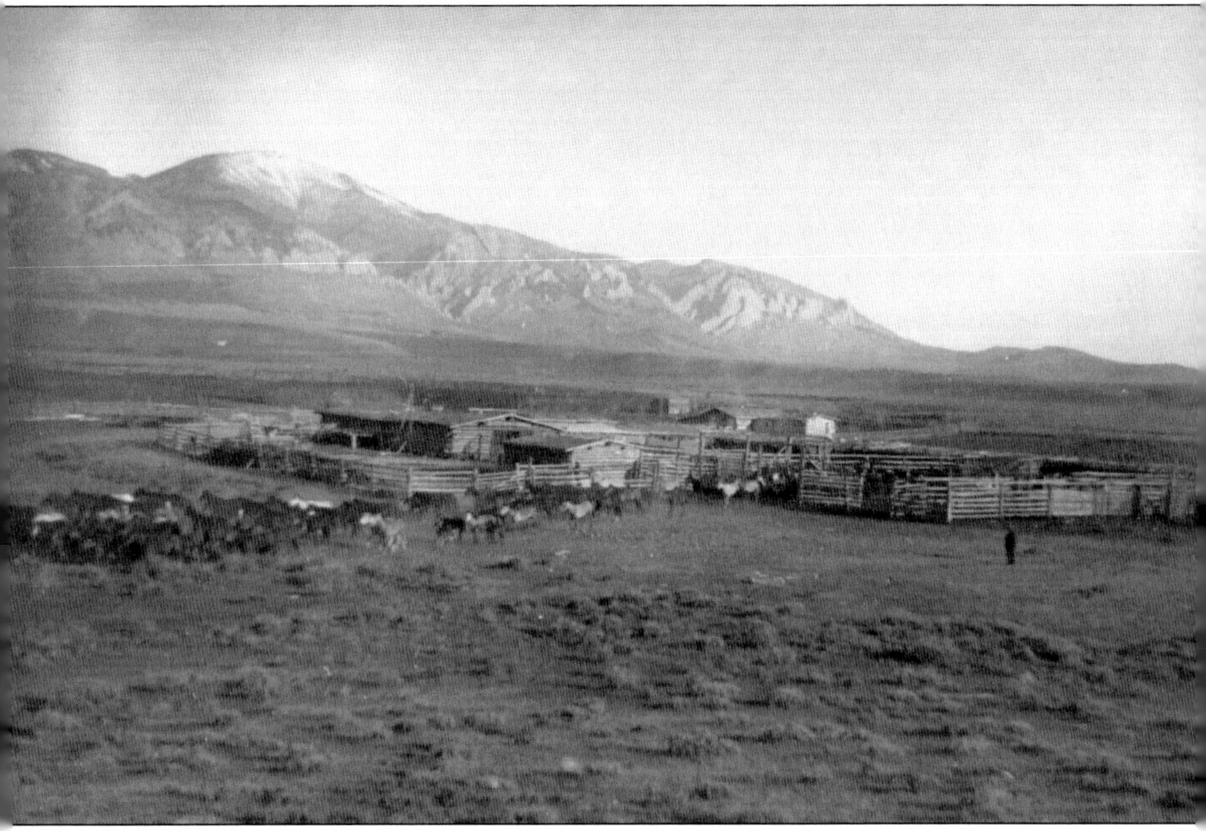

The Dilworth Cattle Company was incorporated under the laws of Kansas and Montana in 1881. One of the shareholders, manager James R. Dilworth, was wintering south of Bozeman in 1881 and trailed east, hoping to get out of the harsh winter country. He landed on what would become Grove Creek and Dilworth Bench east of Red Lodge. A post office was established here along the Meeteetse Trail in 1884, and the ranch maintained the stage stop and fed passengers. The Dilworth ranch ran east to the Yellowstone River, south through the Pryor Mountains into Wyoming, west over the Beartooth Range, and north to current-day Columbus. The cattle herd peaked at about 7,000 head in 1886, when it was the largest ranch in what would become Carbon County. On July 10, 1891, Dilworth was shot by a former employee, Godfrey "Frenchy" Demers, and John Tolman was asked to take over as ranch manager. When this photograph was taken in 1895, most of the Dilworth cattle had been gathered and sold. (Courtesy of Carbon County Historical Society & Museum.)

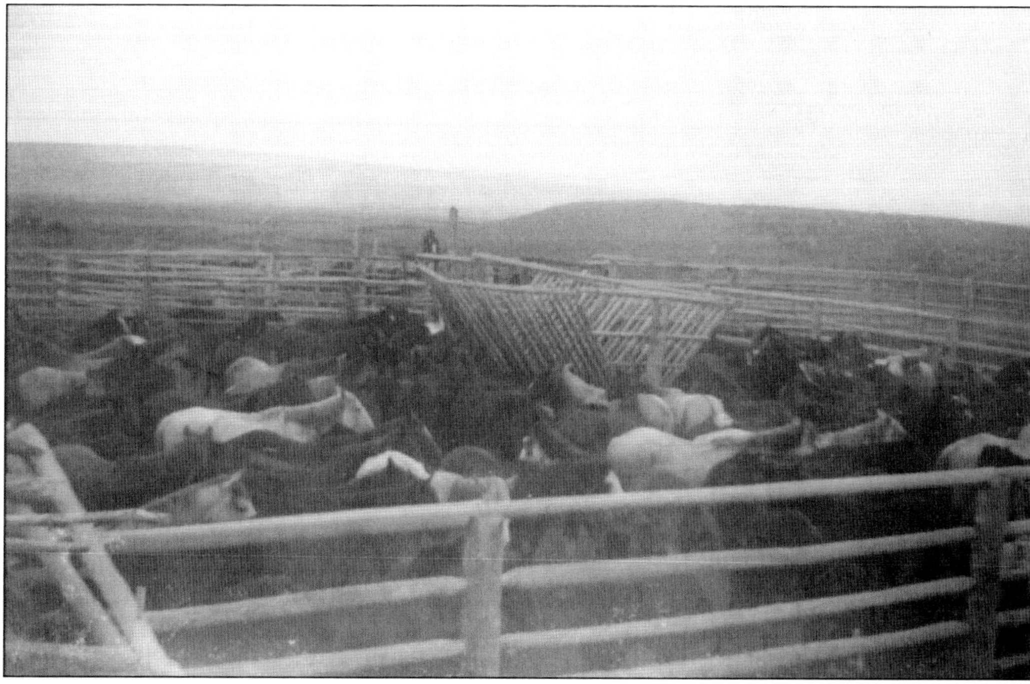

Safely corralled horses were a pleasant sight at the Dilworth ranch, as horse rustling had become a serious problem. Manager John Tolman, in an effort to put an end to horse stealing, addressed strategy in a letter to early pioneer Nelson Story, who also had cattle in the area, detailing his plans to send a circular to every sheriff in surrounding states listing the brands and circumstances and offering a $100 reward. (Courtesy of Carbon County Historical Society & Museum.)

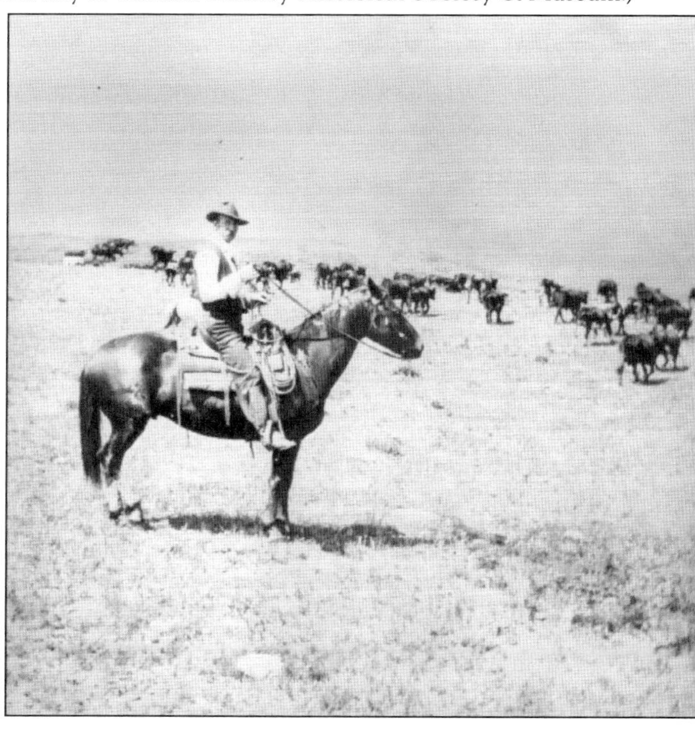

Charles Wright, here on his horse, Fox, worked many years for the Dilworth Cattle Company. He worked his way up to ranch foreman, and in 1896, with his brother Fred, he filed a homestead in the East Rosebud Canyon. In 1900, Wright was elected treasurer of Carbon County. The following year, he married and purchased a ranch near Red Lodge, selling his East Rosebud Canyon holdings to Malcolm S. Mackay. In 1915, Wright was killed by lightning. (Courtesy of Museum of the Beartooths.)

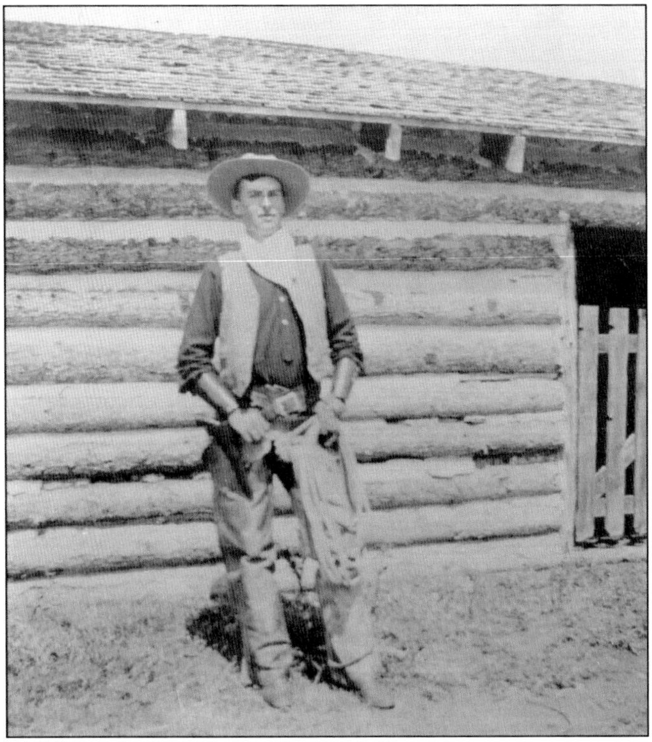

The Lazy EL Ranch, between the East and West Rosebud Rivers, began as the Charles Wright homestead but was purchased by Tenafly, New Jersey, native Malcolm S. Mackay in 1901. Mackay came west to fill his "desire to the see the great cattle country, get into the cattle business and become a rider of the boundless plains." The ranch became home to his new bride, Helen Raynor, in 1907. (Courtesy of Museum of the Beartooths.)

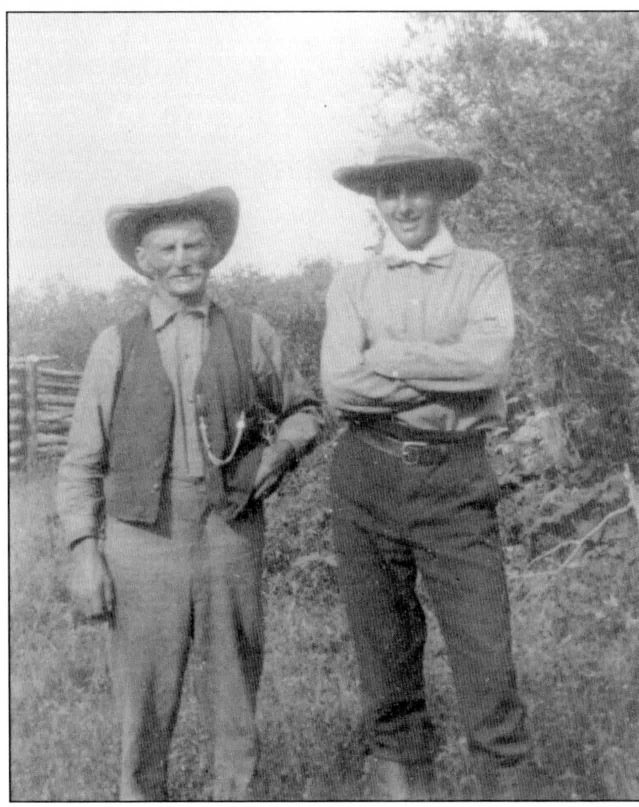

Malcolm Mackay (right) poses with his friend William "Billy" Hamilton. Hamilton led a colorful life as a territorial sheriff in Fort Benton and later as a US marshal. He moved to Yellowstone Valley in 1873 and was employed as a scout. He fought in the battle of the Rosebud on June 17, 1876, with Gen. George Crook. Hamilton was also skilled in Indian sign language, and for a short period, he wrote a descriptive set of lesson plans used in the Columbus school. (Courtesy of Museum of the Beartooths.)

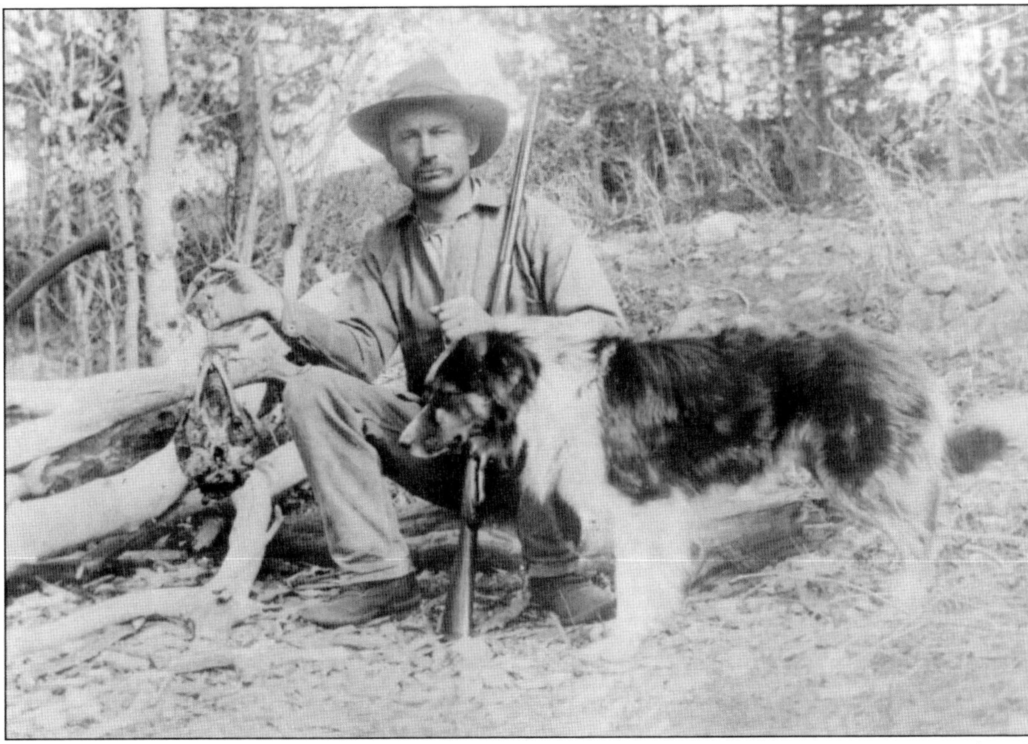

A "foreordained" hunting partner of Malcolm Mackay's was Horace Mullendore, pictured with his dog, Shep. Mackay shot his first bear with Mullendore when the pair vowed to go on the trail of the "wooly boys." They were also hunting together when Mackay shot a seven-point bull elk at the request of his father for the Downtown Club in New York City. Mackay was associated with the Wall Street firm Mackay and Company. (Courtesy of Museum of the Beartooths.)

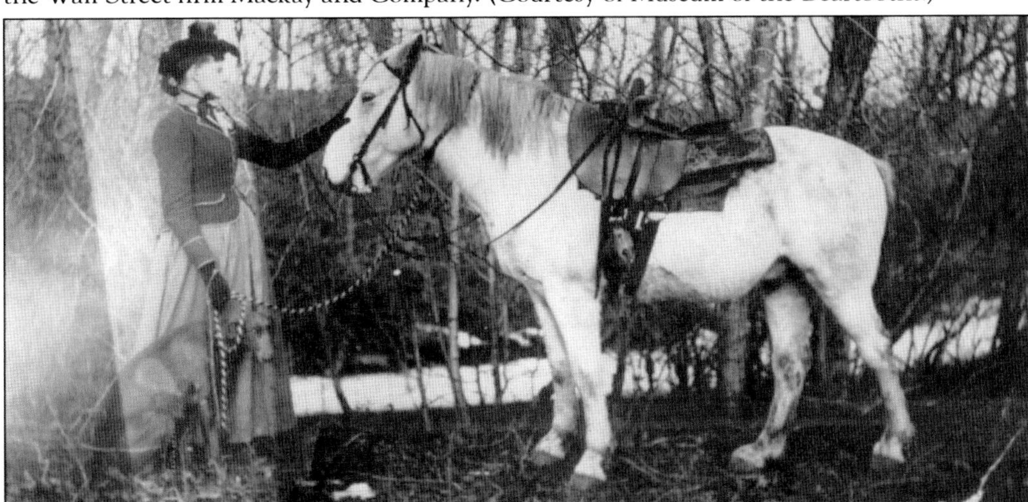

In 1885, Nancy George Brown, the widow of James Brown, married Robert Morris. They settled on the U2 ranch south of Roscoe near the East Rosebud River. Morris also founded the Rosebud Oil Company. Nancy Brown Morris was a highly regarded horsewoman, known far and wide for her hospitality. Her favorite mount, Roscoe, was the inspiration for the town name. She donated her land to be used for the Roscoe cemetery. (Courtesy of Museum of the Beartooths.)

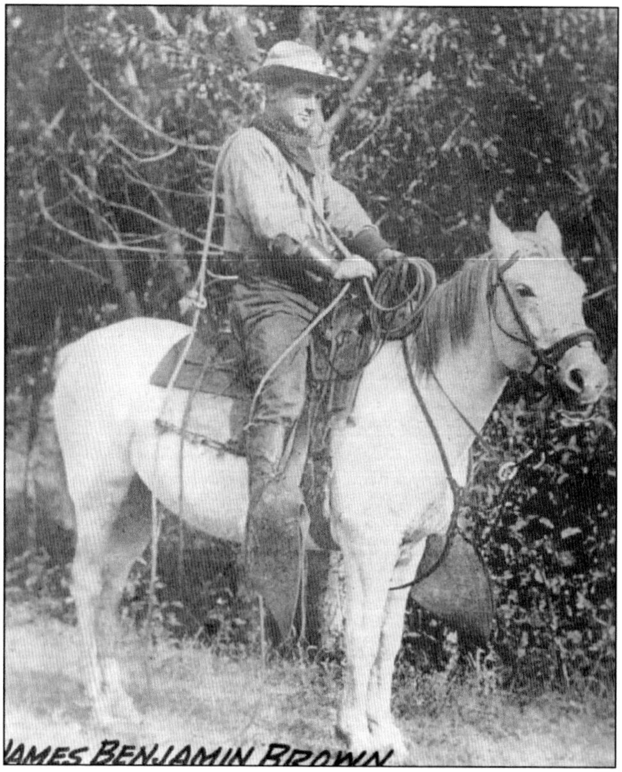

Nancy Brown Morris's son, Ben Brown, poses on horseback. Along with her other children, Sally, Dora, Lulu, and John, Ben was a hand, helping many of the local ranchers along the East Rosebud. Ben Brown married Ella Helenbrook, the first schoolteacher in Roscoe, in 1898, and they had 11 children: George, Fred, Marjorie, Vera, Edna, Hazel, Florence, Violet, Addis, Doris, and Bud. Ben Brown died in the Roscoe flu epidemic of 1918. (Courtesy of Museum of the Beartooths.)

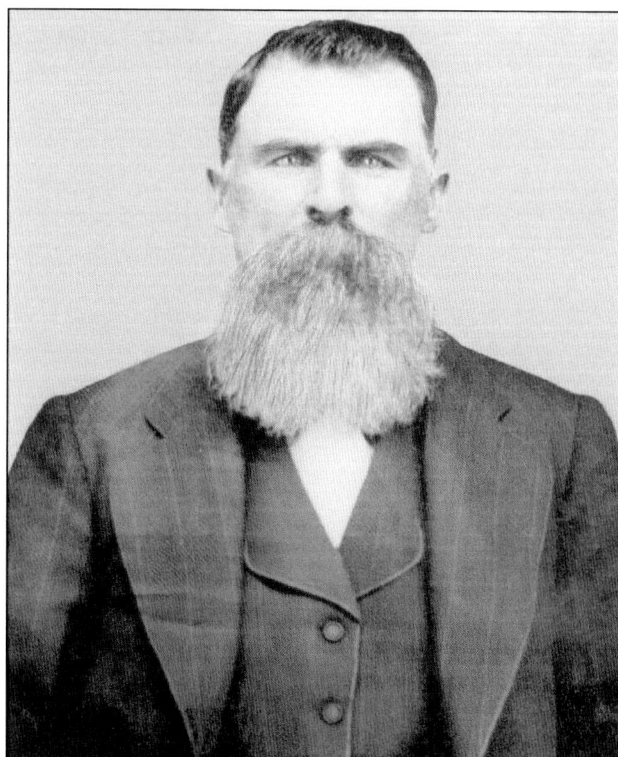

William Franklin McLeod drove 125 head of cattle and 200 horses from Oregon into the Boulder Valley in 1881, when the area was still part of the Crow reservation. McLeod obtained permission from Maj. Henry Armstrong, an Indian agent, to graze on the reservation. McLeod also operated a ferry near Big Timber and cut ties for the railroad. The McLeods had two daughters, Martha and Margaret, and the hamlet of McLeod was named for William McLeod. (Courtesy of Crazy Mountain Museum.)

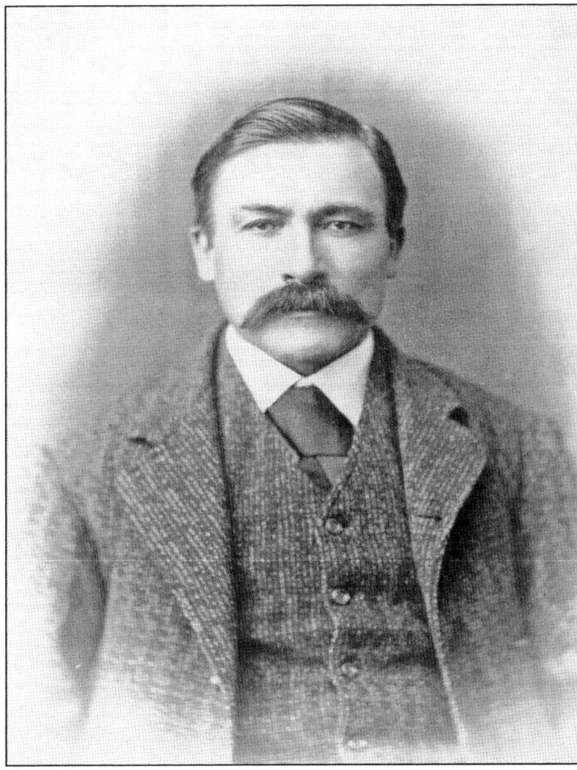

Along the northern face of the Beartooths, near the mouth of Bridger Creek, was the homestead of Thomas Kent. Kent had tried his hand at gold prospecting at Alder and Emigrant Gulch in 1866. By 1872, he was in charge of the beef herd at the Crow Agency near Mission Creek. Settling on his homestead in 1878, he eventually stocked it with 100 head of cattle and 6,000 sheep. Kent married Mary White Shield—whose Crow name was *What She Has Is Well Known*—in 1874. The couple raised five girls—Ella, Mary, Josephine, Elizabeth, and Margaret—in what was considered to be one of the finest ranch residences in the domain as well as the first frame house. (Right, courtesy of Crazy Mountain Museum; below, courtesy of Wanda Wilcox.)

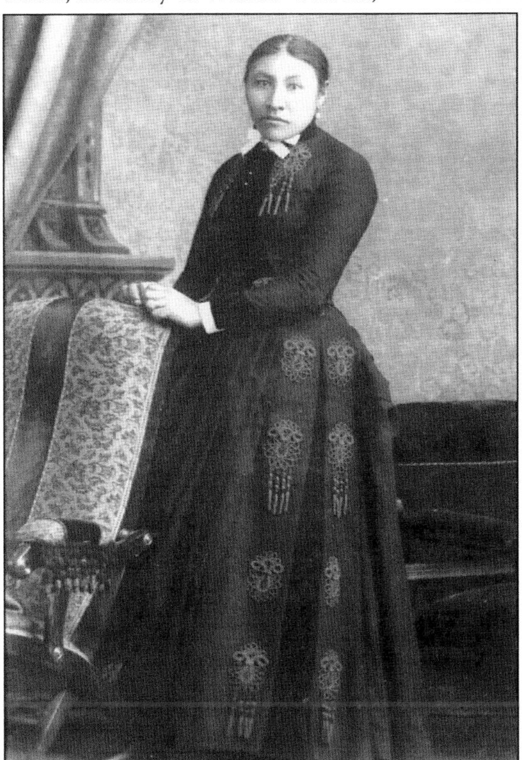

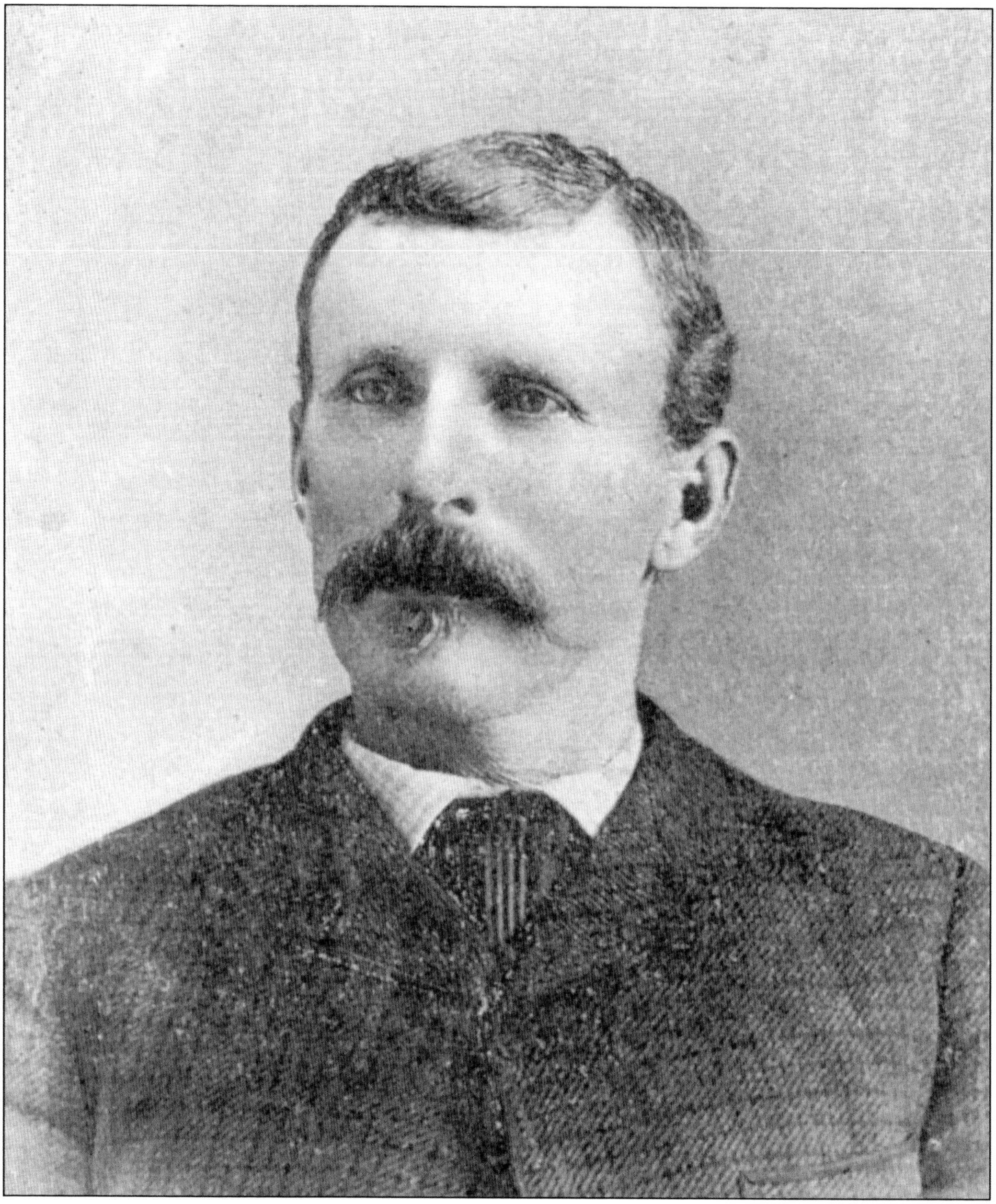

Entering Montana with 1,200 cattle and 80 horses from Oregon in 1879–1880, John Chapman settled with his wife, Alphia, near Pat O'Hara Creek and the Clarks Fork River. The nearest post office at the time was Bozeman, where they went for supplies and mail twice a year. By 1889, his livestock was estimated at 700–800 horses and 3,000 head of cattle, which grazed from present-day Cody to north of Red Lodge. In 1895, he founded the Red Lodge bank along with William Meyer and Paul Breteche; it was known as Meyer and Chapman Bank after Breteche's death, when Chapman became the bank president. By 1900, the Chapmans sold their ranch, and after a short stay in California, they moved to Red Lodge. In 1905, Chapman went into partnership with the Yegen brothers in the resort area along East Rosebud Lake. (Courtesy of Carbon County Historical Society & Museum.)

Seven

Here Come the Dudes

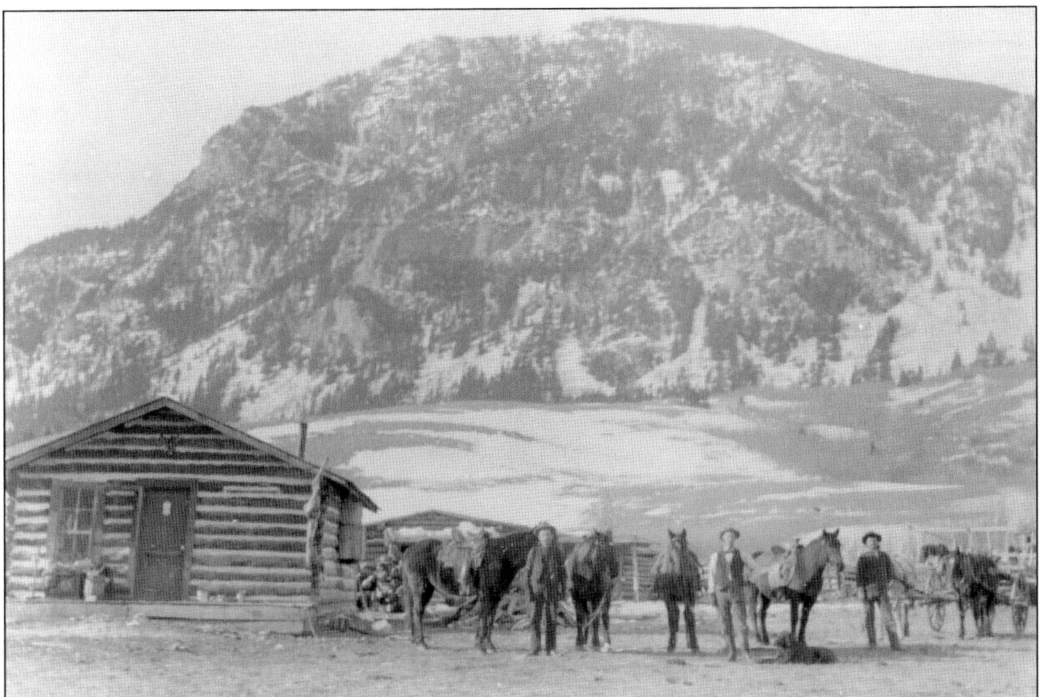

The first patented lands adjacent to East Rosebud Lake were granted to Maj. Henry Armstrong, one in 1894 for 34.11 acres and another in 1895 for 71.76 acres. Armstrong had been the Indian agent at the Crow Agency near Absarokee from 1882 to 1885. The Armstrong cabin was the base for many hunting and hiking expeditions leading from what was once known as Armstrong Lake. Armstrong sold his holding in 1905, and the land is now owned by a private corporation within Custer National Forest. (Courtesy of Carbon County Historical Society & Museum.)

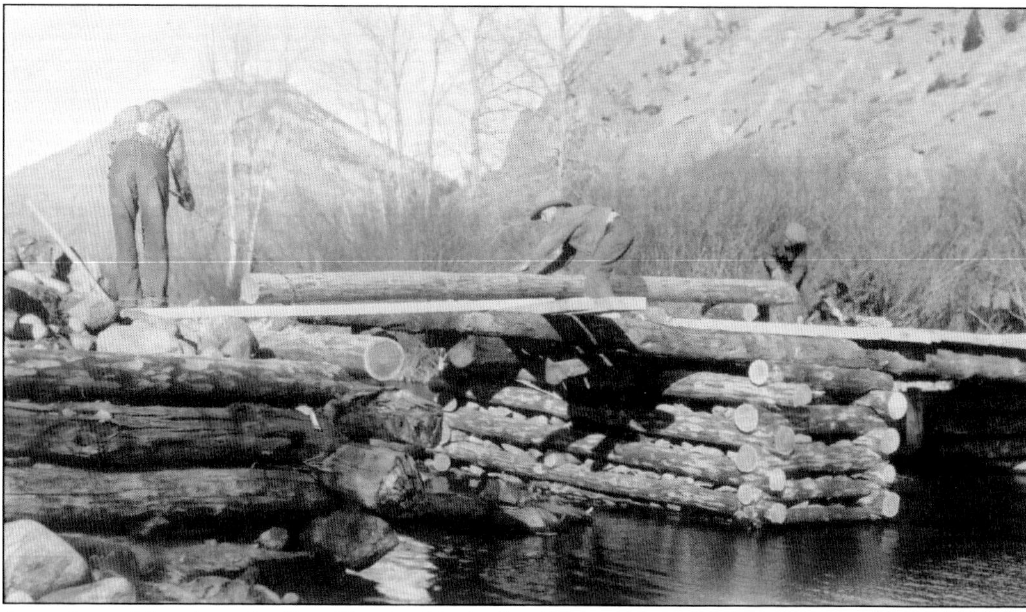

A road was blazed to the East Rosebud Lake by 1908, and in the following year, the first car, followed by a wagon and team for backup, was navigated to the lake. When it was completed, this bridge spanned the East Rosebud River to access the lake. (Courtesy of Special Collections, Montana State University Library, Bozeman.)

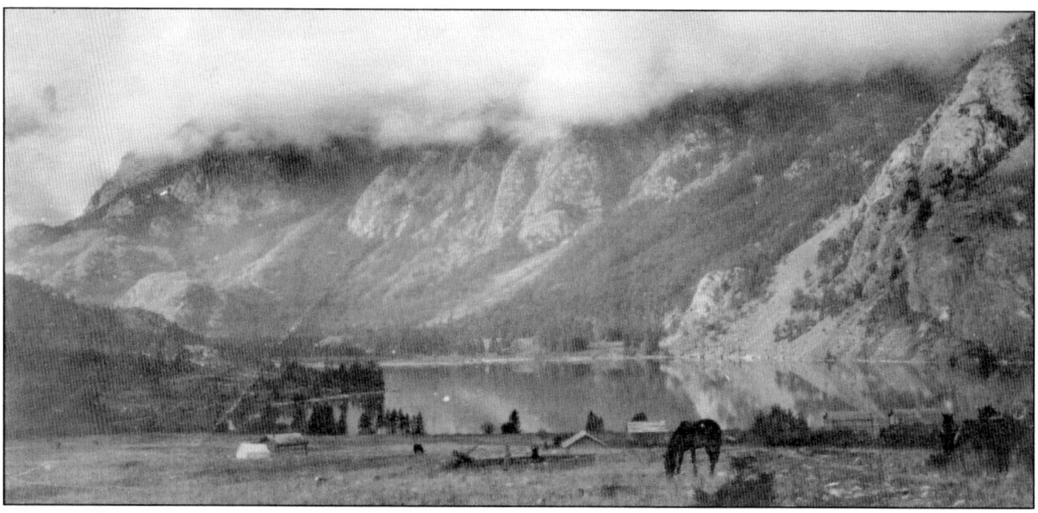

This idyllic setting at East Rosebud Lake was incorporated by the Rosebud Lake Association in 1911 to maintain a pleasure resort for the owners. Plans were also underway for a new road to the lake as well as a rustic hotel. Stockholders were allowed to construct cabins. Known as Alpine, a post office was in operation from 1914 to 1953. (Courtesy of Special Collections, Montana State University Library, Bozeman.)

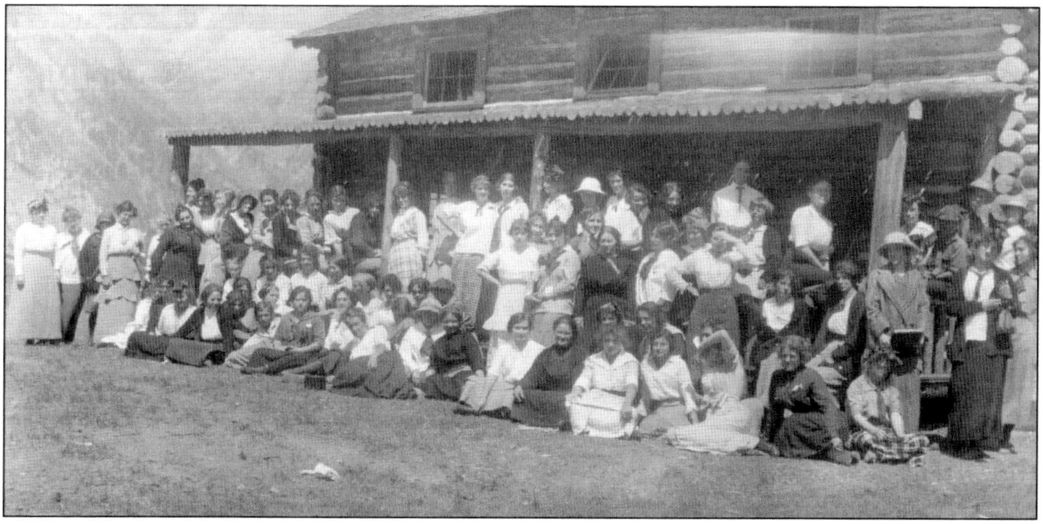

The lodge at East Rosebud Lake was constructed in 1913–1914 from logs salvaged from the fire of 1898. This group of students attends a 1914 normal school session. The cost of the six-week school, including tuition, meals, and tent rental, was $165 in 1919. Courses included reading, geography, and agricultural and nature study. Students also went on hikes, went boating, played tennis, and spent their evenings around a campfire. (Courtesy of Special Collections, Montana State University Library, Bozeman.)

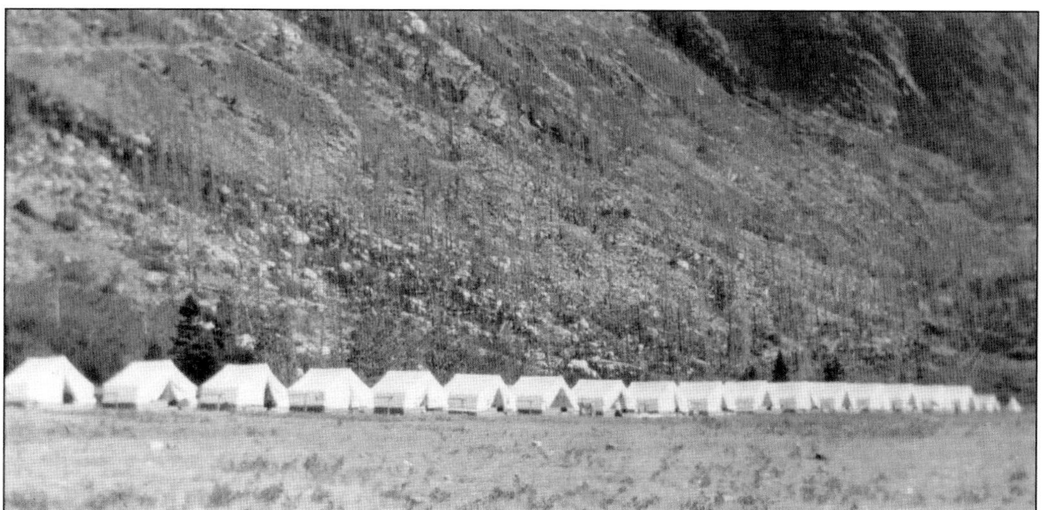

Tents for up to 95 girls were staked alongside a mountain in 1916 at the East Rosebud Camp School, held from 1913 to 1921. This normal school, under the direction of Rosa Dell, was held for a six-week period; later, a 12-week course enabled students to earn their Montana teaching certificate. The girls spent the night in their tents and took classes in the two newly constructed cabins. (Courtesy of Special Collections, Montana State University Library, Bozeman.)

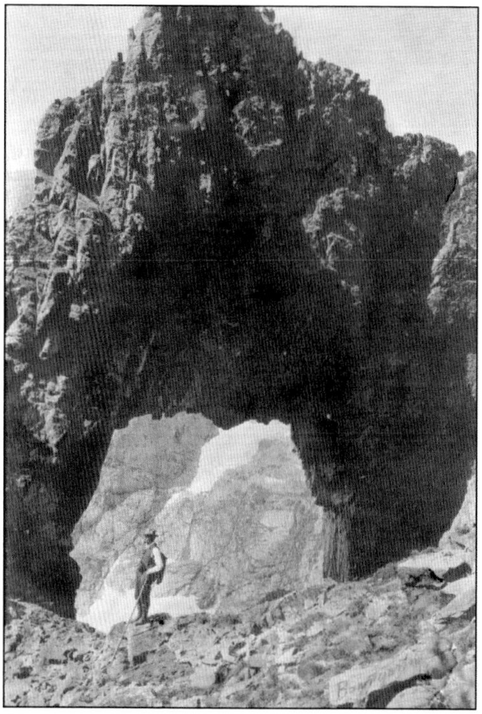

John Branger hikes around Arch Creek along the East Rosebud River in 1908. The Beartooth Mountains reminded Branger of his native Switzerland, and he and his wife, Rosina, decided to homestead in the area after a visit like this. In 1913, Branger built a small cabin near East Rosebud Lake. (Courtesy of the Hash-Branger family.)

Branger's sons, from left to right, David, John Jr., and Christian ride horseback on their homestead. In 1914, the Brangers built a lodge at the lake that was leased from the East Rosebud Lake Association and operated as a dude ranch and summer resort for 18 years. Branger christened the post office Alpine in honor of Switzerland. (Courtesy of Museum of the Beartooths.)

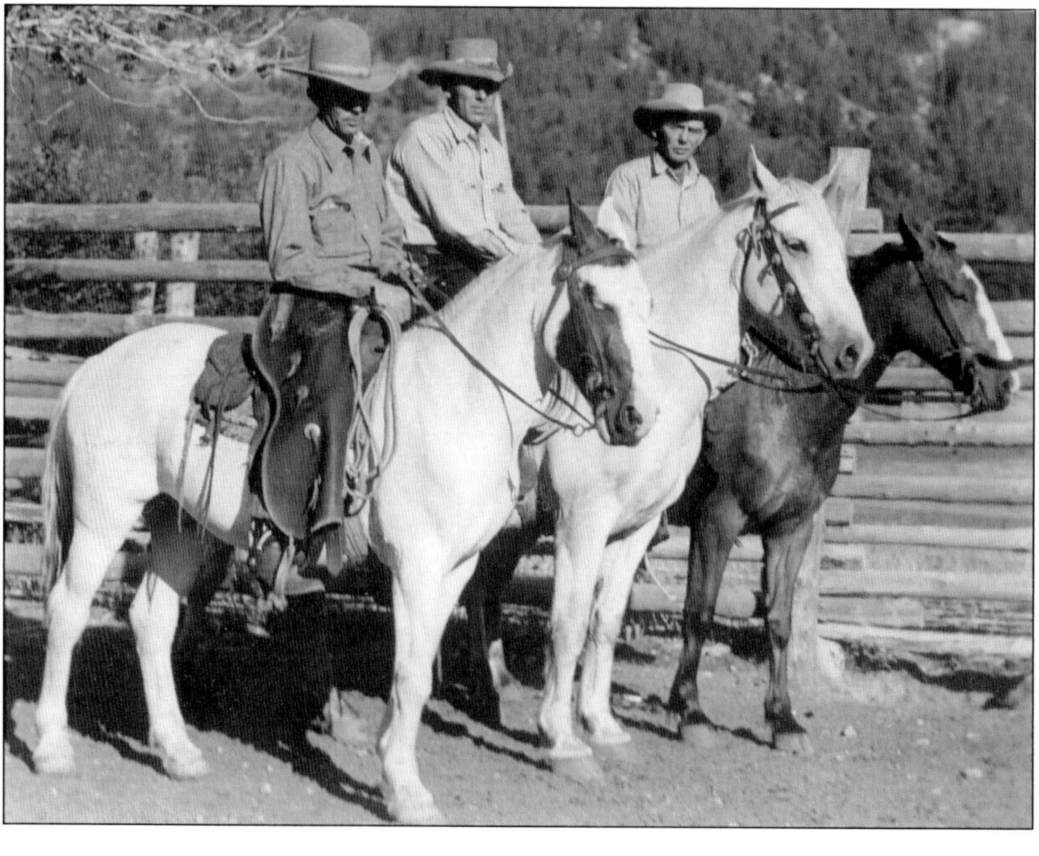

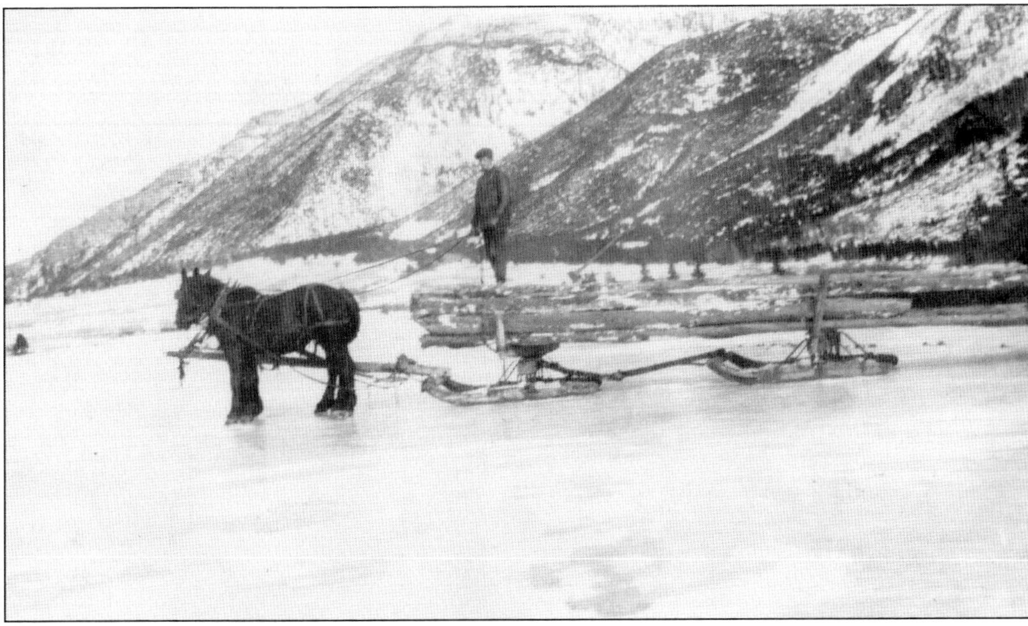

A fire near East Rosebud Lake in 1898 burned over 65,000 acres in the East and West Rosebud drainages. The Branger boys reclaimed the logs and bobsledded them across the frozen East Rosebud Lake to the building site for the lodge, which was completed in 1914. They also crafted furniture and built 41 cabins near the lake for stockholders over an 18-year period. (Courtesy of Museum of the Beartooths.)

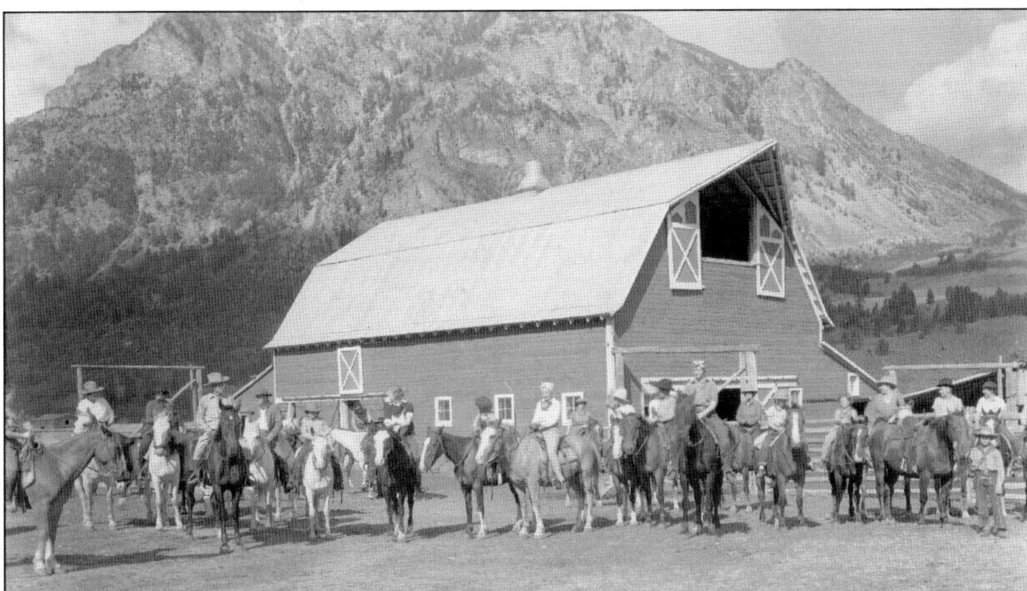

Dudes are mounted in front of John Branger's TO Bar Ranch barn in the early 1920s, after Branger had been focusing on his dude ranch for several years. In addition to the dozens of cabins and outbuildings they built through the years, the Branger boys built a large stone house and this TO barn, which still stands today, in 1920. One fall, David Branger built cages in this barn and raised rabbits, raising more than 200 by spring. (Courtesy of the Hash-Branger family.)

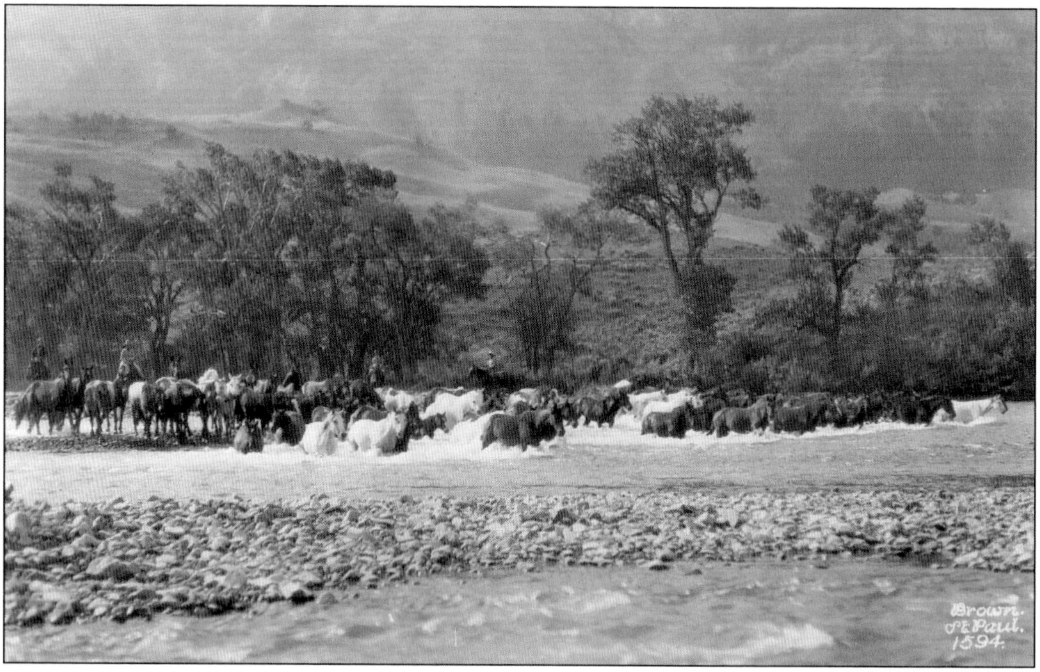

These railroad publicity photographs taken by Bert Brown came as a direct result of the first official meeting of the Dude Ranchers' Association on September 27 and 28, 1926, in Bozeman. Arthur Smith, the passenger manager for the Northern Pacific Railroad, arranged the meeting at the bequest of Max Goodsill and Ernest Miller. Ranchers, railroad officials, and national park executives met to discuss a mutually beneficial opportunity for a relationship between dude ranches and the railroad. Ultimately, the Northern Pacific Railroad would benefit by increasing passengers after promoting dude ranches as new destinations. The ranches received much-needed marketing and increased their number of guests. (Both, courtesy of Parmly Billings Library.)

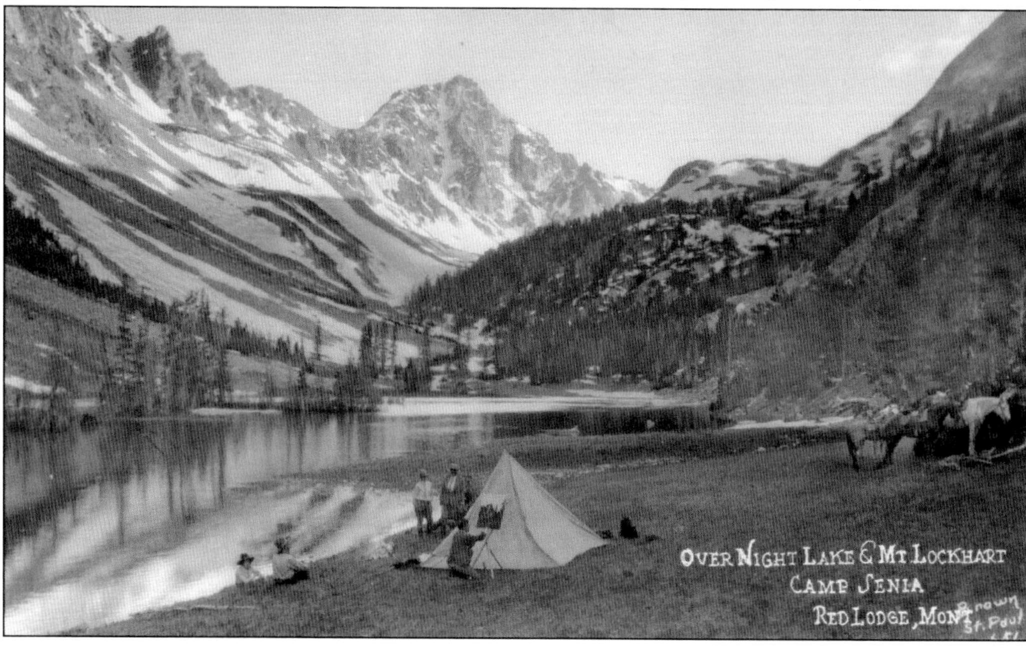

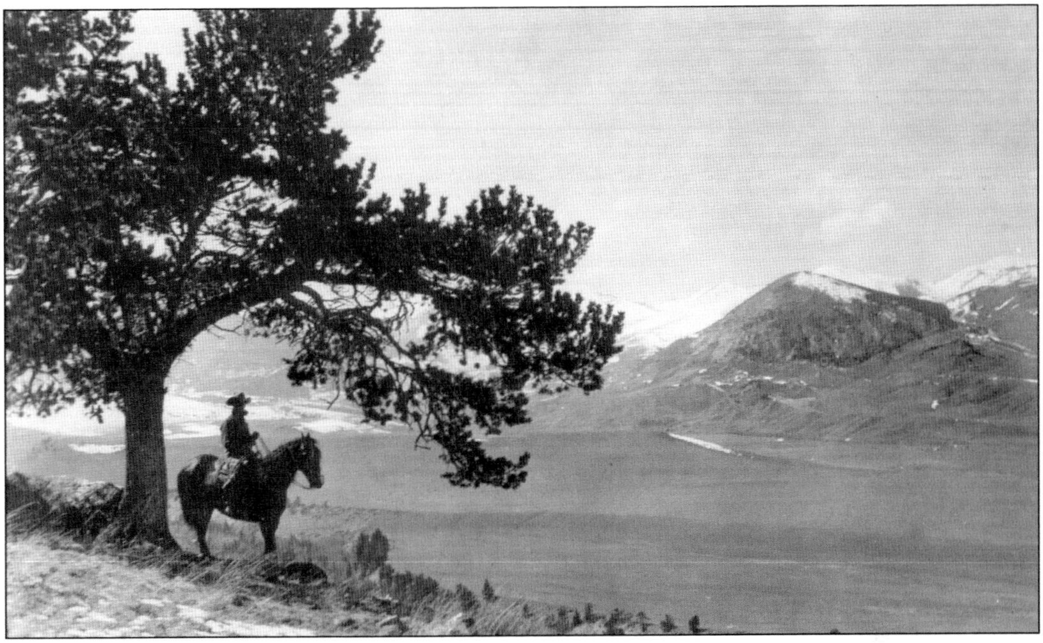

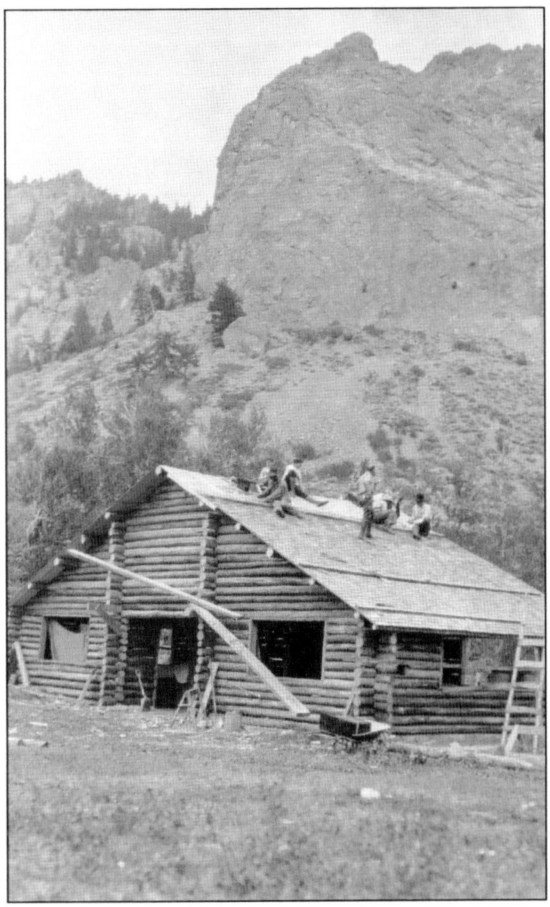

This dude ranch publicity shot was for the Swinging H Ranch near Limestone. The ranch began in 1929 as a partnership between Helen Brooke Herford and her cousin Helen Underwood Wellington. Helen Herford was the daughter of John Brooke "Jack" Herford and Susan Whitney Herford of Yellowstone County, Montana. Following her education in Germany and Massachusetts, Helen returned to Montana, where she taught school in Carbon County and worked on her parents' ranch on the Musselshell River. The Swinging H Ranch operated until 1937, when financial pressures forced Helen Herford to suspend operations and sell. She returned to teaching afterwards and died in Columbus, Montana, in 1972. (Both, courtesy of Special Collections, Montana State University Library, Bozeman.)

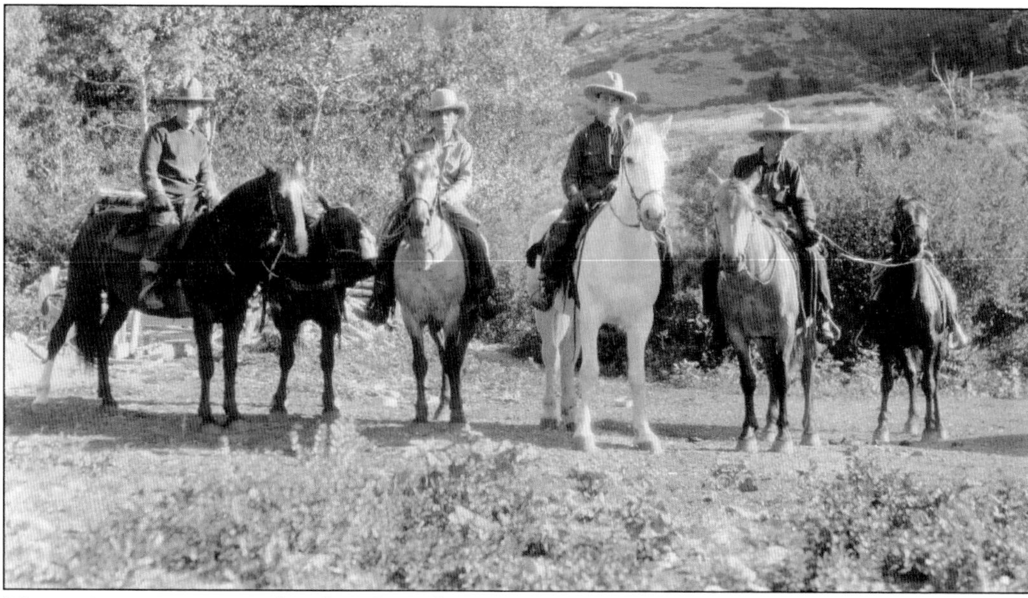

This ambitious group was heading from the Swinging H Ranch near Limestone to the Livingston rodeo. More than likely, they took the Mountain trail system to reach their destination, as did Thomas Leforge while staying at the Mission Creek Crow Agency years earlier. Leforge's journey was for strategic reasons. By keeping in the timber, he hoped to avoid the Sioux while on a mission to locate a band of Crows. (Courtesy of Special Collections, Montana State University Library, Bozeman.)

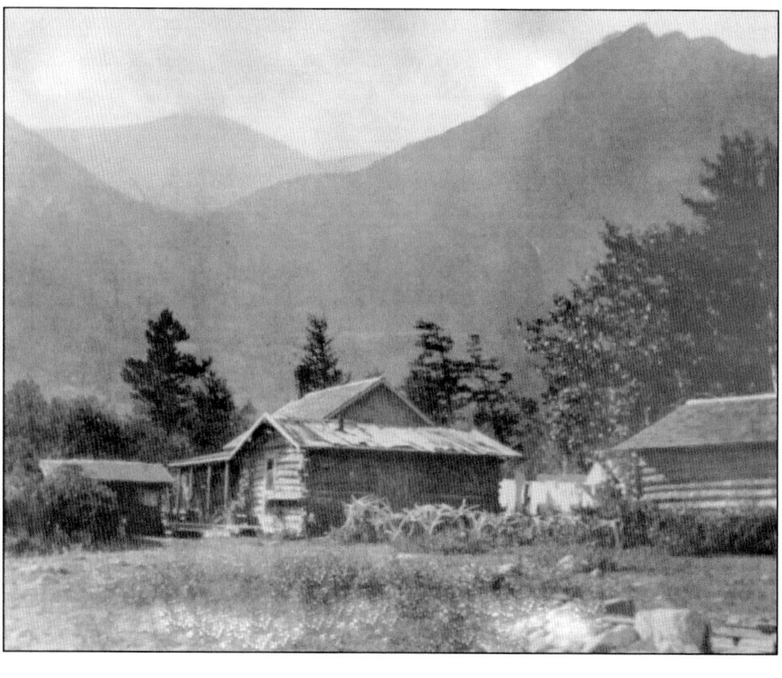

After trying his hand at mining near Cooke City and other camps, Bryon Wood relocated around 1892 to this ranch on the Stillwater River, across from the stream that bears his name, Woodbine Creek. Wood raised cattle before taking in dudes from the local area. In 1921, Ed Ikerman purchased the ranch and renamed it the Beartooth Ranch. (Courtesy of Museum of the Beartooths.)

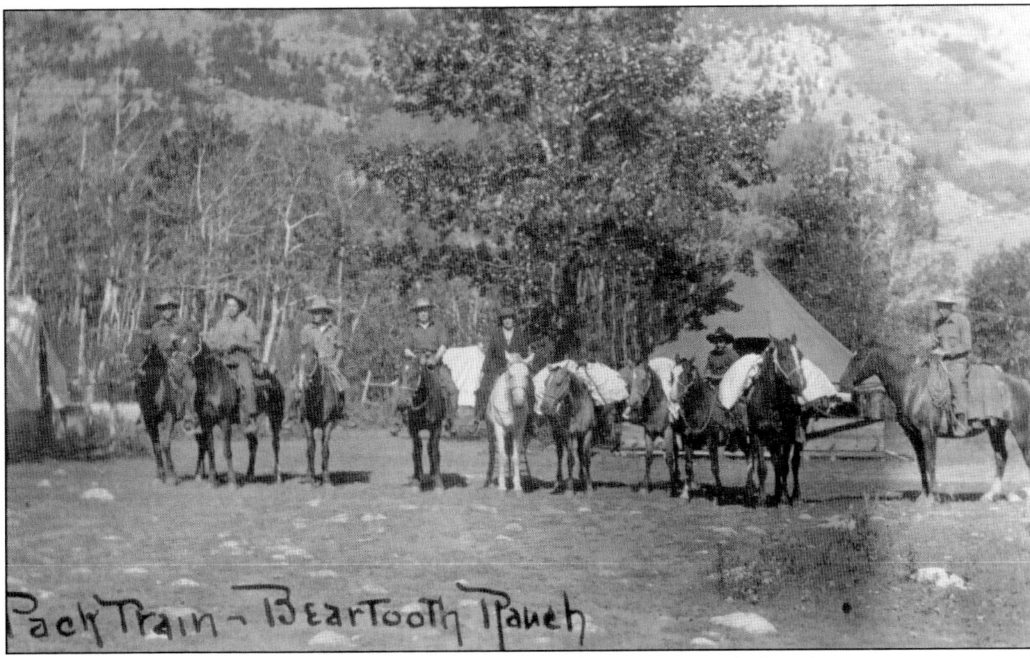

Beartooth Ranch became a center for boys. Physical training, including boxing, was a part of the program, meant to build strong minds and bodies and patriotic men. In later years, Ikerman, with his three girls, Mary Jane, Beth, and Susan, expanded the business to include outfitting and pack trips, and they once hosted John D. Rockefeller and his sons. Jim and Ellen Langston owned and then leased the ranch for many years after; it is now owned by Stillwater Mining Company. (Courtesy of Museum of the Beartooths.)

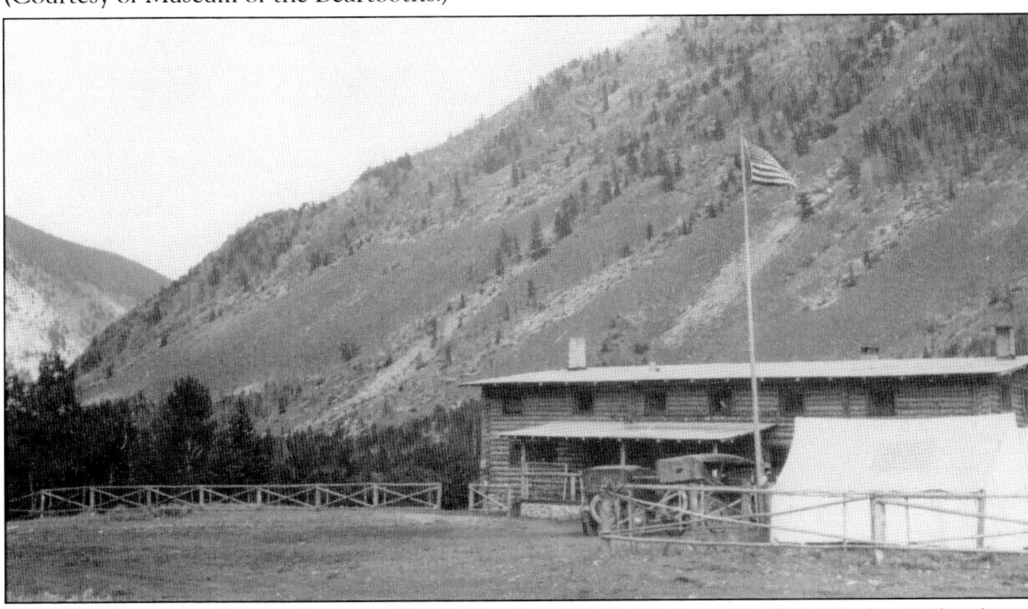

Richel Lodge sat at the confluence of Rock Creek and Lake Fork south of Red Lodge. It developed from a 29-year forest reserve or service lease by Herbert Richel and his wife in 1921. Designed with families in mind, the resort consisted of this recreational lodge, which had a dance hall, dining, and rooms, as well as 13 guest cabins. (Courtesy of Carbon County Historical Society & Museum.)

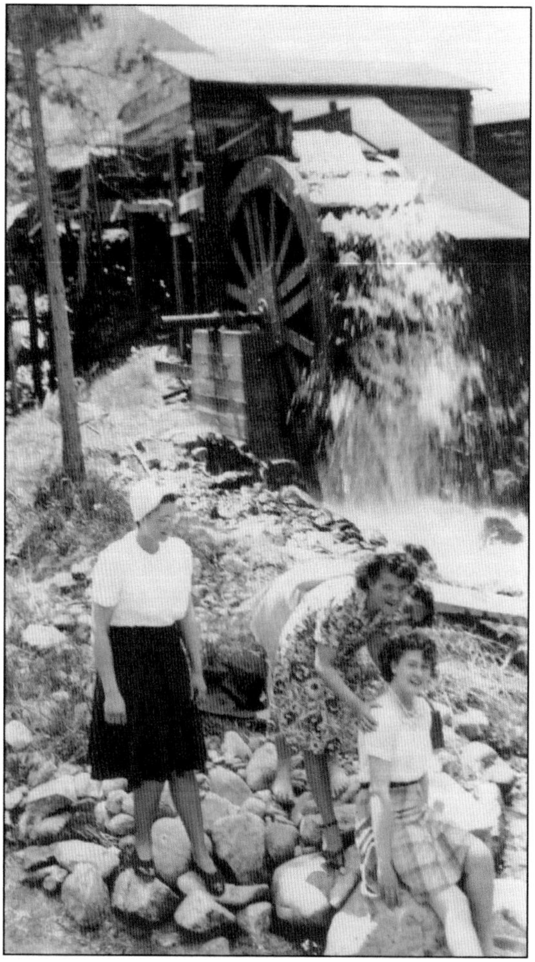

These "dudes" are pictured near the Richel waterwheel, which generated electric power for the complex. The Richels were in attendance at a 1927 dude rancher's convention in Billings, where they discussed how to deal with cancellations, fire insurance, and liability for accidents. A fire in the 1960s burned down the resort, but the wheel was saved and is presently at the Round Barn north of Red Lodge. (Courtesy of Carbon County Historical Society & Museum.)

Jim Redfern's cabin near Beartooth Lake is seen here in 1912. After Redfern left, the Forest Service made use of it as a ranger cabin. Nearby, a special use permit issued in 1927 to Roy Donelson of Red Lodge allowed for the building of his summer home. (Courtesy of Special Collections, Montana State University Library, Bozeman.)

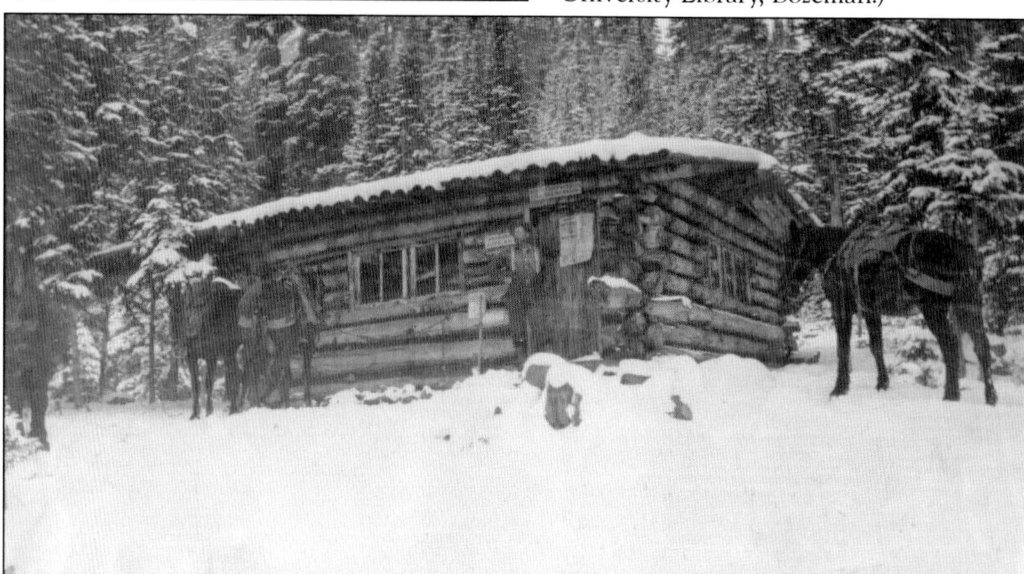

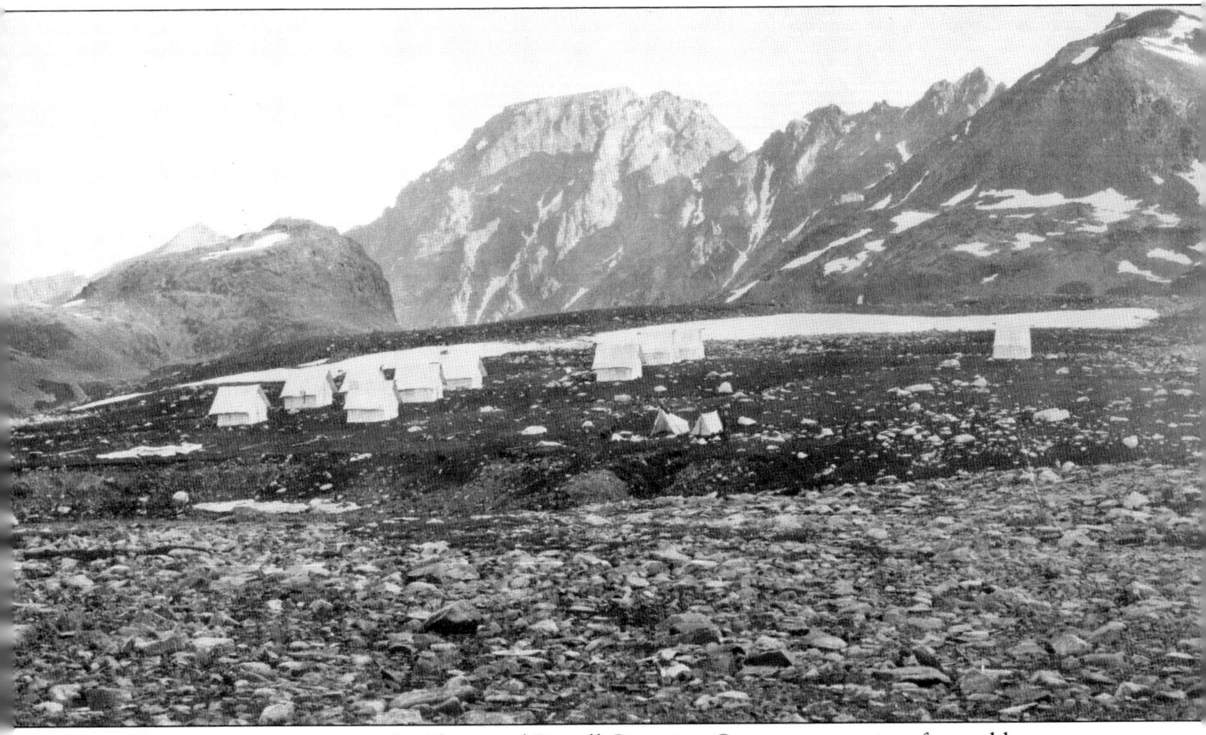

Amos Shaw was a co-owner in the Shaw and Powell Camping Company, a series of movable camps in Yellowstone Park beginning in 1898. His son, Walter, assisted with this operation and continued the tradition, building Shaw's Camp on Goose Lake, along the trail to Grasshopper Glacier. The trail to the glacier was 12 miles long and required 10 to 12 hours for a round trip on horseback. Savvy guests could spend the evening at Shaw's camp and have more time to enjoy amazing views of Grasshopper Glacier. Walter Shaw also maintained a guide service in Cooke City. In June 1925, he drowned in the Gardiner River, and his brother, Chester, took over the Cooke City operations. (Courtesy of Special Collections, Montana State University Library, Bozeman.)

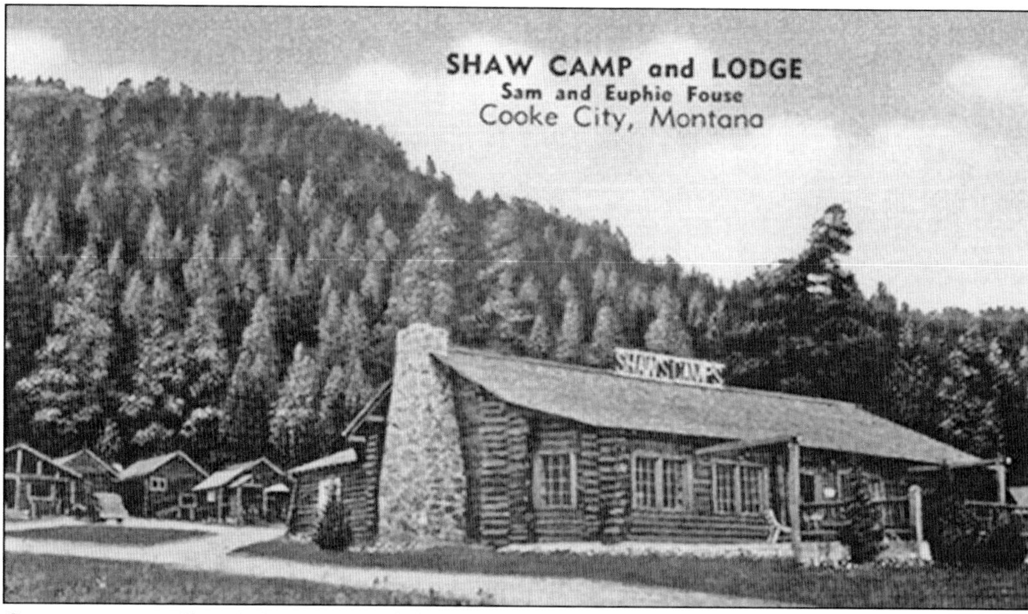

Guests arrive at Shaw's Camp, one of the first tourist facilities in Cooke City. Dignitaries such as western artist Wilhelm Heinrich Dethlef "W.H.D." Koerner relaxed here. The Northern Pacific Railroad employed Walter Shaw during the winters as a promoter traveling through the East giving lectures on the beauties of the region. Today, Shaw's camp is home to the Antlers Lodge. (Courtesy of Antlers Lodge.)

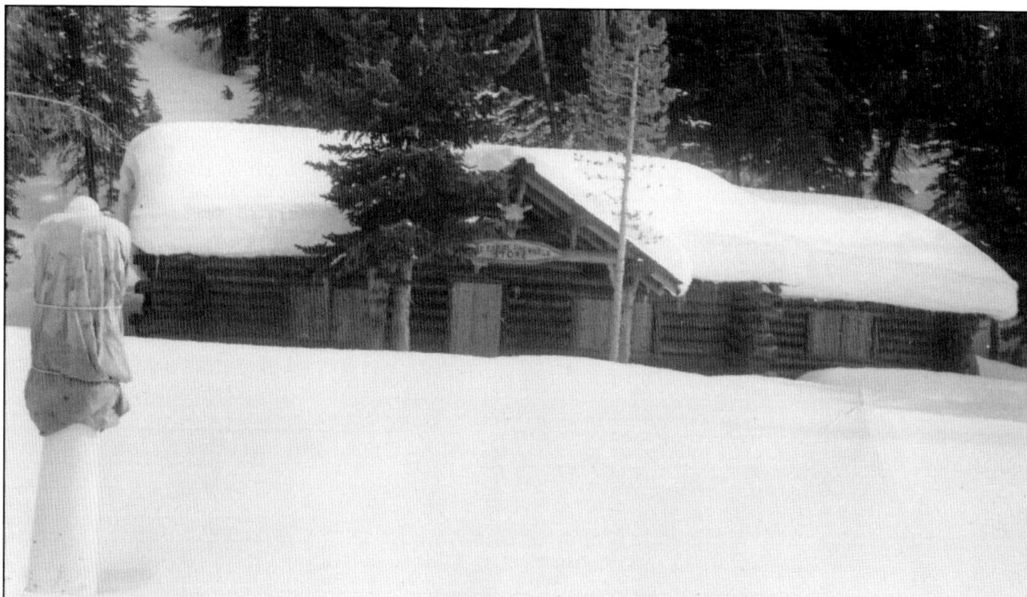

Around 1933, Roy Hicox built Beartooth Lake Lodge. Guests would get off the Northern Pacific train in Red Lodge and travel 12 miles by car and then 22 miles on horseback. They were housed in tents until the 1940s, when Herb Flatt obtained the lease and added 16 cabins and this curio shop, the Top of the World Store. In 1966, the permit was terminated by the Forest Service, and the buildings were moved to Cooke Pass. (Courtesy of Marlene Donelson.)

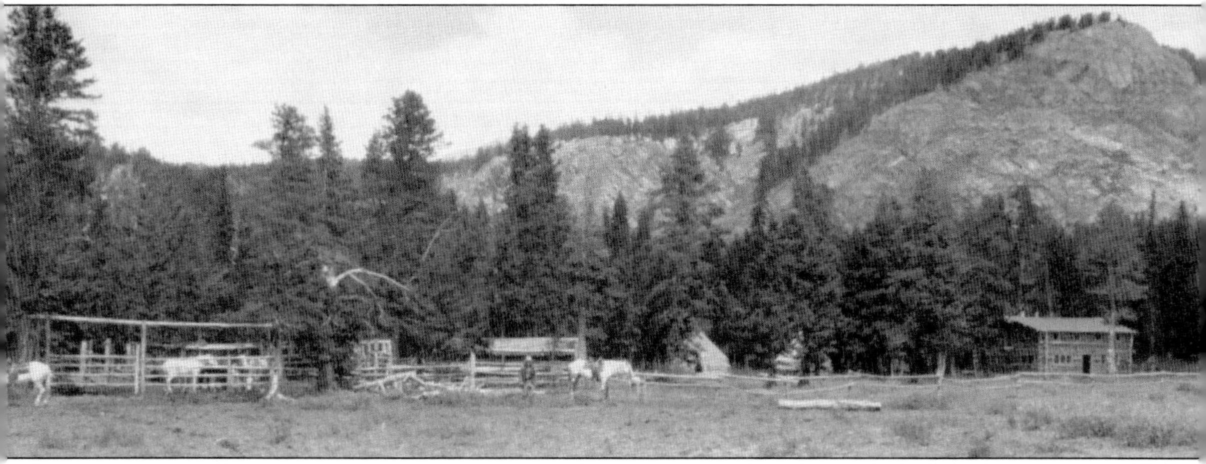

F.I. Johnson found this spot at the base of Sawtooth Mountain to build Camp Sawtooth in 1921. Without a road, he packed 40 board feet per packhorse to build it. Reservations could be made with the Northern Pacific Railway with rates of $75 per week. Guests would be driven 16 miles from Red Lodge along Rock Creek to the end of the road. From there, it was 11 miles to the camp by saddle horse; the motto was, "Do not get in a hurry on the trail." At 8,500 feet, the camp was open from July 1 to September 15. Johnson touted that there was "trout at every meal" because of the more than 20 lakes within four miles of the camp. After Johnson retired in 1937, the camp had a handful of owners, including Luther and Harriet Bradshaw, who purchased it in 1958. However, the Bradshaws had to give up their lease in the mid-1960s, and the lodge, the five cabins, and the corrals were burned by the Forest Service in 1970. (Courtesy of Parmly Billings Library.)

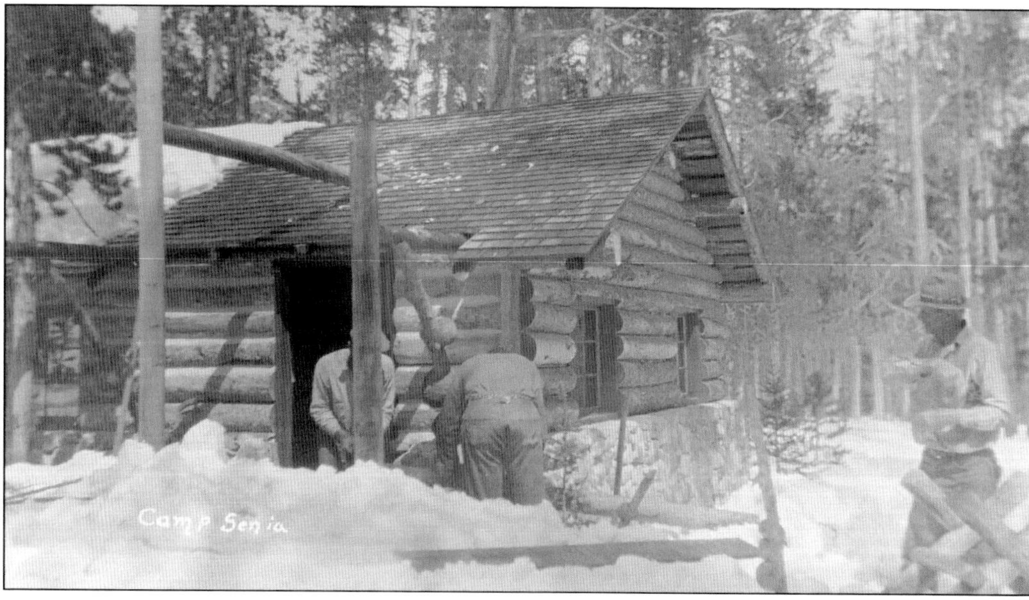

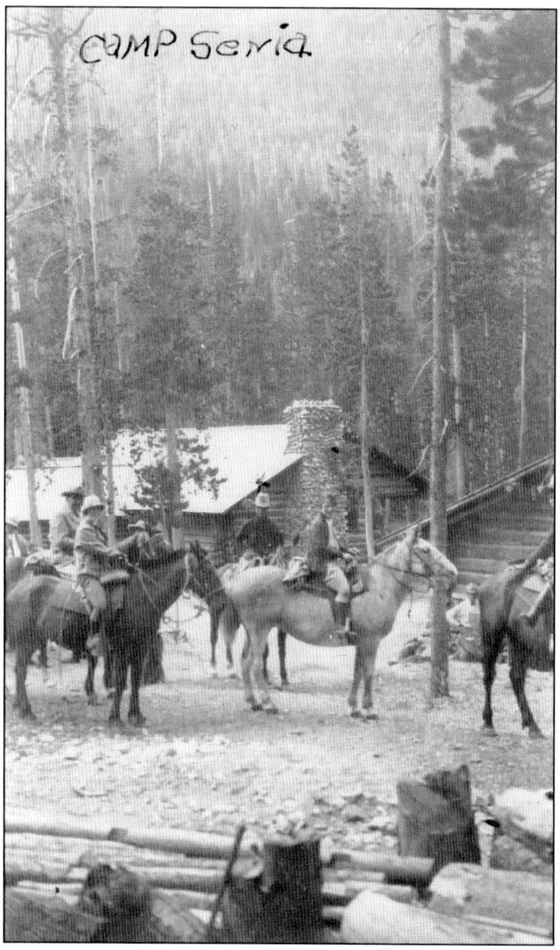

At 8,000 feet in the west fork of Rock Creek Canyon, Camp Senia was a dude ranch owned and operated by Alfred Croonquist and his new bride, Senia, after whom the property was named. In 1919, the first building, the main lodge "lobby," was completed, and throughout the next decade, 19 buildings were crafted by a group of Finnish friends from Red Lodge. All materials were brought 15 miles from Red Lodge. Guests would arrive in Red Lodge and take a wagon nine miles before getting on a "trusty saddle horse" to the camp. It was suggested that guests pack their duffel with wool underwear, outing shirts, canvas leggings, and stout shoes so that it could be put into an old flour or grain sack, which made for excellent saddle bags on a packhorse. Hauling steamer trunks to camp was an extra charge. (Above, courtesy of Museum of the Beartooths; left, courtesy of Carbon County Historical Society & Museum.)

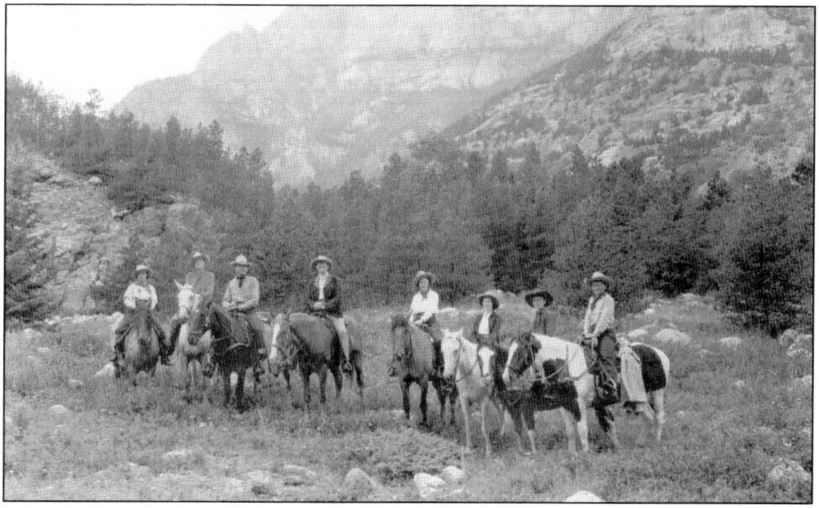

Senia Croonquist was in charge of the day-to-day operations and was the chief camp cook for up to 40 guests. Early rates were $100 a month, $25 per week, or $4 per day and climbed to $45 a week in the mid-1920s. Horses were provided for each guest, a Victrola provided music, and newspapers and mail were brought in daily. Many trails and side trips were offered, including a 10-day trip from camp. In 1926, Al helped organize the Dude Ranchers Association, serving as vice president from 1926 to 1931. He also initiated the Dude Ranchers Magazine. Camp Senia failed during the Depression, but new investors kept the resort functional from 1933 to 1935, when the Yellowstone-Bighorn Research Association rented the facilities. In 1938, Camp Senia Corporation purchased the camp, making the cabins into private residences leased from the Forest Service. (Above, courtesy of USFS, Custer National Forest; below, courtesy of National Register of Historic Places.)

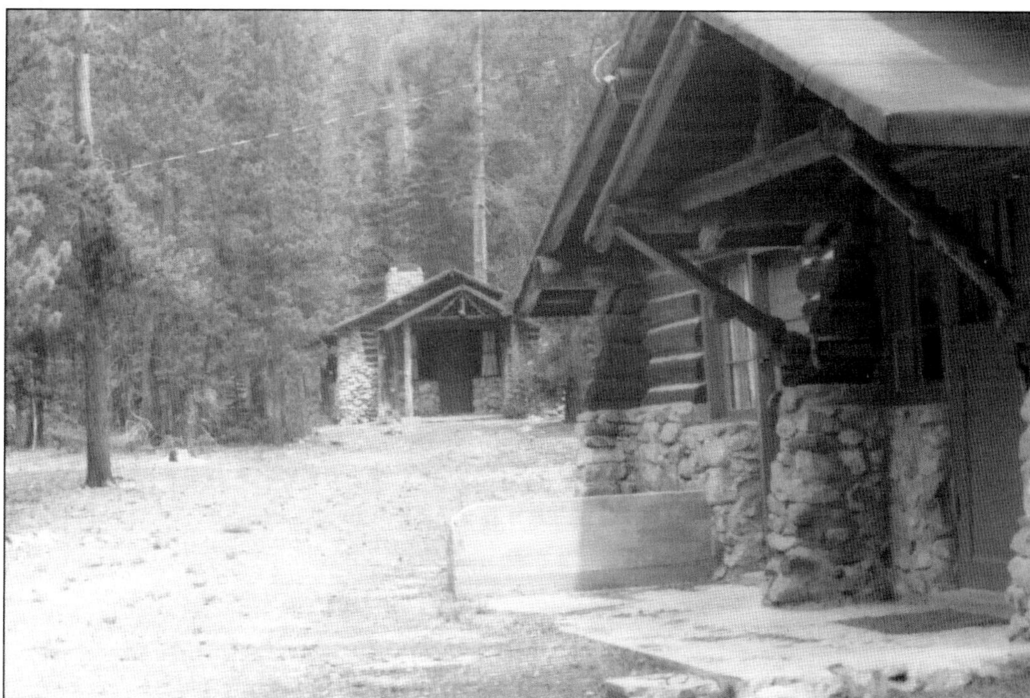

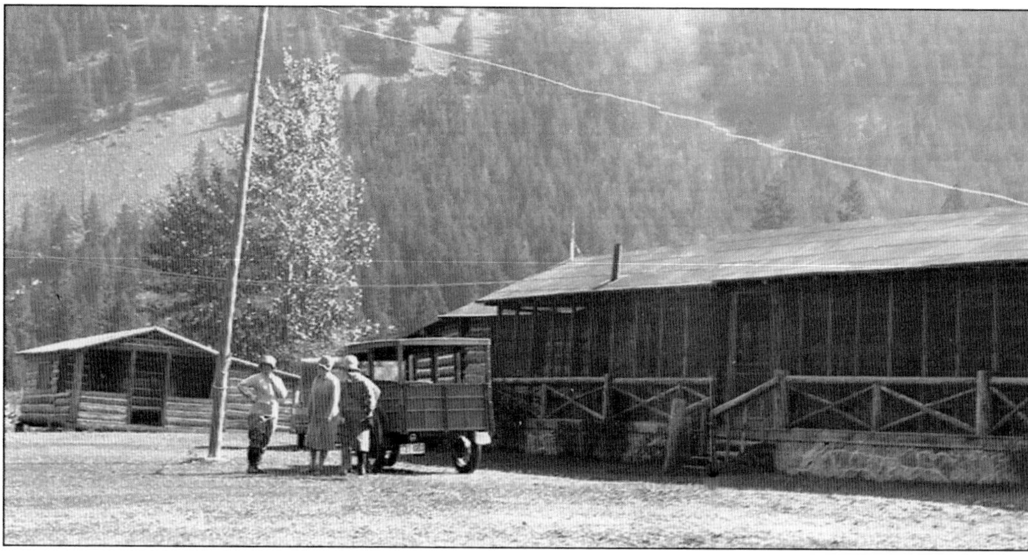

In 1920, J.W. Kirwin started the Kirwin Dude Ranch along the Boulder River. He later renamed it the White Bear Ranch in an attempt to attract more guests. The Kirwins staged a rodeo for guest enjoyment once a year. Clyde and Violet Bowen of Billings, who were frequent guests, eventually purchased the property. (Courtesy of Special Collections, Montana State University Library, Bozeman.)

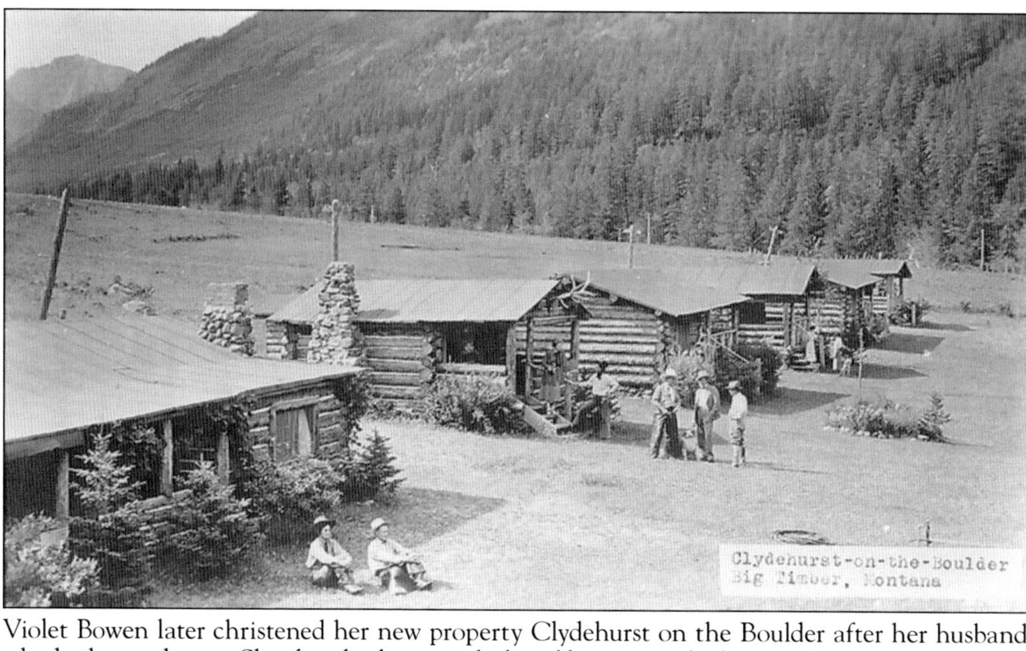

Violet Bowen later christened her new property Clydehurst on the Boulder after her husband, who had passed away. She then built a nine-hole golf course and advertised 21 cabins for use. In 1943, it was sold to a church camp, and it is now home to Clydehurst Christian Ranch. (Courtesy of Brian Sullivan.)

Joe Keeney catches trout in the river. In 1896, Keeney purchased land holdings near Contact from Sam Cowan. By 1900, he opened this property, Gould's Resort, as a haven for hunters and fishermen. Noted artist Edward Paxon was a frequent guest, and another guest, Walter Aller, liked the property so much that he purchased the 650-acre operation in 1918. (Courtesy of Crazy Mountain Museum.)

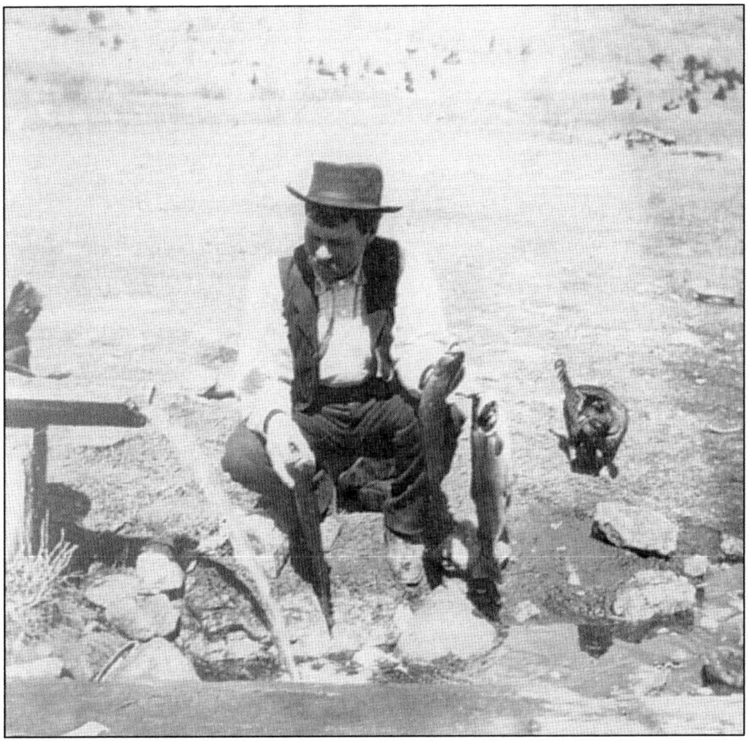

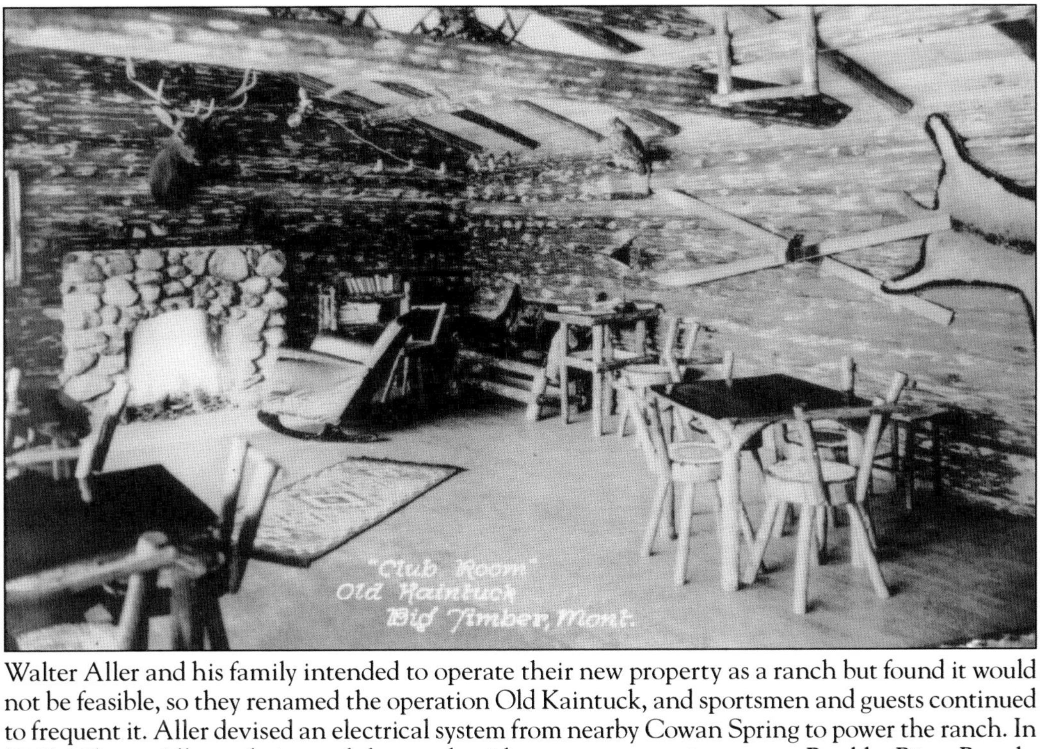

Walter Aller and his family intended to operate their new property as a ranch but found it would not be feasible, so they renamed the operation Old Kaintuck, and sportsmen and guests continued to frequent it. Aller devised an electrical system from nearby Cowan Spring to power the ranch. In 1947, Gilman Aller rechristened the ranch with a more appropriate name, Boulder River Ranch, which is still in operation today. (Courtesy of Crazy Mountain Museum.)

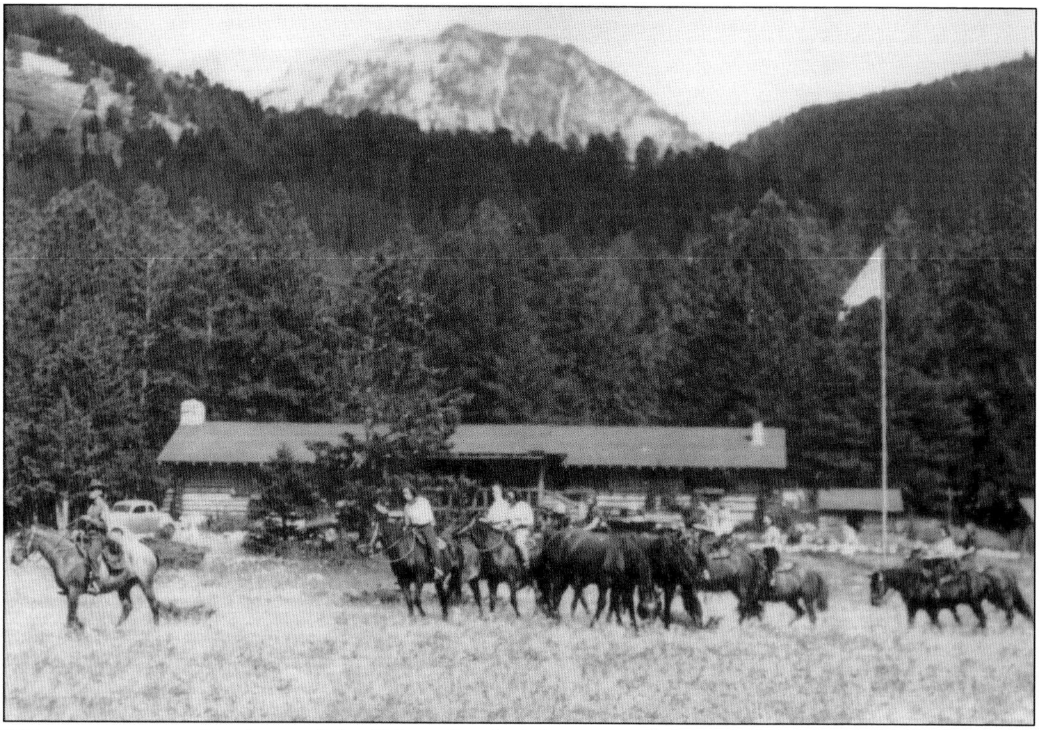

Riders are mounted in front of the Ethan Cowles's homestead, located on the Boulder River near Hicks Park. Upon Cowles's death, his son, Don (left), and Don's wife, Julia (right), inherited the property. Julia named the ranch Bar Lazy DA. A lodge, dormitory, and cabins were constructed in the early 1930s. Guests were met at the Northern Pacific rail depot in Livingston, and riding lessons and pack trips to Independence, Yellowstone Park, and other destinations were offered. Don Cowles passed away suddenly in 1933, after which the ranch was leased out for several years. After World War II, his son, Don Jr., waving his hat in between his parents, maintained the ranch until 1954, when a portion was sold to the Lutheran Bible Camp. It is now home to the ministry program Christikon. (Both, courtesy of Don Cowles Jr.)

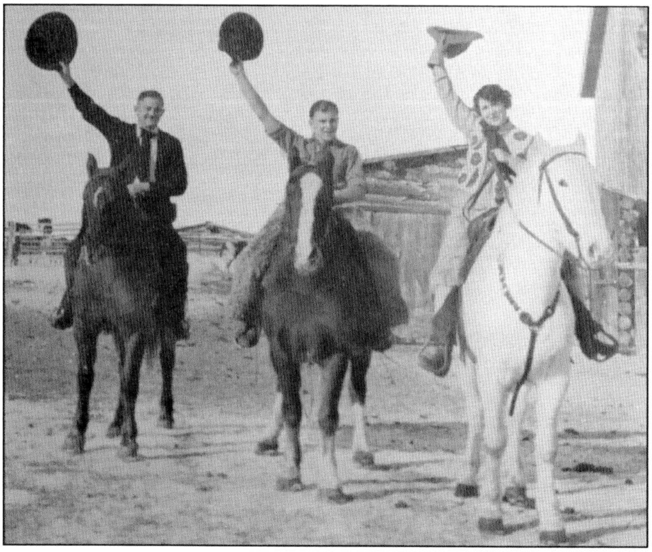

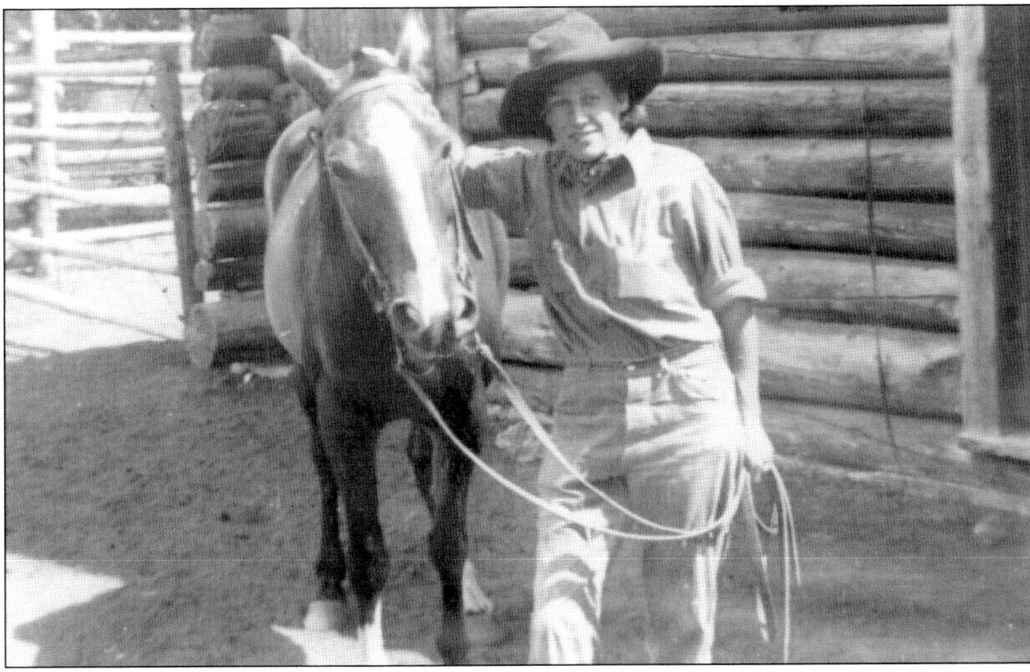

Florence Antonia Ames, born in 1898 in Munich, Germany, was a descendent of the Schirmer music publishing family. At an early age, she learned to sing, dance, and play the piano. After the sudden death of her parents, "Tony" and her brothers were shipped back to the United States. Eventually she fulfilled her dream of owning a dude ranch, running the Bar TA on the East Boulder River from 1939 to 1954. (Courtesy of Crazy Mountain Museum.)

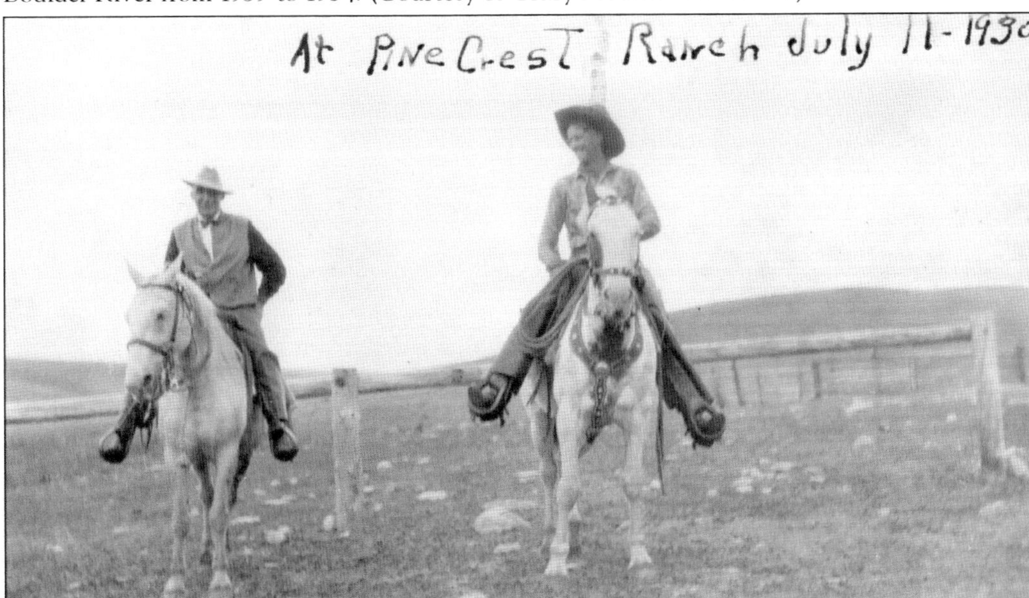

Located just west of Luther at the head of Butcher Creek, the Pinecrest Ranch was operated by Lawrence Rankin. From Red Lodge for a fee of $2.50 or from Columbus for $5, guests were transported by ranch cars to Pinecrest. Spring bear hunts and seasonal small game and bird hunts were also provided, all for $5 a day. (Courtesy of Museum of the Beartooths.)

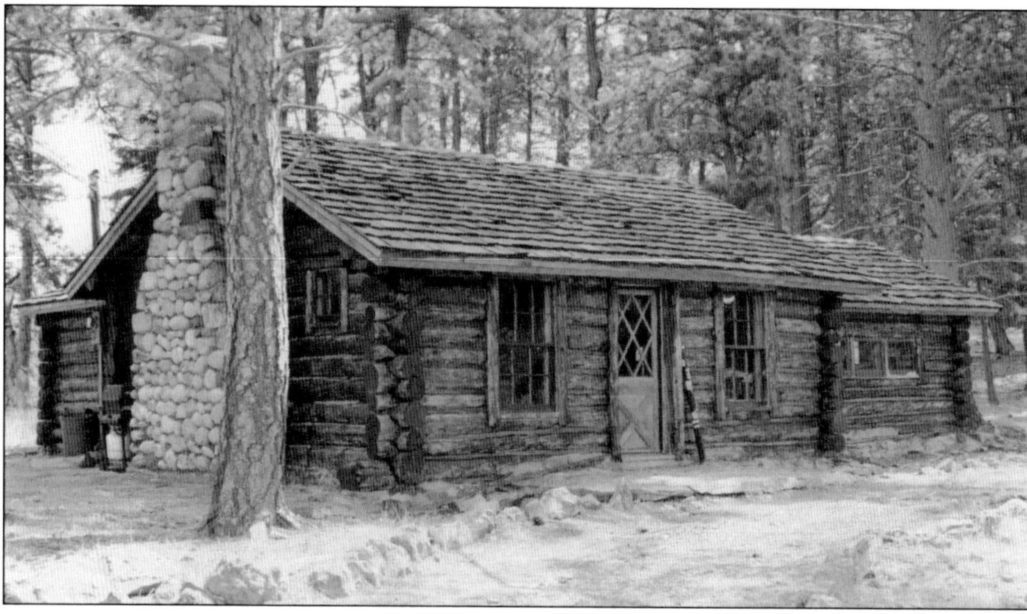

Beginning in 1896, Charles Fisher squatted for seven years on land that would eventually become the 4K Ranch. He received a patent to the land in 1904 but sold out four years later. Elliot "Ed" Keene purchased the acreage in 1919 from F.E. Runner, and Keene ran livestock and developed the property with a nine-hole golf course. The winner of a golf tournament in 1927 was given the honor of naming the ranch. He named it Keenes Kozy Kountry Klub, or 4K. Guest cabins were constructed in the same year, and a large log lodge was completed by 1932. Keene was a member of the Dude Ranchers Association until 1937, when he sold out to Frank Book, Gordon "Mickey" Cochrane, and Elmer Holmgren, who made efforts to promote the dude operation. Eventually, the property passed through the hands of the Moreheads and the Wilsons. Today, it is on the National Register of Historic Places and is privately owned. (Both, courtesy of National Register of Historic Places.)

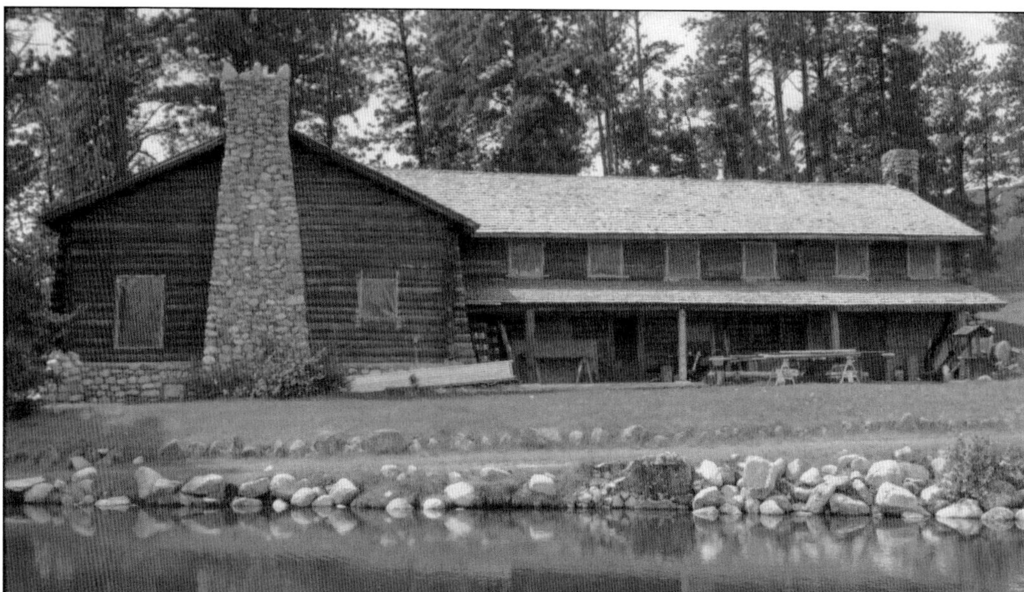

Eight

Forest

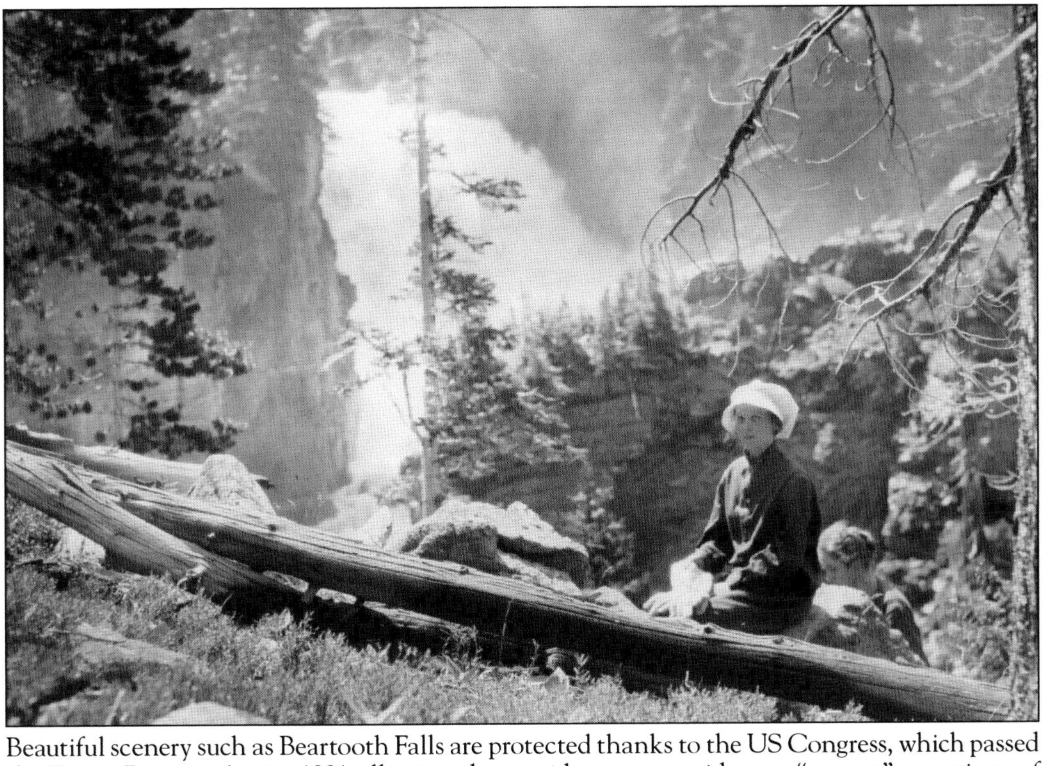

Beautiful scenery such as Beartooth Falls are protected thanks to the US Congress, which passed the Forest Reserve Act in 1891 allowing the president to set aside—or "reserve"—portions of public domain for the protection of natural resources. On March 3, 1891, Pres. Benjamin Harrison established the nation's first forest reserve, the Yellowstone Park Timber Land Reserve, which included the entire Beartooth Mountain Range. In 1902, the Absarokee Forest Reserve and the Yellowstone Forest Reserve were established as reserves as well. In 1905, under the leadership of Pres. Theodore Roosevelt, congress designated the forest reserves as national forests under the US Department of Agriculture. (Courtesy of Carbon County Historical Society & Museum.)

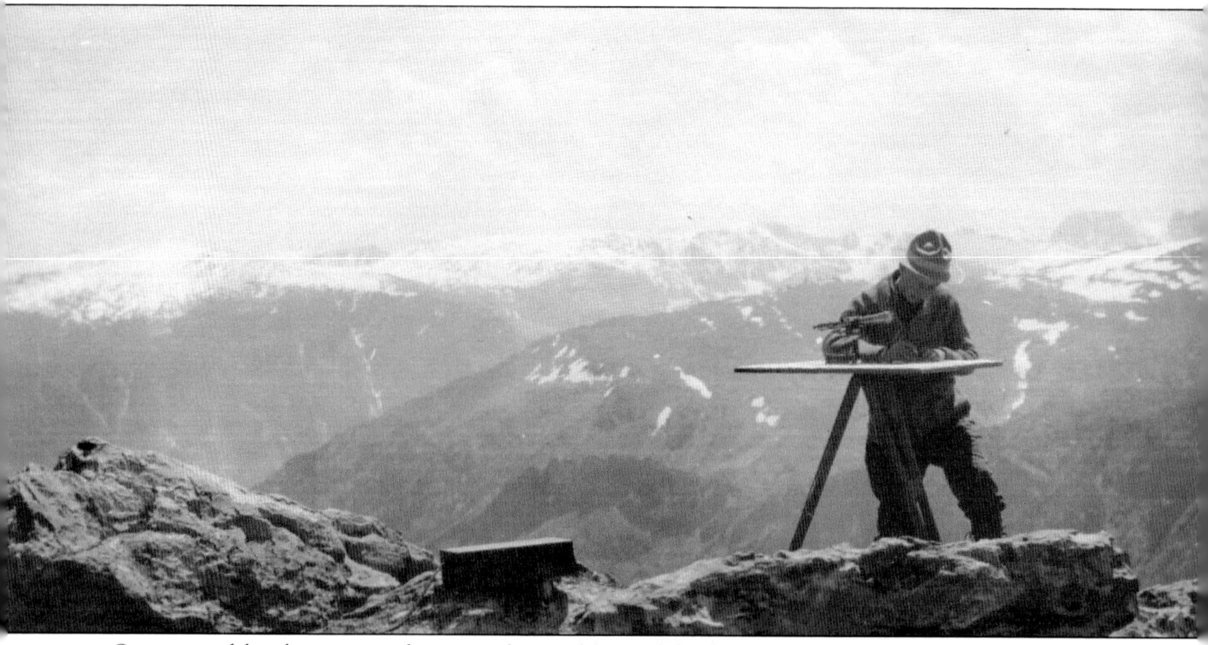

Surveyors, like this one performing plane table work high on a mountain, played important roles in establishing boundaries. In 1908, the Beartooth National Forest and Absarokee National Forest were created from the Yellowstone National Forest Preserve. That same year, Custer National Forest was established from the Otter Forest Reserves. In 1932, Beartooth Forest became part of the Custer National Forest, and the 230,000-acre Beartooth Primitive Area and the 64,000-acre Absarokee Primitive Area was established. In 1945, the Gallatin National Forest was created from the Absarokee National Forest and a portion of Custer National Forest. On March 27, 1978, Pres. Jimmy Carter signed the Absaroka Beartooth Bill, establishing 920,310 acres as wilderness to be preserved for future generation and administered by Custer, Gallatin, and Shoshone National Forests. (Courtesy of Special Collections, Montana State University Library, Bozeman.)

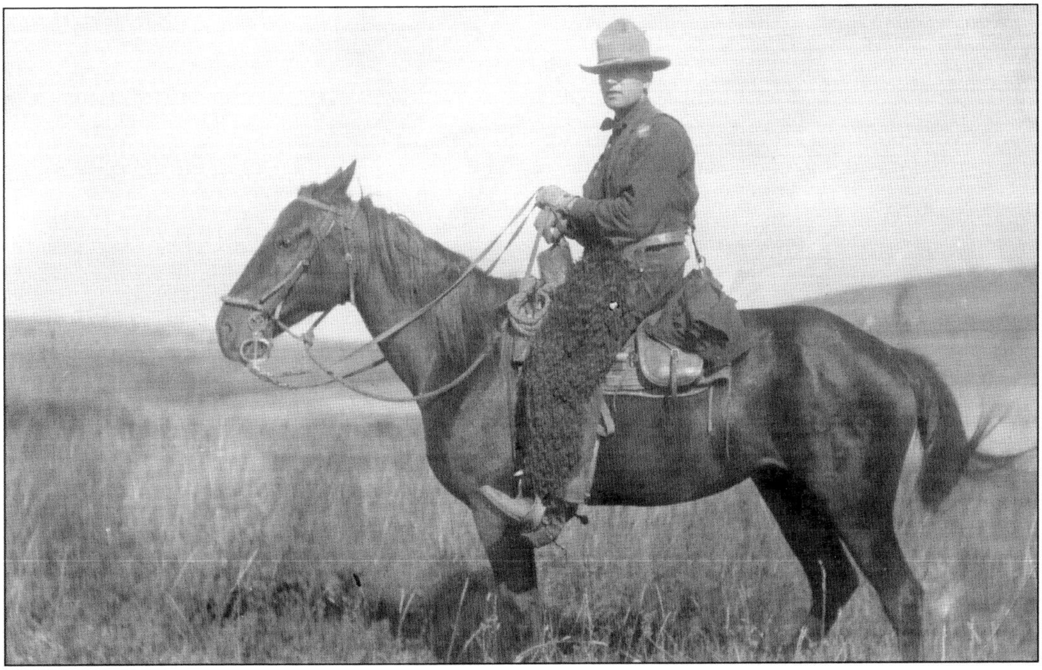

Harry Kaufman signed on as a guard ranger in 1903 and was assigned to the Absaroka Division of the Yellowstone Forest Reserve. As a prerequisite, he had to provide two horses, pack outfits, camp equipment, and his services 24 hours per day in exchange for $60 a month. In 1904, Kaufman crossed a mountain pass from the Myers Creek Ranger Station to establish a new ranger station on the Boulder River. In 1905, he constructed a 14-foot-by-14-foot cabin. For almost 40 years, this Boulder Station was the headquarters and residence for Kaufman, his wife, Coral, and their children, Harry Jr. and Betty. Harry administered the activities for about 300,000 acres of national forest lands and was responsible for cruising timber, issuing permits, fighting fires, surveying homesteads, and enforcing poaching and trespass laws. (Both, courtesy of USFS, Big Timber Ranger District.)

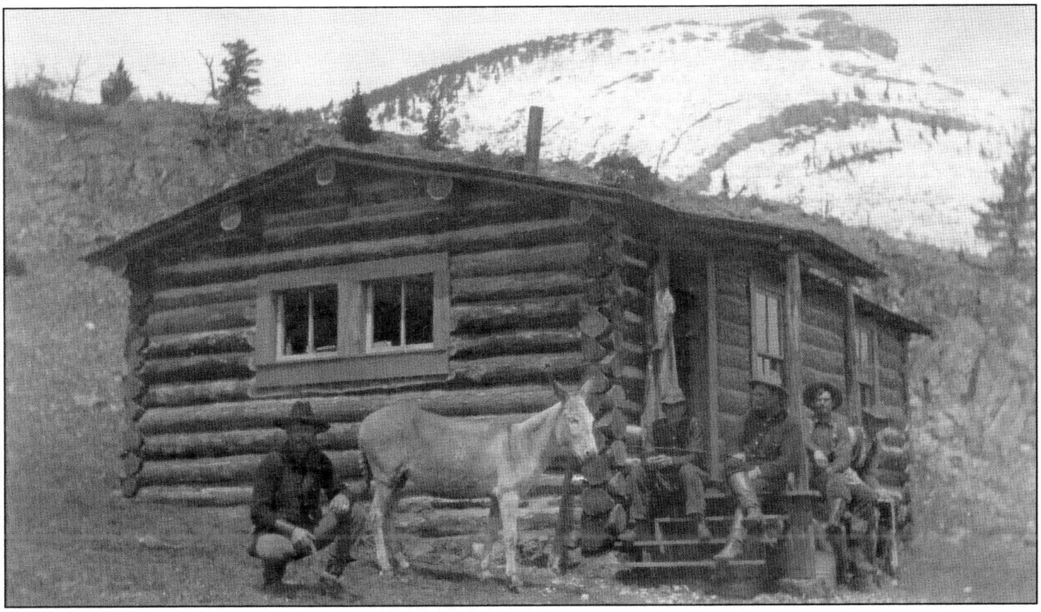

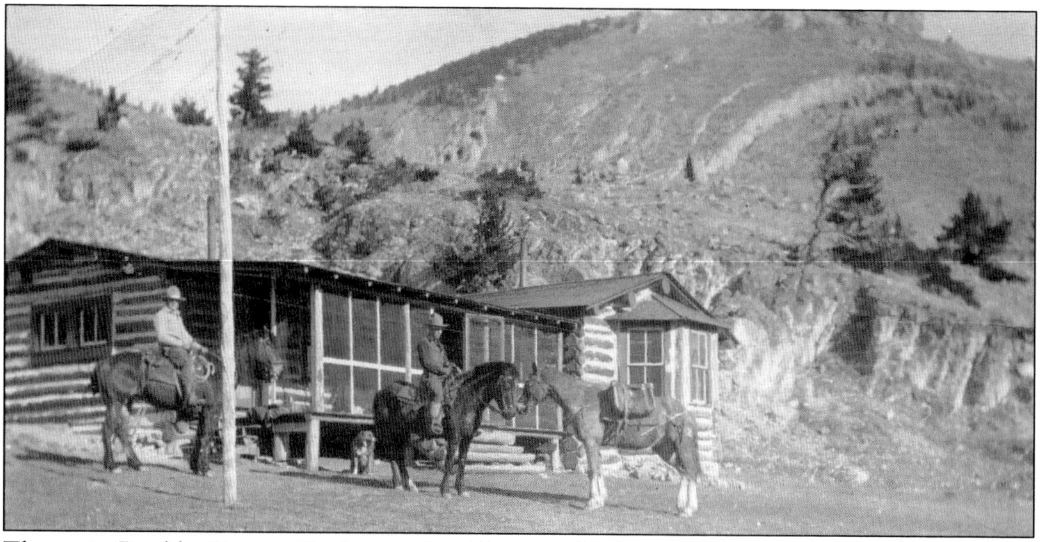

The main Boulder Ranger Station, with additions added in 1907 and 1933, may represent the oldest facility in the Forest Service system. The station has been restored and is open for summer visitation. Other stations on the Boulder included Four Mile and Box Canyon, which are now used as administrative sites. The ranger headquarters moved to Big Timber when the Absaroka National Forest was consolidated into part of the Gallatin and Custer National Forests in 1945. (Courtesy of USFS, Big Timber Ranger District.)

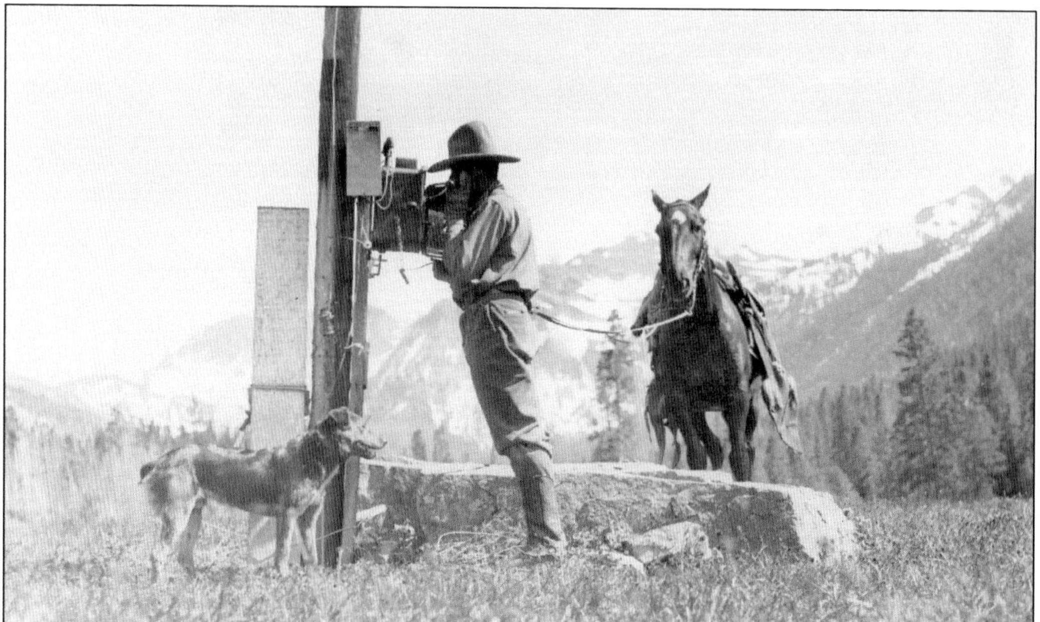

Horse and dog by his side, Harry Kaufman makes a call from the patrol phone box. In 1907, area ranches, various Forest Service cabins, mines, and post offices, and the towns of Big Timber and Livingston were connected via patrol phone boxes. The switchboard for these remote phones was located at the main Boulder Ranger Station. The Forest Service was responsible for erecting and maintaining all the poles and lines, which were on national forest lands. (Courtesy of USFS, Big Timber Ranger District.)

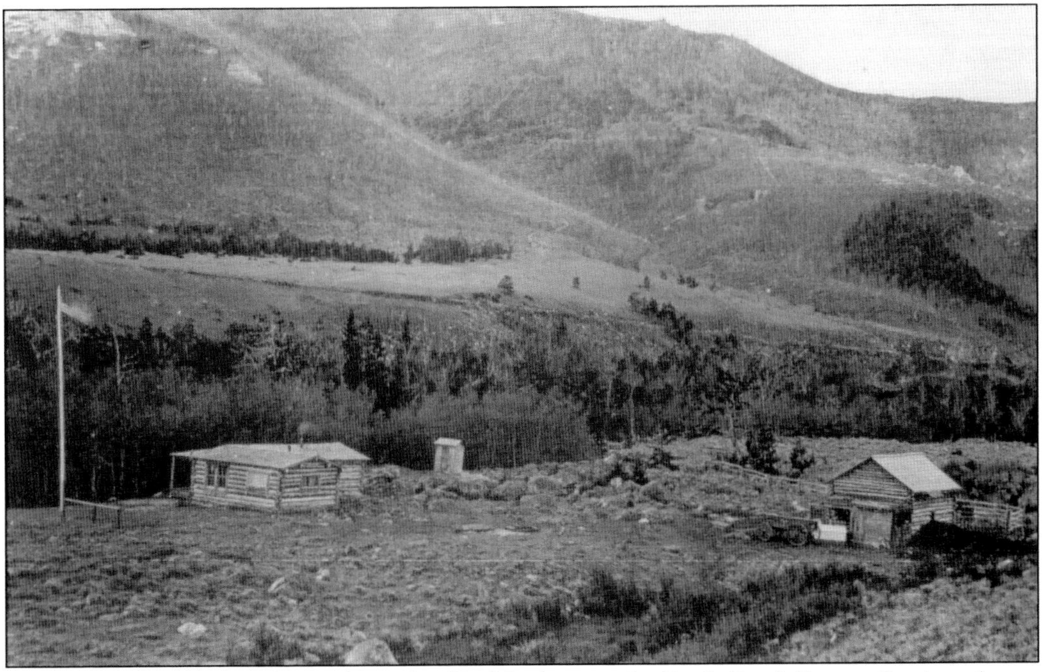

On the West Fork of Rock Creek south of Red Lodge was the Rock Creek Ranger Station, shown here a few years before the Beartooth National Forest and Absarokee National Forest were established from the Yellowstone National Forest Preserve in 1908. The lack of timber is due to fires, which burned more than 138,000 acres in the Beartooth Mountains from 1870 to 1904. Today, the ranger station is an administrative site. (Courtesy of USFS, Beartooth Ranger District.)

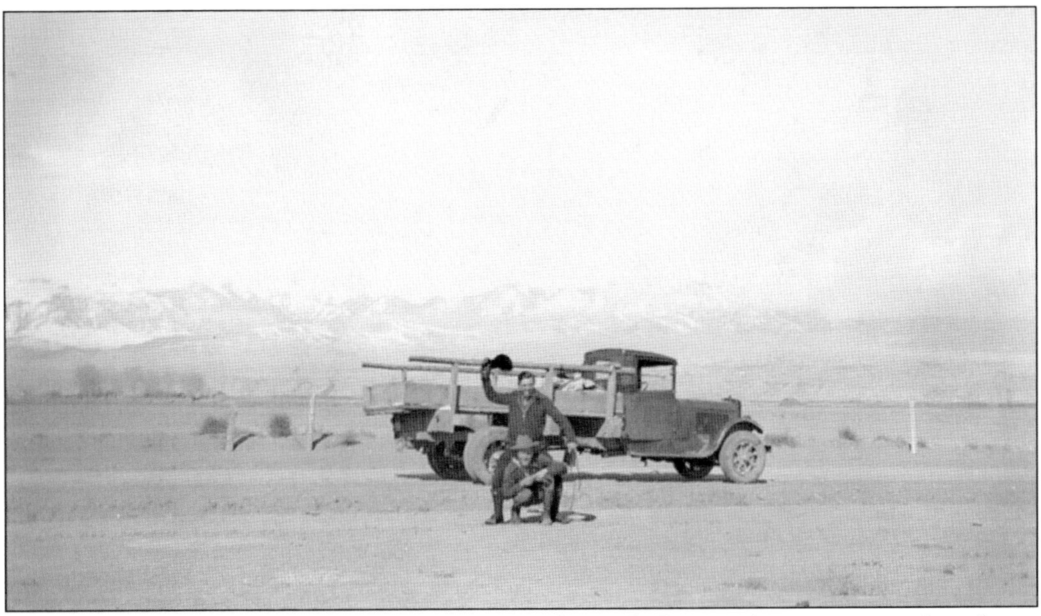

Dale Jennings and Hariam Baretta pose in 1936 in front of a Reo truck on game patrol southeast of Line Creek near Clark, Wyoming. (Courtesy of USFS, Custer National Forest.)

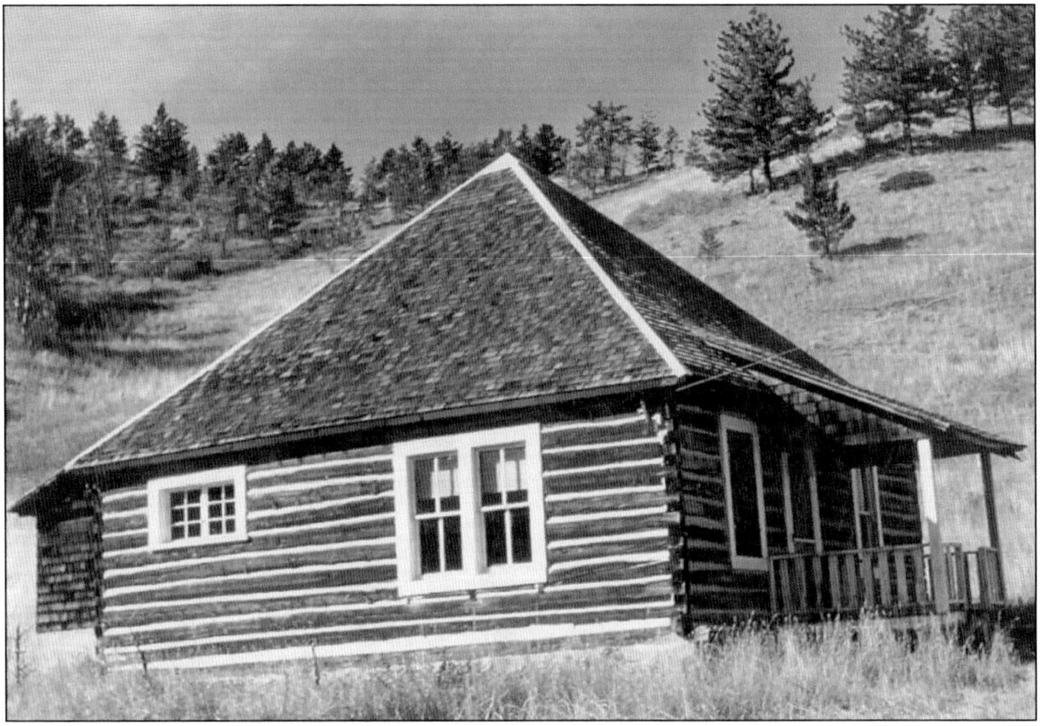

Located on Red Lodge Creek south of Luther was the Red Lodge Creek Ranger Station. Stations were typically located approximately 10-12 miles or a one-day horse ride apart. In 1924, Ranger W.W. Larsen oversaw four miles of road construction and improvements between Luther and this post. This station was removed in 1954. (Courtesy of USFS, Beartooth Ranger District.)

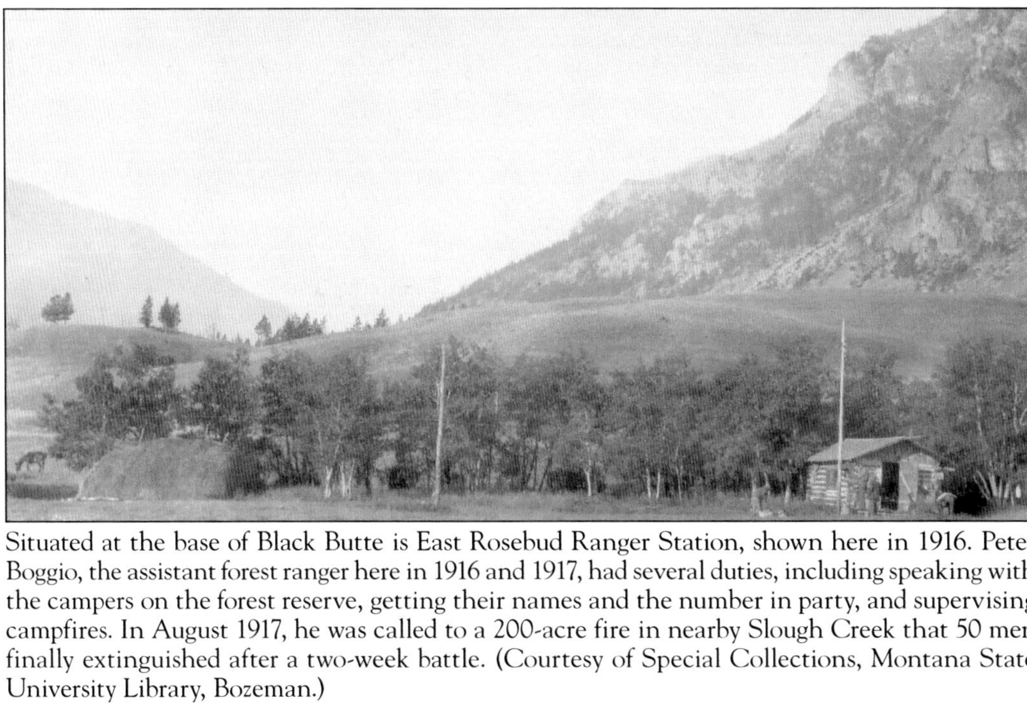

Situated at the base of Black Butte is East Rosebud Ranger Station, shown here in 1916. Peter Boggio, the assistant forest ranger here in 1916 and 1917, had several duties, including speaking with the campers on the forest reserve, getting their names and the number in party, and supervising campfires. In August 1917, he was called to a 200-acre fire in nearby Slough Creek that 50 men finally extinguished after a two-week battle. (Courtesy of Special Collections, Montana State University Library, Bozeman.)

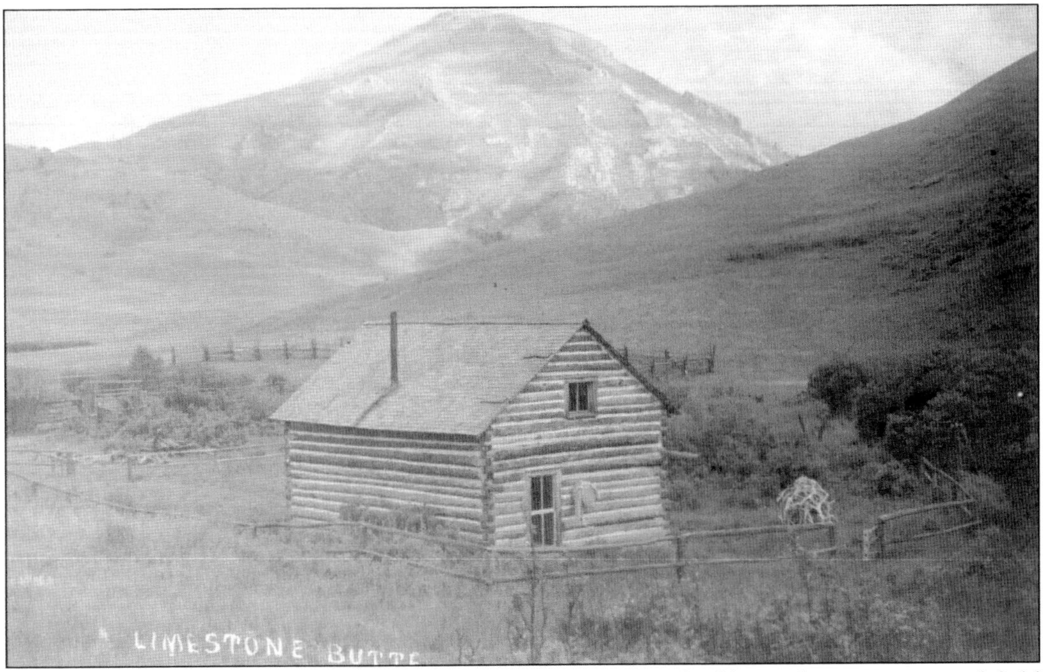

In 1908, the Forest Service began a program of obtaining or building administrative and field offices for local on-the-ground control. Many old homesteads and mining cabins, including the Myers Creek Ranger Station, shown here in 1907, were converted into field offices. Rangers patrolled the forests on foot and on horseback to administer mining and grazing permits and protect against forest fires. (Courtesy of Museum of the Beartooths.)

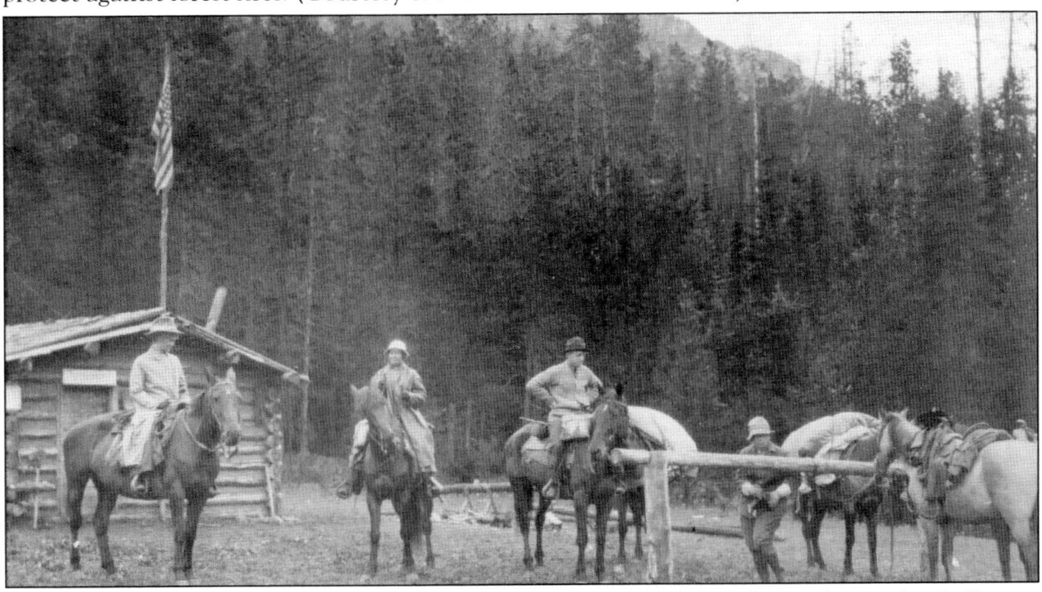

Unidentified riders saddle up at the Big Park Ranger Station, located 12 miles up the Stillwater Trail. Rangers were responsible for cruising timber, issuing special and free permits, fighting fires, surveying homesteads, and enforcing poaching and trespass laws. The Big Park Ranger Station burned in the Yellowstone fires of 1988. (Courtesy of Special Collections, Montana State University Library, Bozeman.)

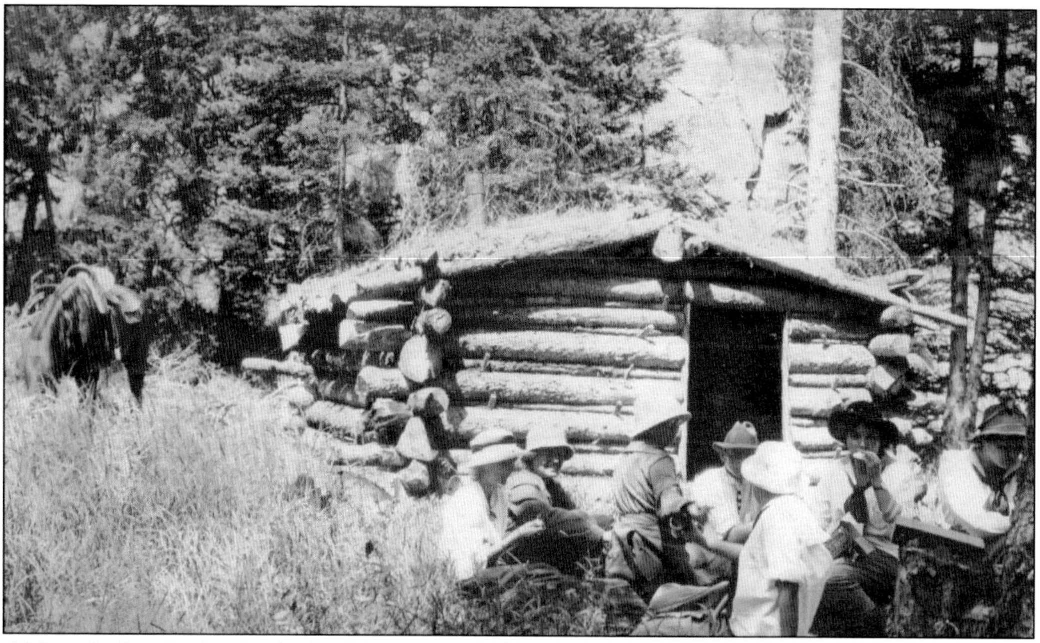

Although they had to bushwhack to get to it, this party enjoyed this trapper's cabin at Elk Lake along the East Rosebud in 1916. It was not until 1921 that the Forest Service began construction of the East Rosebud Trail, most likely in an effort to expand recreation opportunities in the area at the urging of local cabin owners along the lake. Two miles of pathway were built that year at a cost of $40. (Courtesy of Special Collections, Montana State University Library, Bozeman.)

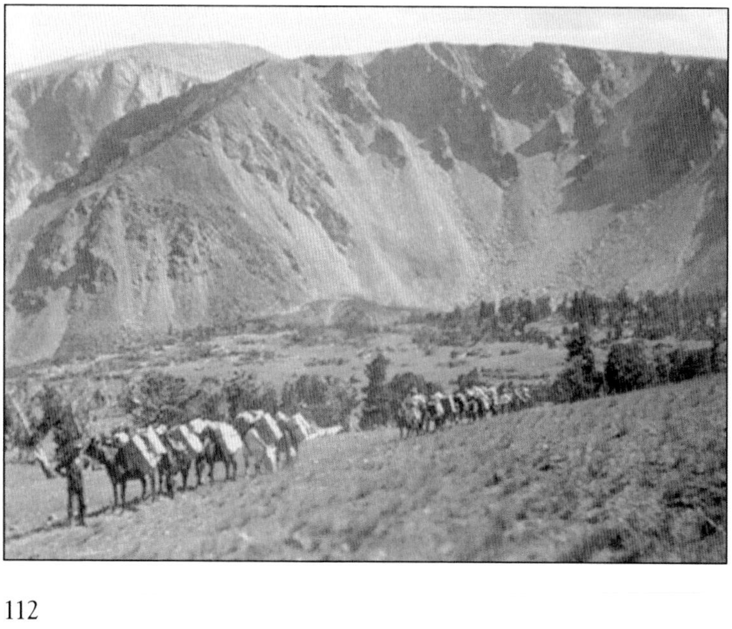

Horses and mules were the typical mode of transportation for packing tools and supplies for the trail crews. In 1939, the Civilian Conservation Corps (CCC) established a camp at East Rosebud Lake. The 10-man CCC crew was to build four miles of trail, but times had changed since 1916, the first mile cost $3,170. Three more miles were completed over the next two years. (Courtesy of USFS, Beartooth Ranger District.)

Wayne Cunningham, a former trail cook and army veteran, takes a rest on a rock cairn topped with a buffalo skull between the East and West Rosebuds in 1936. World War II halted construction along the East Rosebud Trail. Although it was resumed in 1947, a portion of the trail was relocated across the river, abandoning 1.7 miles of path. By 1949, a 6.7-mile trail had been built at a cost of $23,523.34. (Courtesy of USFS, Beartooth Ranger District.)

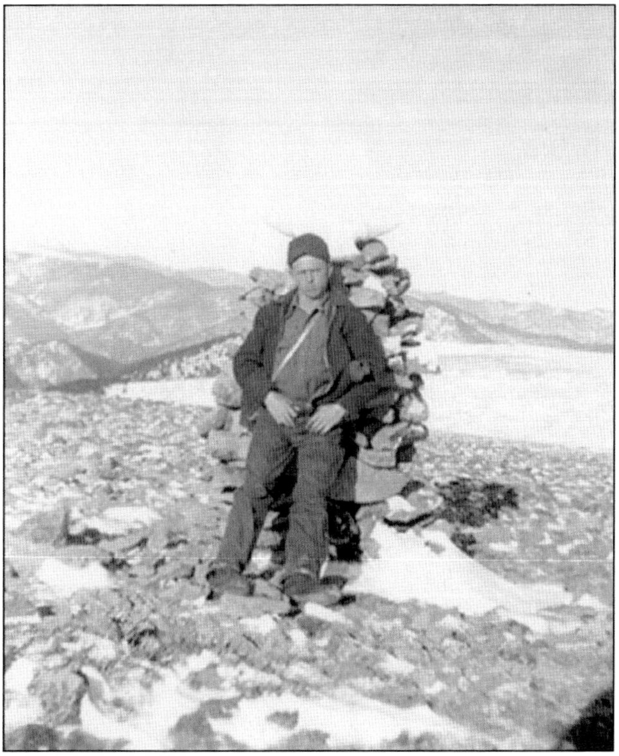

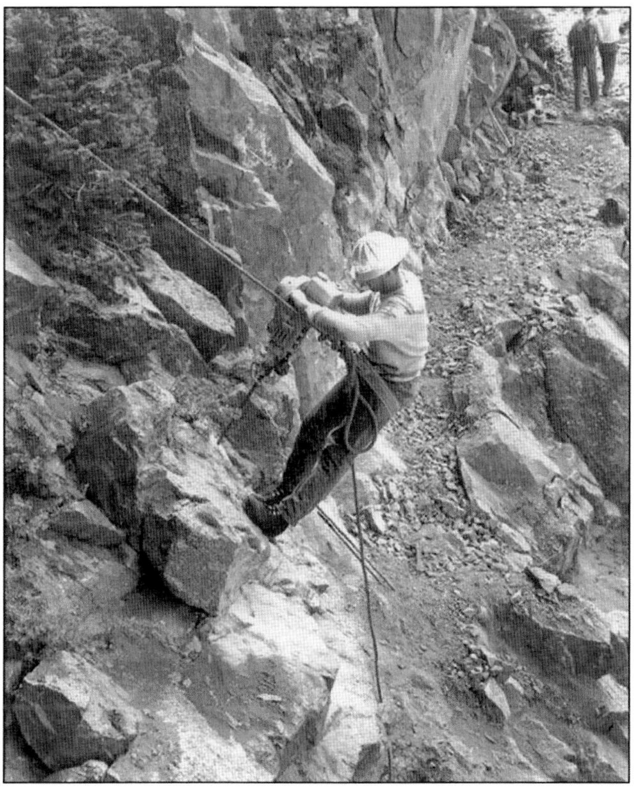

A worker operates a gas-powered jackhammer to help build a trail. He was one of 10 men working under crew foreman Blasé DiLulo. This crew dangled from ropes on sheer ledges, drilling and setting 100 charges of explosives each day. On September 10, 1964, Al Knox drove a golden spike into the ground that tied the trail together, creating the 26-mile path from East Rosebud Lake over the 10,000-foot Beartooth Plateau and dropping to the Clarks Fork of the Yellowstone. (Courtesy of USFS, Custer National Forest.)

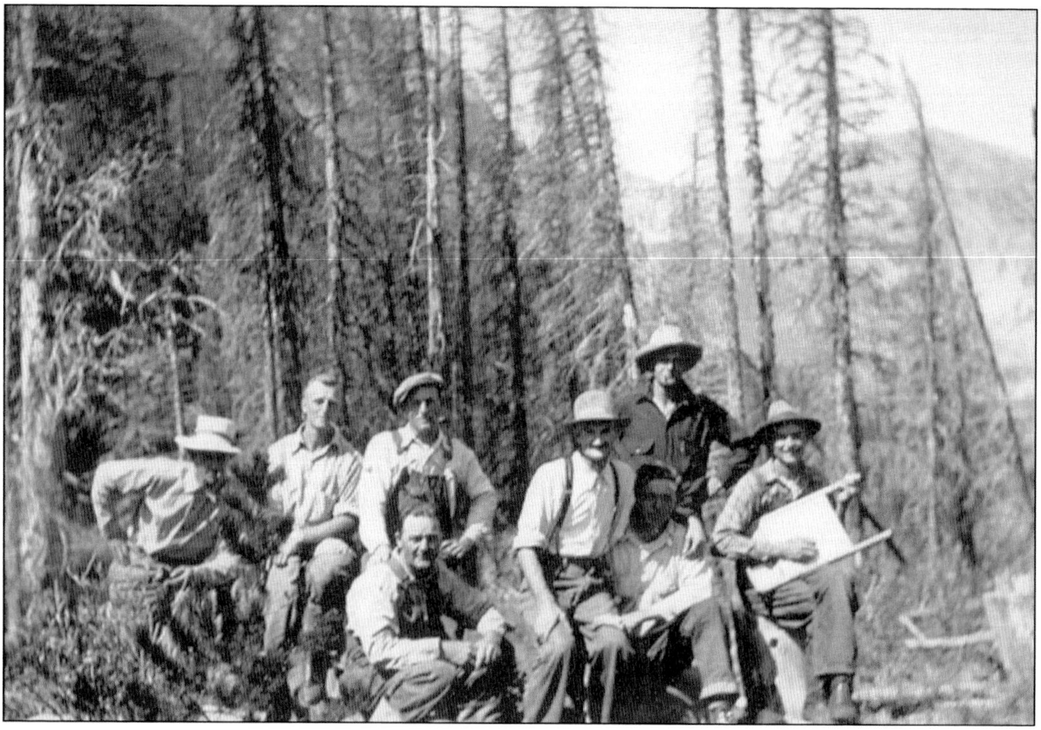

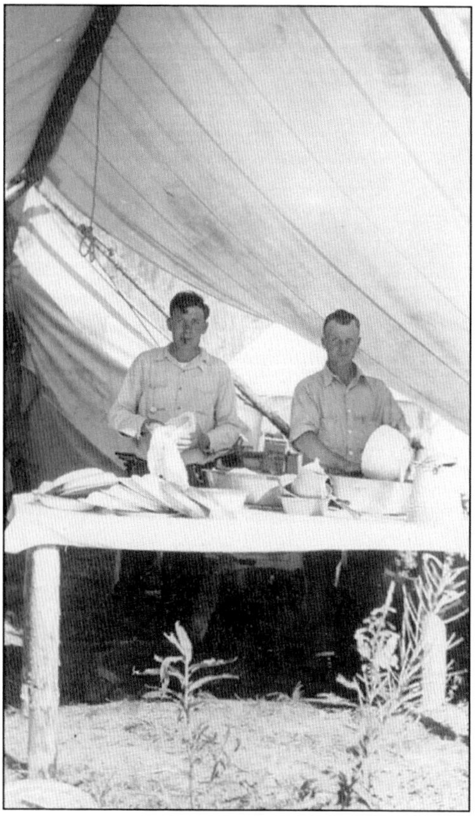

In 1936, money was appropriated for construction of 32 miles of trail in the Stillwater division. This included the 12-mile stretch between East Rosebud Lake over the divide to Mystic Lake at an approximate cost of $350 per mile. Shown are two contrasting views of trail life. Above is the crew hamming it up along the shores of Slough Lake in the Phantom Creek drainage; from left to right Mio Backovitch, Joe Papez, John Orler, Bill Parker, Lloyd Theil, Henry Loumis (seated left front), Ray Ramsey (seated in shadow), and Sam Thorp (with washboard). At left is Sunday kitchen duty, also on the Phantom Creek trail; Pat Dorn is at left, and Joe Papez is at right. (Both, courtesy of USFS, Beartooth Ranger District.)

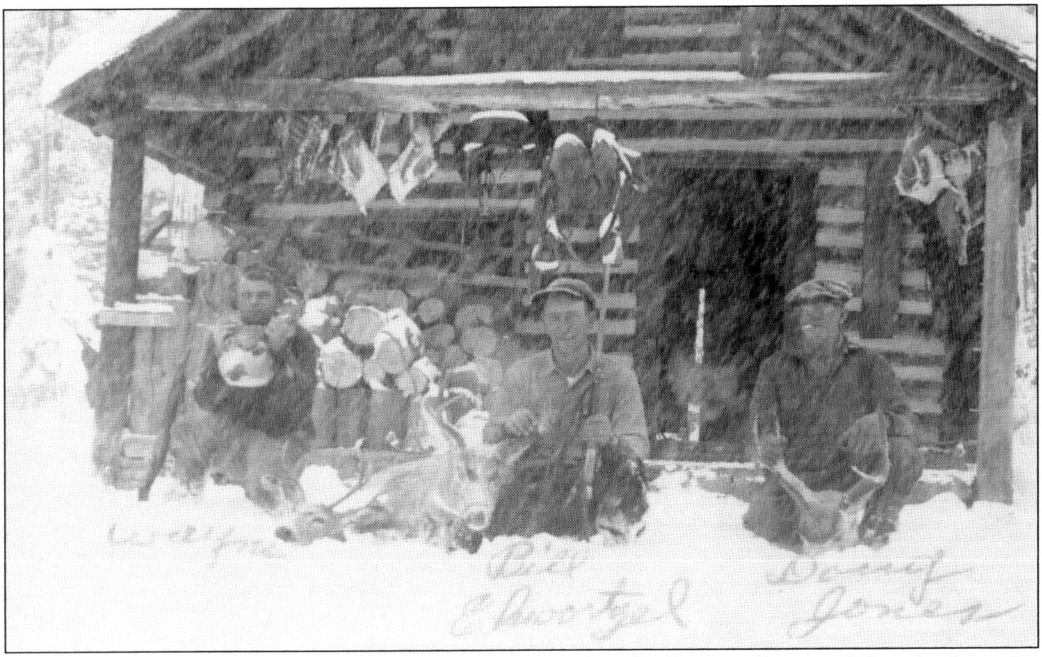

Wayne ?, Bill Ekwortzel, and Davey Jones are pictured at the Dayton Farmer Cabin, built in the mid-1920s along the Stillwater Trail. The Stillwater Trail may have been used as a mail route in the early 1880s. However, Forest Service trail work along the Stillwater River to Cooke City began in 1923. In 1978, Congress created the Absaroka-Beartooth Wilderness boundaries. The cabin was removed in 2002. (Courtesy of Museum of the Beartooths.)

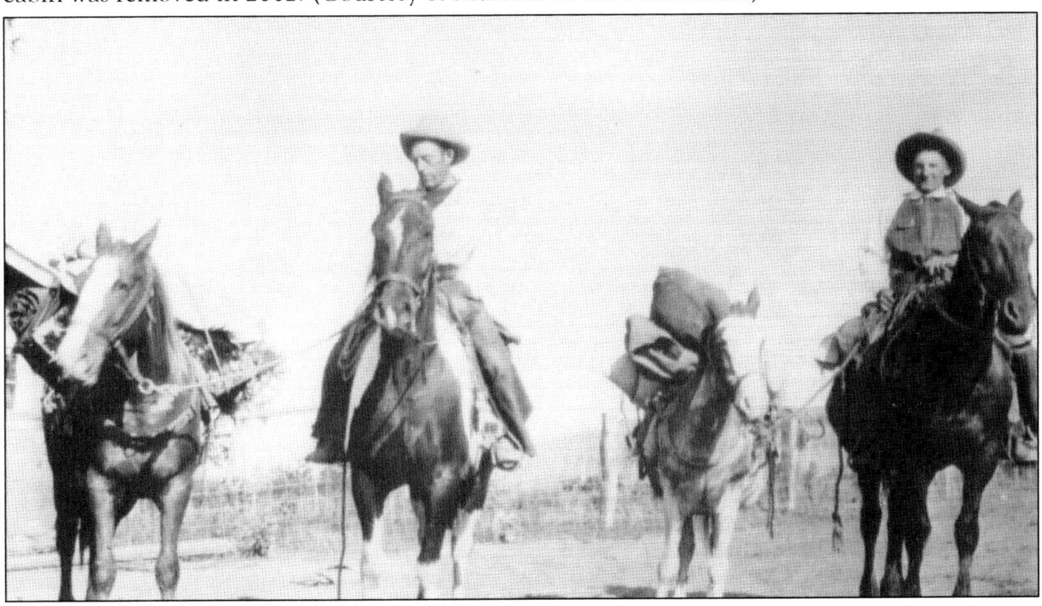

George McKinsey (left) and George Schwenneker head for Wounded Man Creek. According to material collected by Dudley White, Wounded Man Creek, a Stillwater tributary, is named for Peter Ginsterblum, who was killed in 1887 or 1888 in a forest fire during a railroad survey in the region. He suffered a skull fracture and was taken by stretcher to Nye City. Dr. Line was sent for, but Ginsterblum died before he could be reached. (Courtesy of Museum of the Beartooths.)

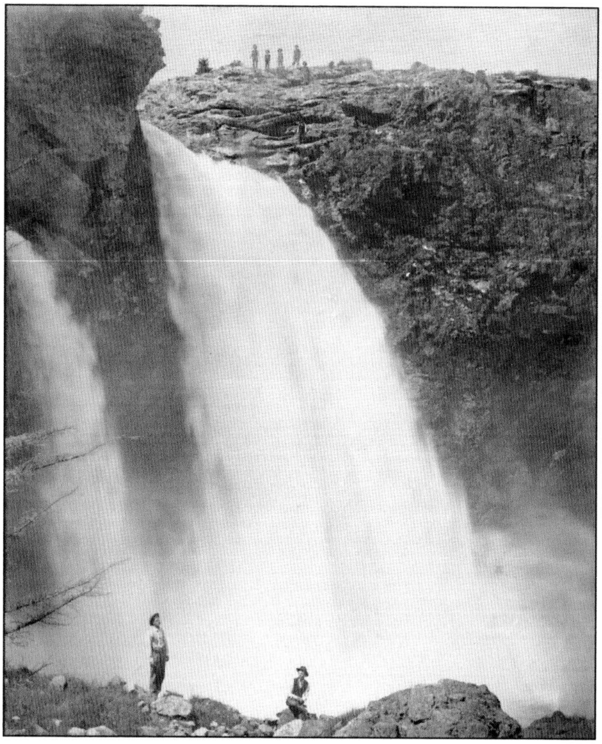

Natural Bridge Falls, which now features a picnic area, is caused by a 100-foot drop in the Boulder River. There used to be a natural bridge spanning the river at this spot, but unfortunately the bridge collapsed in 1988. Indians called this the place of "diving water." Around 1883, when the Boulder River was used to float timber downstream, one of the holes that formed the bridge became plugged with logs. (Courtesy of Crazy Mountain Museum.)

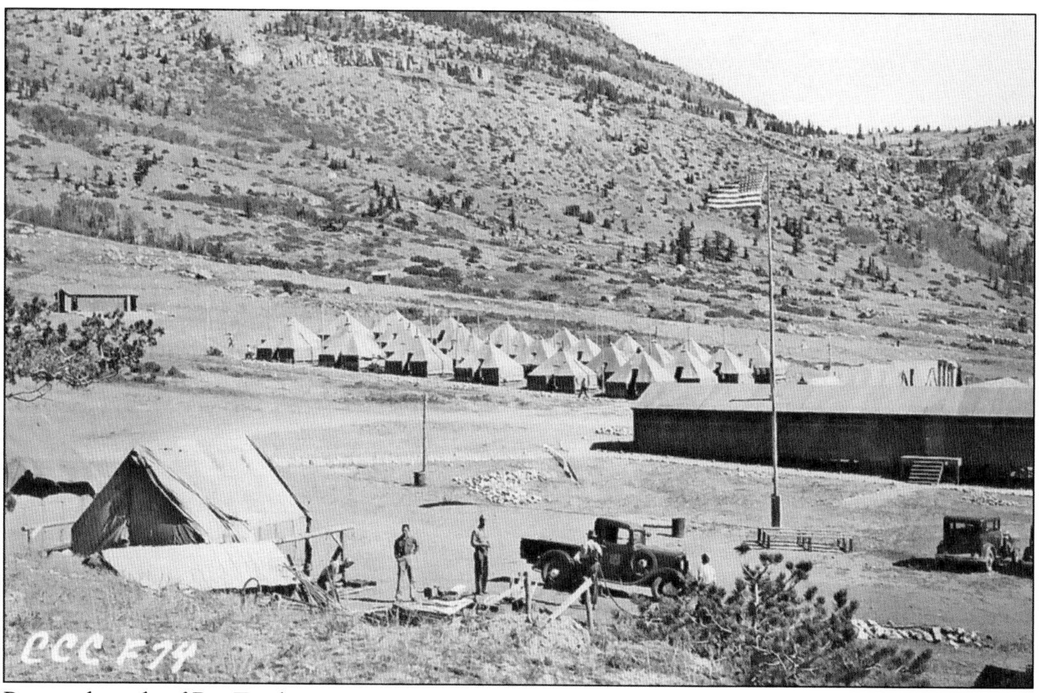

Pictured south of Big Timber is Camp Boulder F-74, a CCC camp from the 1930s that stationed men from Delaware, New Jersey, and New York. Work included relocating the Boulder road, building the suspension bridge at Natural Bridge Falls, and constructing Aspen and Falls Creek campgrounds. (Courtesy of USFS, Big Timber Ranger District.)

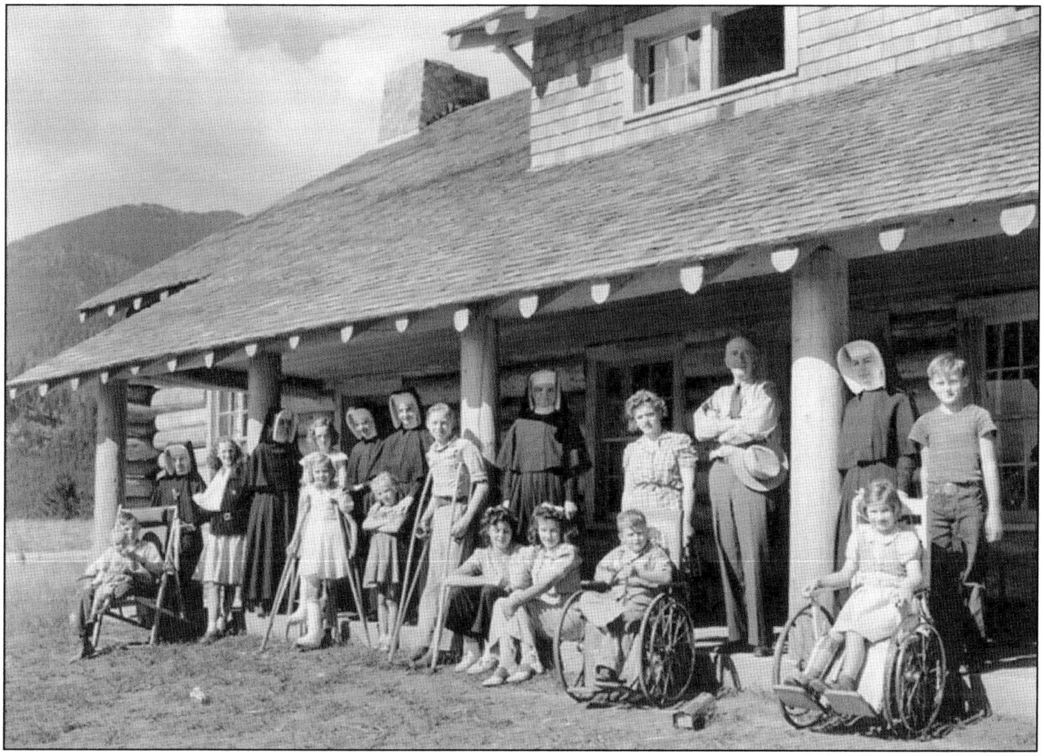

On the West Fork of Rock Creek south of Red Lodge, the Billings Rotary Club built a recreational retreat for youth. When this photograph was taken, in 1932, it was known as Camp Rotary and run in cooperation with Dr. Allen and St. Vincent's Orthopedic Hospital, giving polio patients and the handicapped the opportunity to enjoy mountain vacations. The CCC also assisted with building projects such as this Jelly Bean wading pond. In 1970, the camp was transferred to the Treasure Trails Girl Scout Council and renamed Timbercrest Girl Scouts Camp. It is operated under a special-use permit from Custer National Forest. (Both, courtesy of USFS, Custer National Forest.)

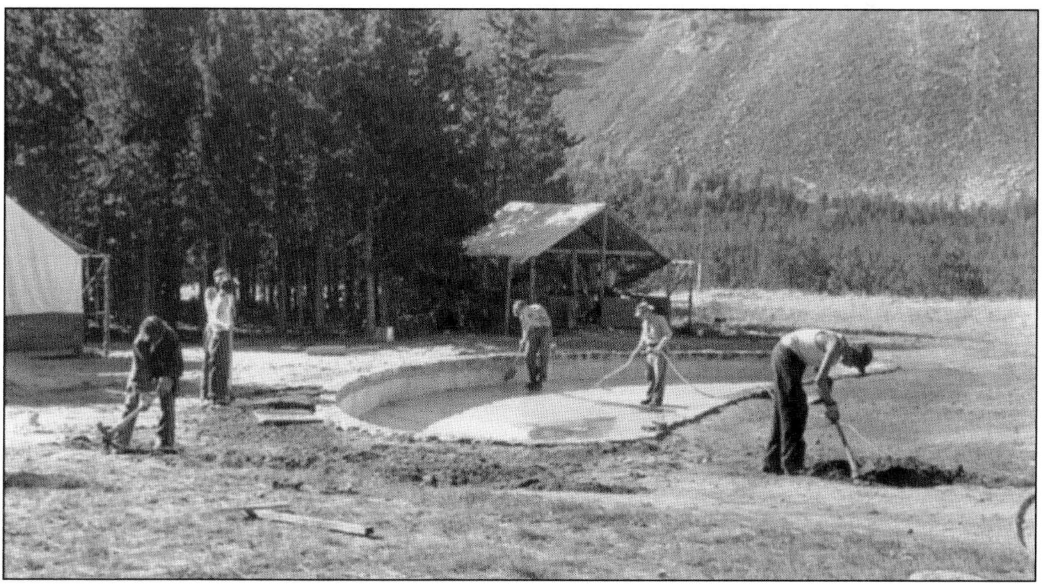

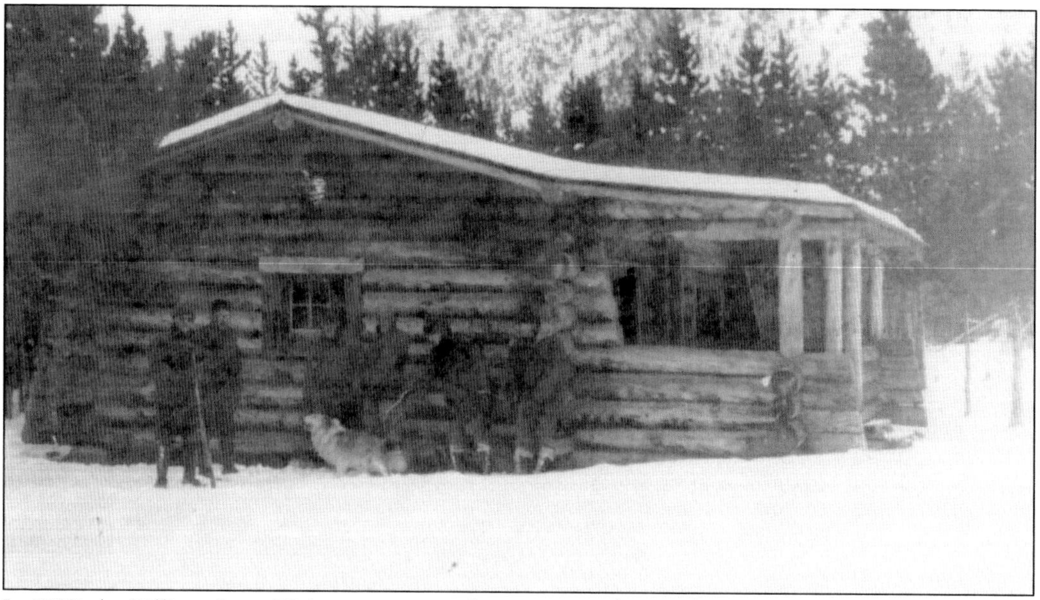

In 1927, the Billings Lion Club set up its youth camp 10 miles south of Red Lodge. The Boy Scouts soon joined the Lions in building the facilities. In the mid-1930s, CCC Company 1223, along with project F-11, built water lines, furniture, and housing. Today, the Lions' Beartooth Mountain Youth Camp boasts 22 buildings with facilities to serve up to 130 people from June through August and is operated by special permit with Custer National Forest. (Courtesy of Lions Club.)

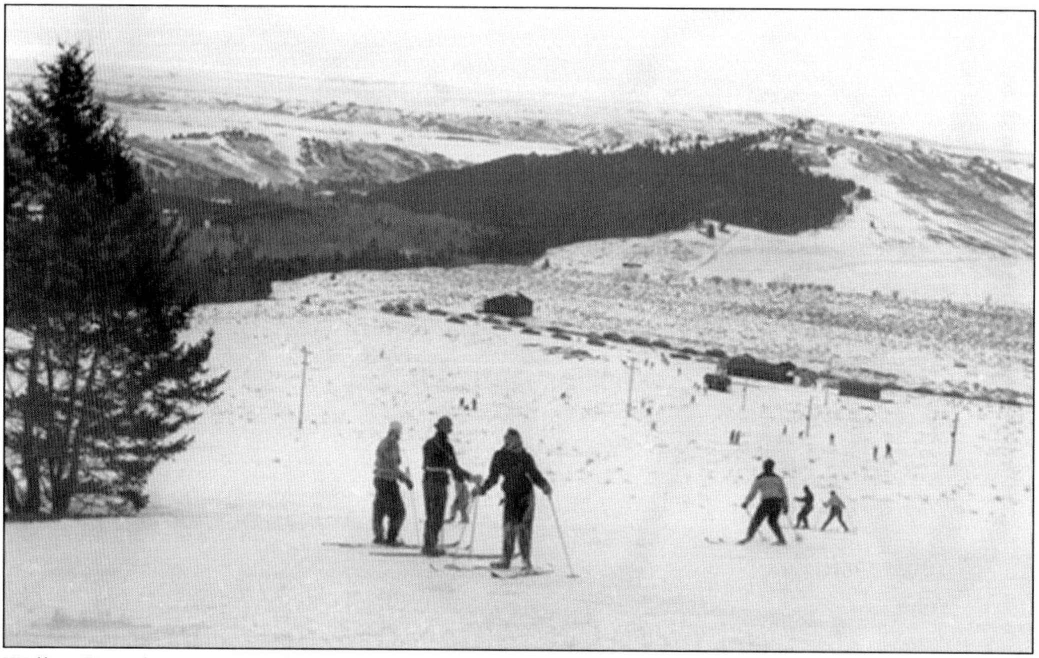

Willow Run ski area, near the current access road to Red Lodge Mountain, was a project developed by the CCC around 1939. Red Lodge had two CCC camps: the Palisades Camp, near the base of the Palisades, and Rock Creek Camp, on Rock Creek. There was also two "spike camps" in the East Rosebud, one near the present-day Sand Dunes picnic area and the other near the trailhead to Sylvan Lake. (Courtesy of USFS, Custer National Forest.)

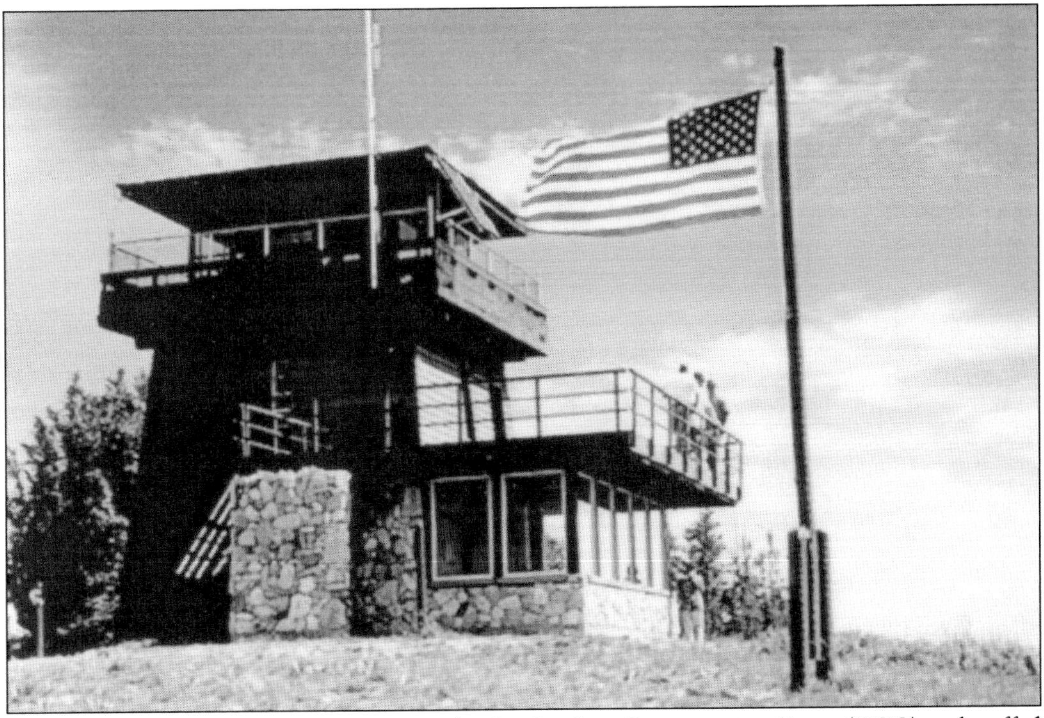

The Clay Butte Lookout was built in 1942 by the Civilian Conservation Corps (CCC) and staffed until the 1960s, when aircraft proved a better tool for fire detection. Because of its popular scenic vantage point and proximity to the Beartooth Highway, Clay Butte continues to be used as a visitor information site. It was remodeled in 1962 and has been staffed since 1975 by volunteers. The focus of Clay Butte today is to give visitors a glimpse of how fire lookouts functioned 60 years ago. (Courtesy of the US Forest Service.)

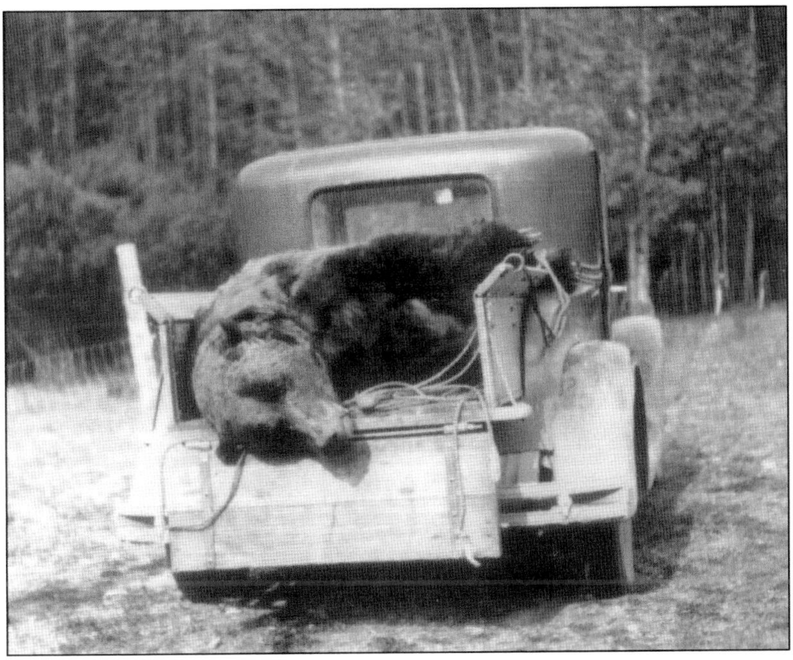

"Old Scar Face" was finally trapped near the Jarrett cabin in August 1933 by a government trapper named Johnson and was towed away in the pickup bed of Floyd Bailey's truck. The massive bear was a terror in the upper Boulder River area. It was presumed he wandered in from Yellowstone Park and quickly learned to find the food stored in cabins. (Courtesy of Crazy Mountain Museum.)

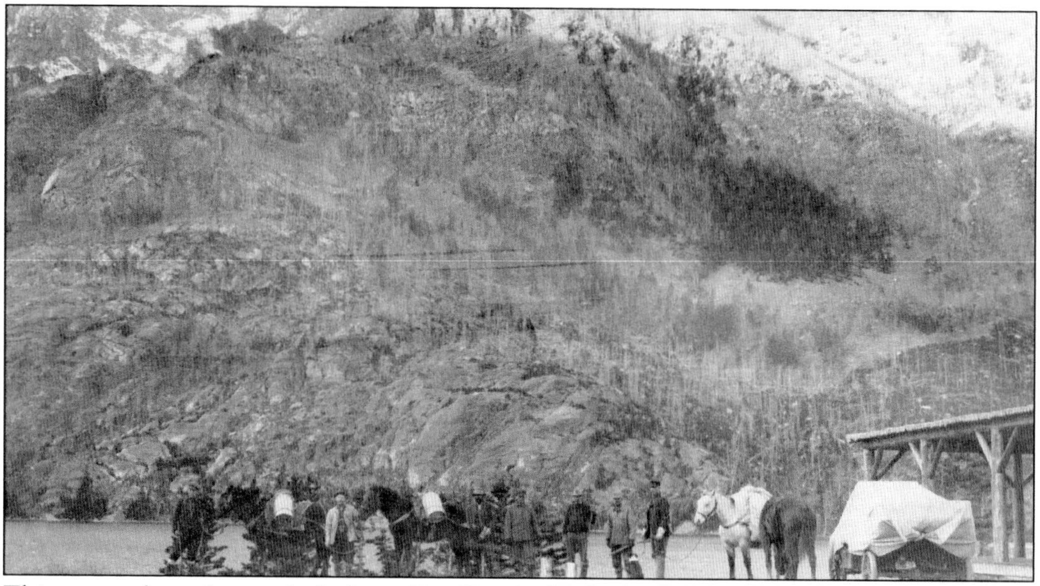

This group of men leaves the lodge at East Rosebud Lake leading pack horses loaded down with milk cans full of fish to stock the East Rosebud lakes and drainages. Rainbow trout were first stocked in Rainbow Lake in 1915 by John Branger, Martin Simmon, Albert Newman, and J.C. Witham. Branger hoped to name the lake "Rosina" after his wife, but he relented to christening it Rainbow Lake after the fish species they planted. (Courtesy of Special Collections, Montana State University Library, Bozeman.)

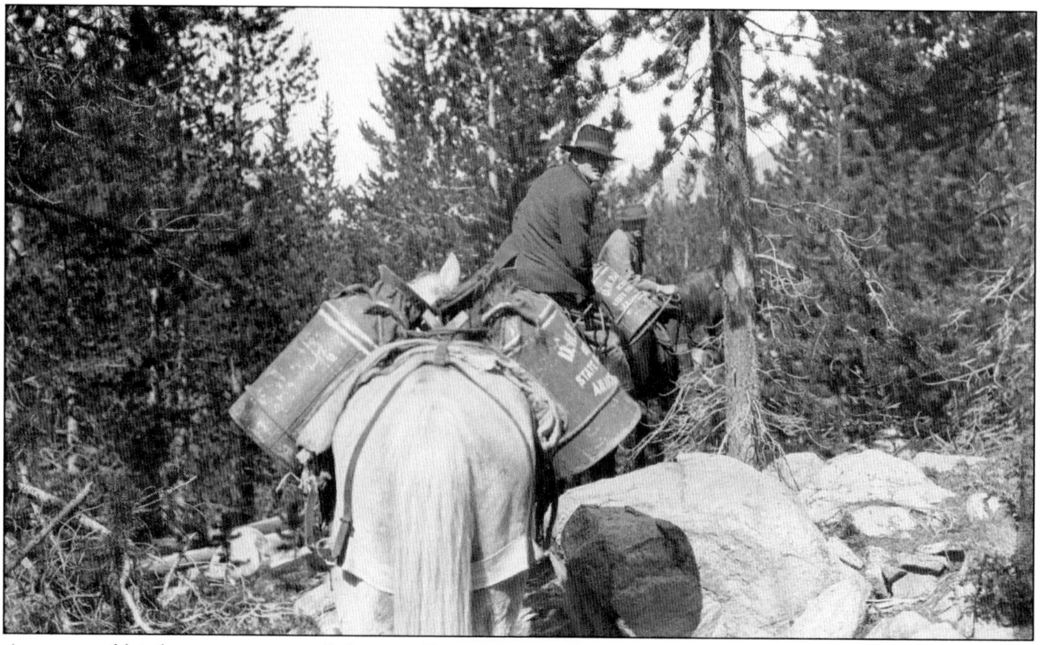

A man and his horse transport fish in milk cans to stock Crow Lake in 1924 or 1925. Al Croonquist brought the fish from a holding area near Richel Lodge through Lake Mary to Crow Lake. Otto Jalmer "O.J." Salo assisted Croonquist and other forest personnel in stocking many lakes. He named Lake Gertrude after his wife, while Mount Salo (Spirit Mountain) is named after him. (Courtesy of Carbon County Historical Society & Museum.)

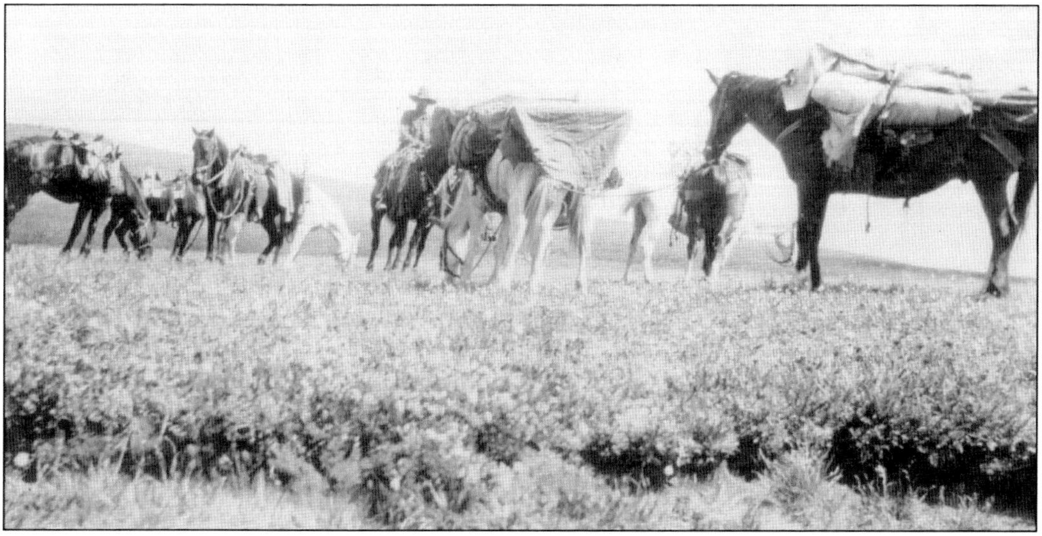

Whitetail Peak, between the headwaters of the Lake Fork and the West Fork of Rock Creek, was first recorded on maps in 1947. A long white snowfield on the mountain may have led to its name, but local legend states that Ben Greenough, a local hunter and guide known as "Pack Saddle Ben," coined the name after he shot the tail off a whitetail deer that was out its normal habitat near this mountain. (Courtesy of Museum of the Beartooths.)

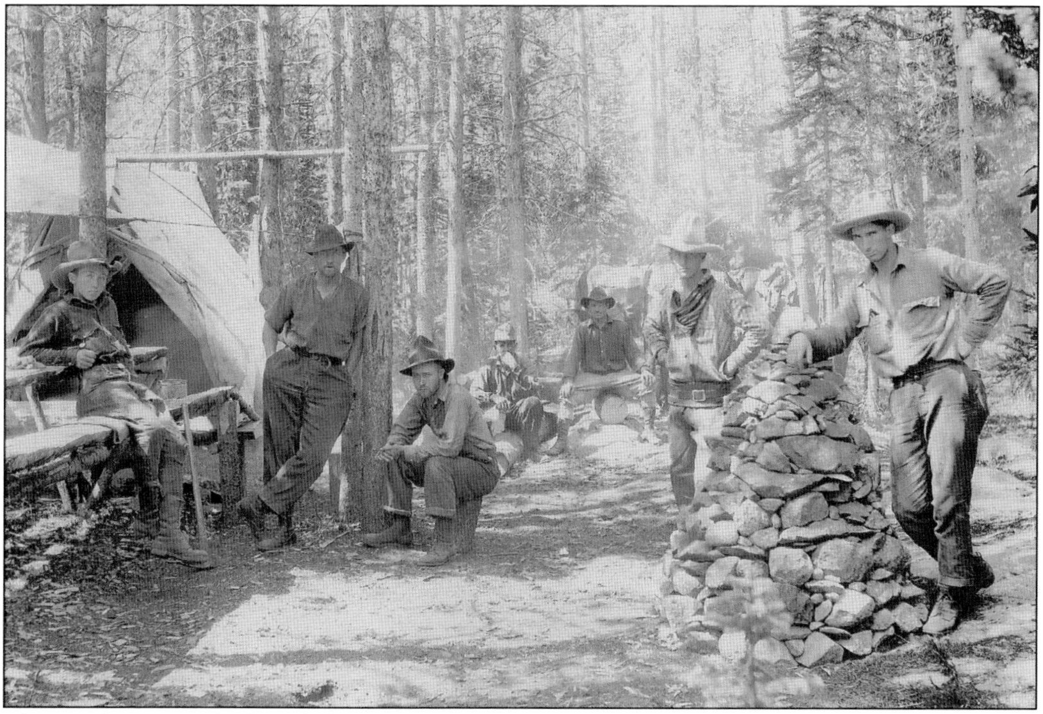

This trail crew, with, from left to right, Wesley Danees, David Kjell, Howard Thomason, O.L. Blacken, Frank Kuehn, Ben Coster, and Ranger Wallace Larsen, camped near Sentinel Falls for two months during trail construction on the West Fork of Rock Creek in 1922. Kjell used his strength and vitality in another way during the flu epidemic of 1918–1919, going to victims' homes to stoke their fires, cook meals, and ventilate their homes. (Courtesy of Mavis Carrithers.)

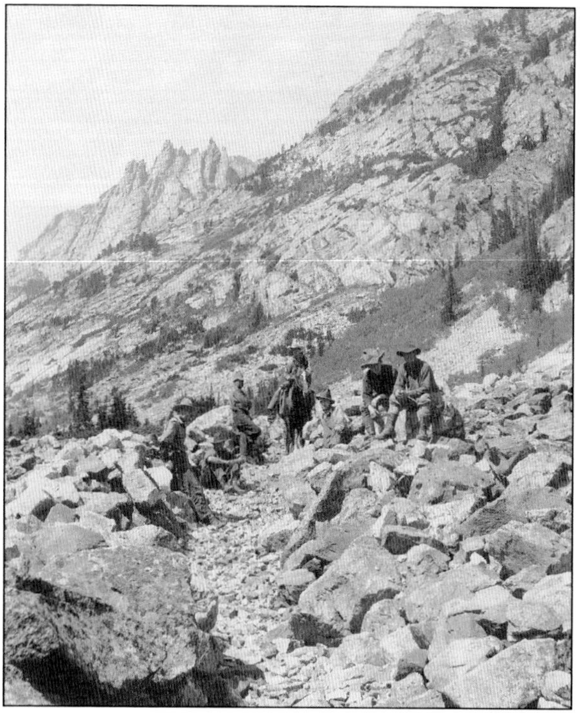

David Kjell, known as "the Galloping Swede," worked on this portion of trail in the West Fork of Rock Creek in 1922. After a long day of building the trail with "man power," Kjell could still appreciate the granite rock "which sure is perty after a shower." Kjell was also an adept mountain climber, once leaving the trail crew camp at Sentinel Falls early on a Sunday morning, scaling the 12,343-foot peak of Bowback Mountain, and returning by 3:00 p.m. He was looking for a check that Al Croonquist, the first to climb Bowback, had placed there two years before. The $25 check was wrapped in tinfoil and placed under a rock monument with this inscription written on the back: "Some view from here, eh Boy!" (Both, courtesy of Mavis Carrithers.)

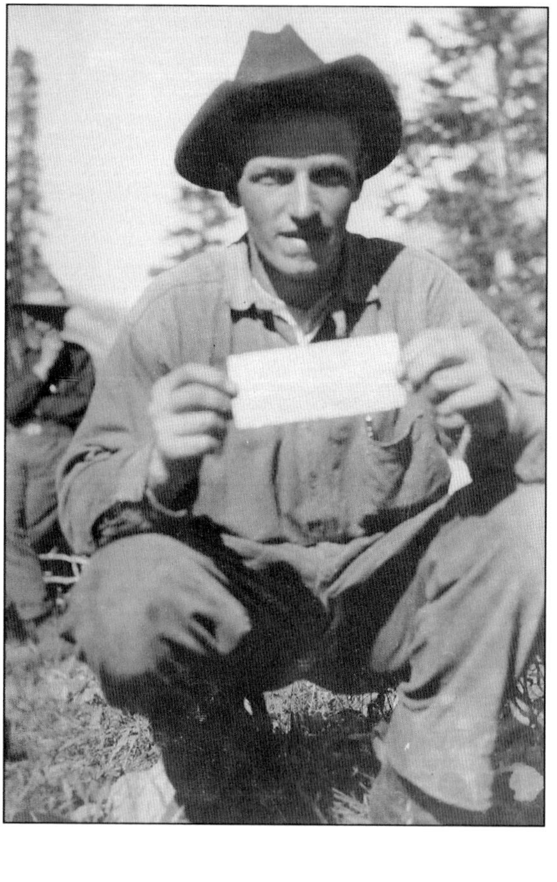

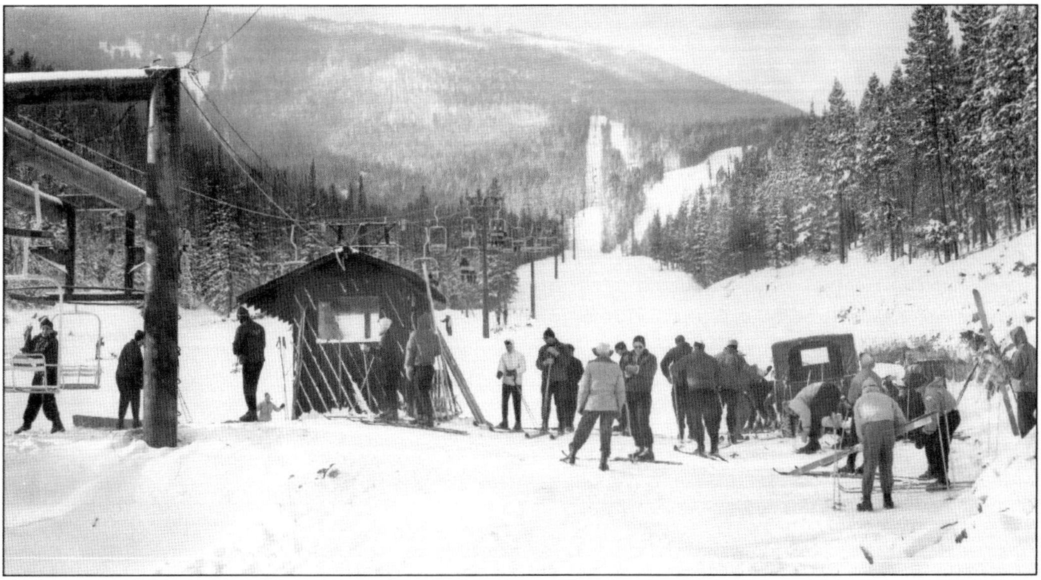

Today's Red Lodge ski culture began with several early ski areas. The Princeton Camp, south of town, was the first in 1939, but when a snowstorm made it difficult to access a year later, it was closed. From 1941 to 1958, skiers flocked Willow Creek near the foot of Red Lodge Mountain. Shangri-La, located 15 miles up Rock Creek canyon, became the dominant ski destination in 1947, but a forest fire destroyed it a year later. Developed in 1965, the Sundance ski area also closed after one season. In 1958, Grizzly Peak, Inc., offered stock certificates to provide funding for a new location and resort. Shown here, it opened in February 1960 with one chairlift and three runs. Renamed Red Lodge Mountain in 1965, the hill celebrated its 50th anniversary in 2010 under the ownership of JMA Ventures and operated under a special permit from Custer National Forest. (Both, courtesy of Carbon County Historical Society & Museum.)

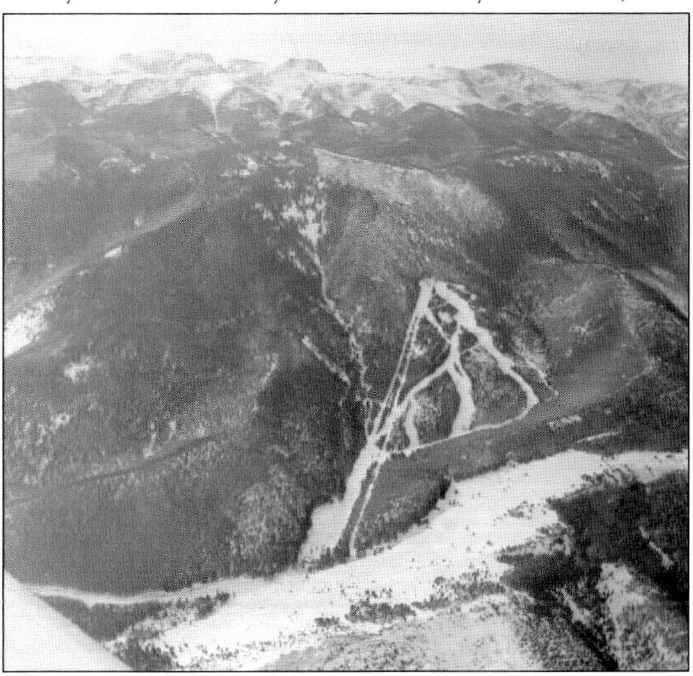

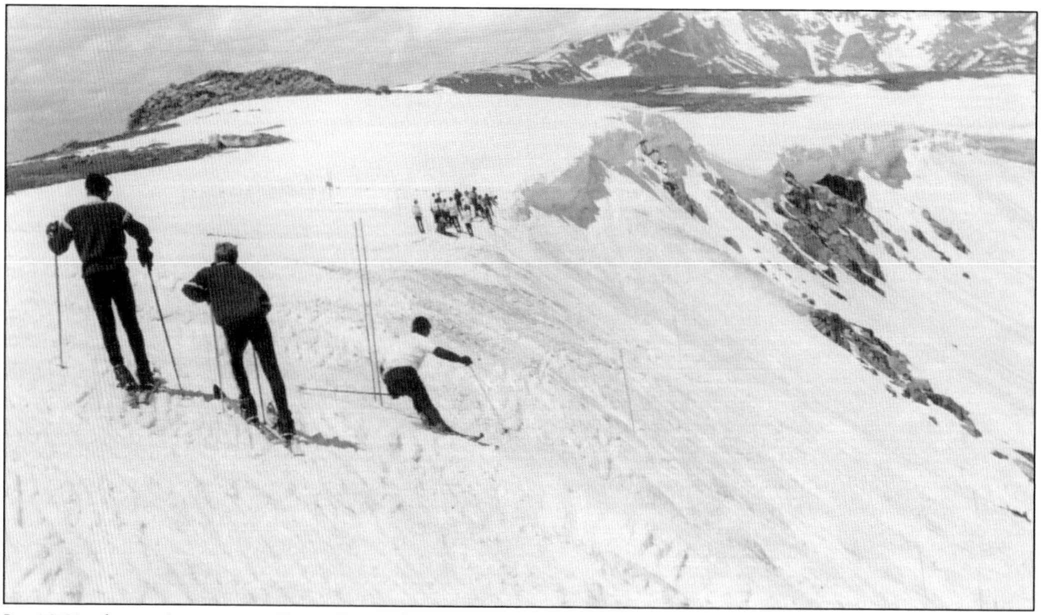

In 1961, three Austrians, Pepi Gramshammer, Eric Sailer, and Anderl Molterer, established the Red Lodge International Ski Camp at the Twin Lakes Headwall on the Beartooth Pass. Several past participants have made the US Olympic team. One such hopeful in 1968 was Tom Molinaro, the brother of the author, but his dreams were ended after he sustained a broken leg. The camp is now operated by Justin Modroo, Austin Hart, Joseph Maxwell, and Kurt Hallock. (Courtesy of Carbon County Historical Society & Museum.)

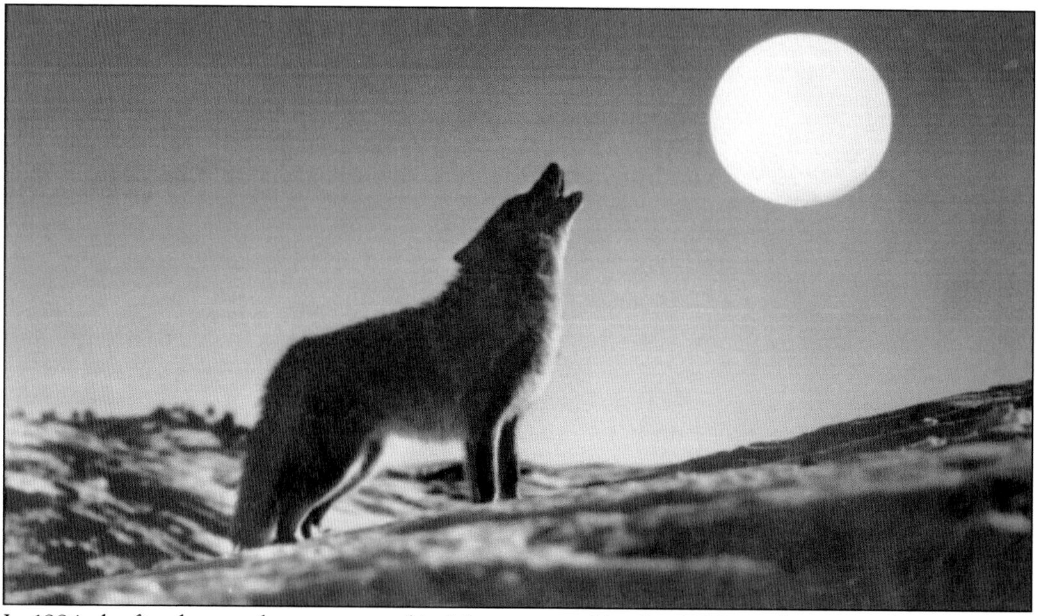

In 1884, the first bounty law was passed in Montana, and by the 1930s, wolves were almost extinct in the state. In 1995, fourteen wolves were captured in Canada and transported to Yellowstone National Park. Shortly after, two of the wolves, No. 9 and No. 10, found their way to Red Lodge. No. 10 was shot, but No. 9 gave birth to eight puppies near Mount Maurice. Wolves remain a controversial issue in the region. (Courtesy of Carbon County Historical Society & Museum.)

Nine

Slough Creek

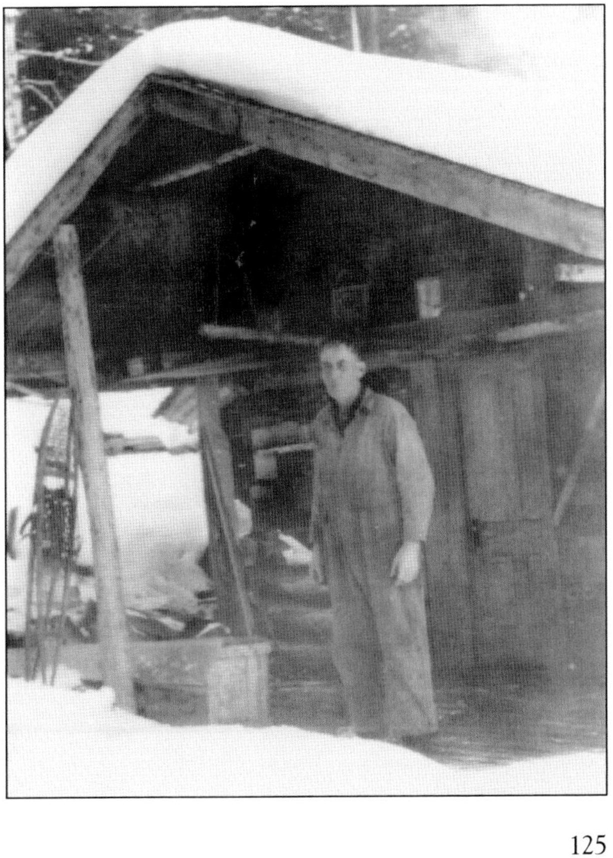

Warren Hutchings poses for the camera at the Slough Creek Ranger Station. Hutchings, with fellow ranger William Dehnhoff, found the body of Joseph "Frenchy" Duret, the victim of a grizzly bear. The pair returned with boards from the ranger station to make a coffin. The Slough Creek Station, built in 1913, was named after the nearby creek, so dubbed by Ansel Hubble, a member of Lou Anderson's prospecting party in 1867. Hubble's remark that the creek was "but a slough" was proven wrong when other prospectors came along and found it a rushing torrent. The Buffalo Fork Station, to the west, is also located along its namesake creek and plateau. In the spring of 1870, Bart Henderson found many buffalo grazing nearby and named the area "Buffalo Flat," since changed to Buffalo Plateau. Both stations serve as administrative outposts today. (Courtesy of Yellowstone National Park, No. 43898.)

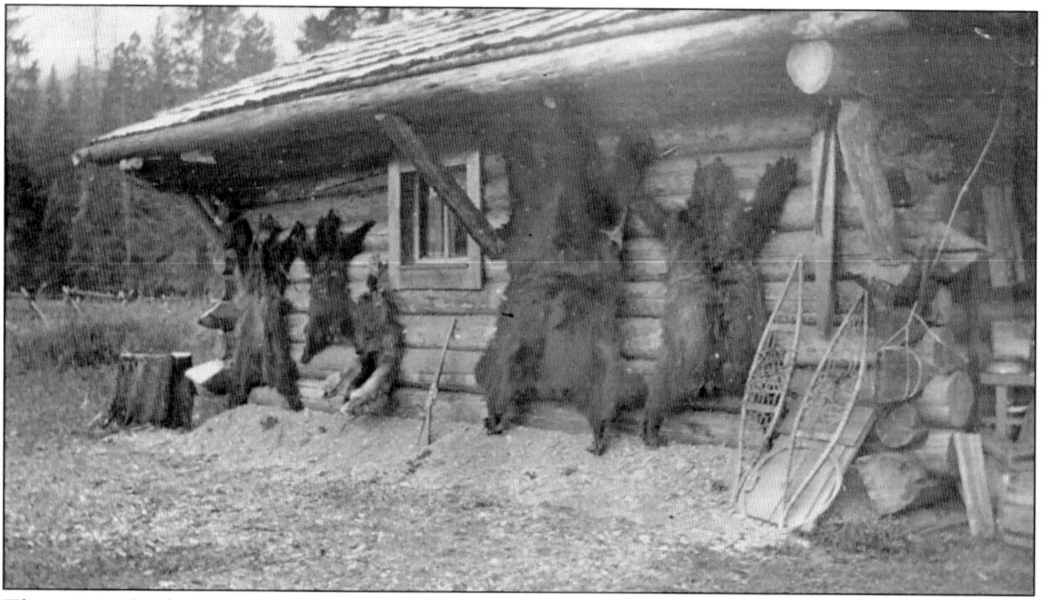

The original Silver Tip Ranch consisted of 157.2 acres adjacent to Yellowstone National Park in the Slough Creek valley where G. Milton Ames applied for his homestead on September 16, 1913. On the back of this photograph, he wrote, "First year on my homestead. Shot eight bears that spring." Ames remained there for five years before selling to Burton Lacombe and Charles Smith in 1918. (Courtesy of the Yellowstone Gateway Museum of Park County, Montana.)

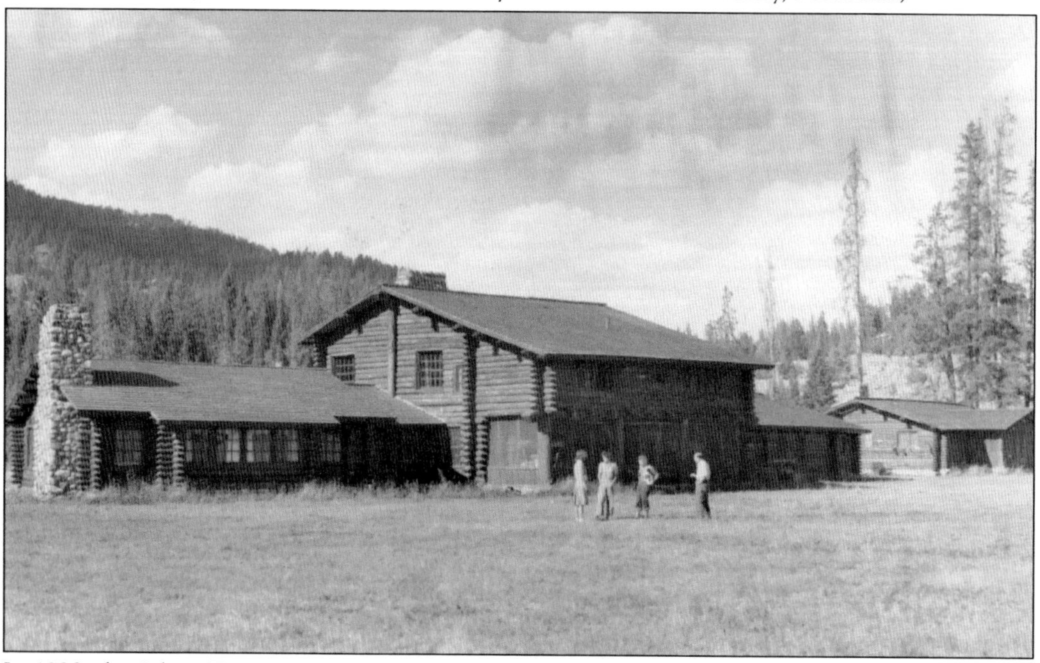

In 1923, the Silver Tip came into the hands of Cornelius Bliss, who used it as a vacation retreat for family and friends for 60 years, managed by Jim Anderson. Hung on the wall of the rustic lodge beside the massive stone fireplace was the No. 6 Newhouse bear trap and Winchester Model 1895 rifle that belonged to Joseph "Frenchy" Duret. (Courtesy of Special Collections, Montana State University Library, Bozeman.)

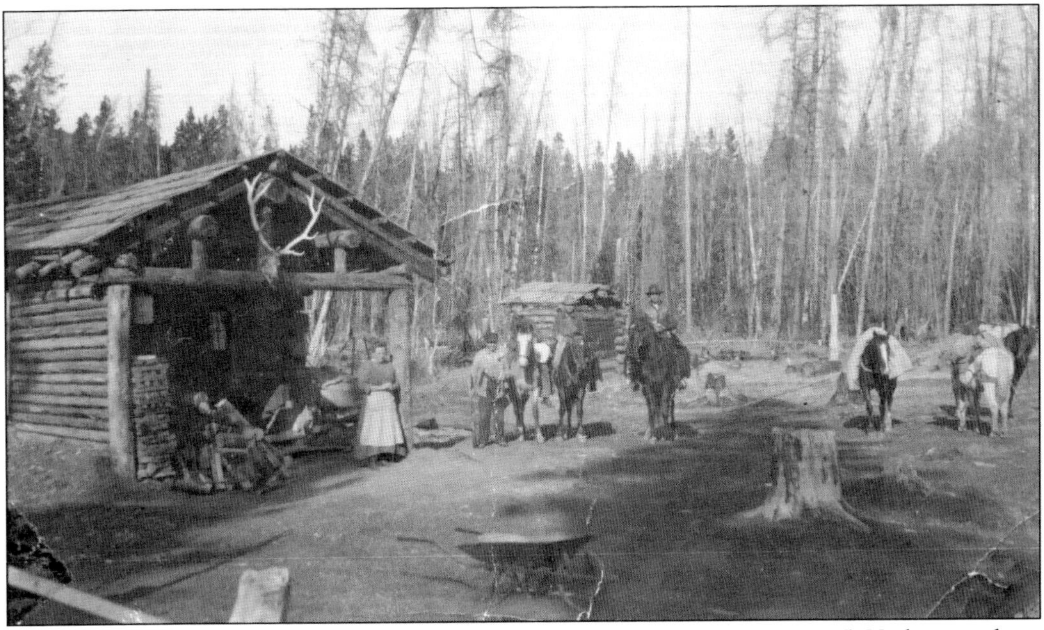

Joseph "Frenchy" Duret was a prospector in the early days of Nye City in 1885. He later took up hunting and trapping. Around 1900, he selected this homesite near Slough Creek in a prairie now bearing his name, Frenchy's Meadows. In front of his cabin are, from left to right, Jennie Duret and Dewey Whited; (riders) Ambrose French, Jake Schwenneker, and Robert Hudson. In 1913, at the age of 52, he married Jennie McWilliams, who also had a homestead and cabin in the meadows. He claimed to have killed over 250 bears while living on Slough Creek, but one eventually got him. On June 22, 1922, he was the victim of a grizzly bear that broke loose from his trap. Frenchy was found mutilated two miles away from the trap and buried on the spot. Jennie Duret sold the ranch, which was later purchased by Cornelius Bliss, who had just bought nearby Silver Tip Ranch, in 1923. In 1988, the Forest Service obtained a conservation easement on Frenchy's Meadow that provides public access. (Above, courtesy of Museum of the Beartooths; below, courtesy of Special Collections, Montana State University Library, Bozeman.)

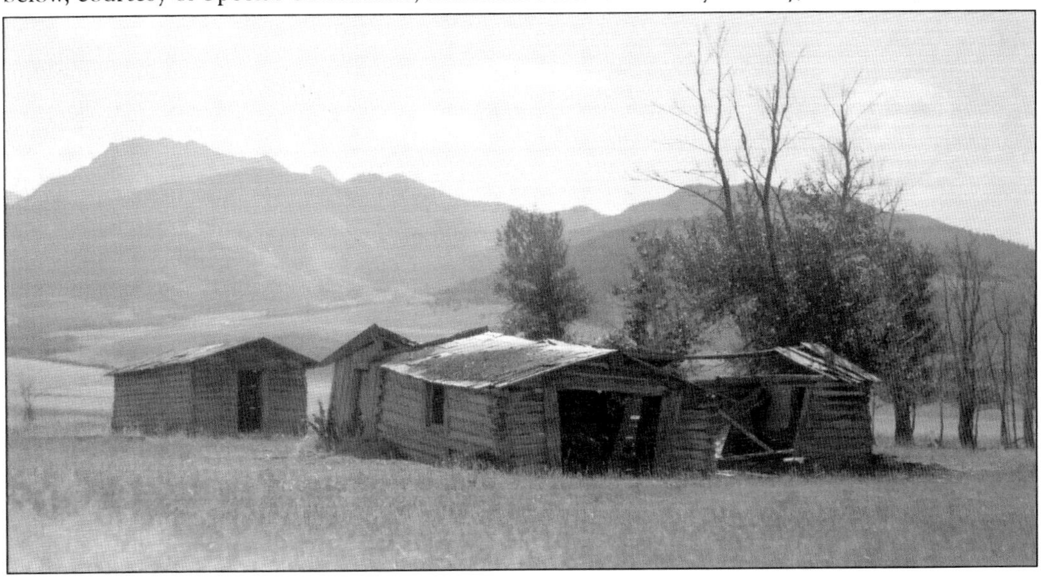

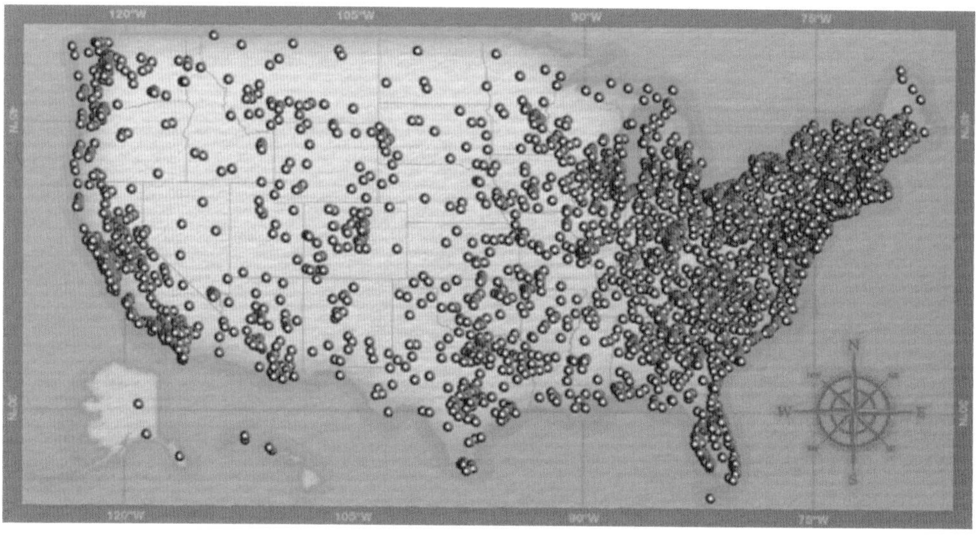